HOPE FOR GOD'S PEOPLE

Commentary on Ruth

Books also written by Dr. Carolyn Donner ...

HOPE FOR GOD'S PEOPLE (Commentary on Ruth)

Bible Word Hunting – Old Testament

Bible Word Hunting – New Testament

The Tale of Two Brothers
   (Ancestors and Descendants of John and Joseph Bay)

Future books to look for by the same author ...

Activity Book based on Ruth (for children)

Bible Word Hunting – Women of the Bible

The History of the Showalter Family of Kentucky

The History of the Perkins Family of Kentucky

Available on amazon.com and from the author.

HOPE FOR GOD'S PEOPLE

Commentary on Ruth

Dr. Carolyn I. Donner, M.Div, D.Min.

First Edition published 2010 by Darda Publishing
Second Edition published 2019 by
Donner's Country Crafts, LLC

Unless otherwise stated, scripture used in this book is taken
from the Modern English Version (MEV). Copyright © 2014 by
Military Bible Association. Used by permission. All rights
reserved.

Publisher Cataloging in Publication Data

Donner, Carolyn
    Hope for God's People (Commentary on Ruth).

    Includes bibliographical references.
    ISBN 978-0-9834458-4-5
    1. Bible. O.T. Ruth – Commentaries. 2. Ruth
3. Redemption – Biblical Teaching. 4. Christian Women. 5. Moab –
History. I. Title.
222.35
BS1315

DEDICATION

This book is lovingly dedicated to the memory of my grandparents,

Valentine and Nannie Bay

who gave me my first Bible. They also inspired me to go to Bible College and encouraged me from my childhood and up to study the Bible. Thank you, Papaw and Grandma.

Table of Contents

LIST OF CHARTS, MAPS AND ILLUSTRATIONS

ACKNOWLEDGEMENTS

No book is ever completed with the work of just one person. The author writes, but others provide important support throughout the process. That is true of this book as well and I would like to say a few "thank you's" to those people who helped with this commentary on Ruth.

My husband Gary has been a very valuable encourager to me. He encouraged me to go back to school and work on my Doctorate, which led to the writing of this book. Also, for patiently waiting for the book to be finished before proof reading it and offering valuable suggestions.

While I was finishing up the book, I decided to have several people proofread it to get a feel for how it would be understood and, of course, to correct my spelling, grammar, and punctuation. I want to thank Doug and Dottie Keiffer, and Jerry and Dot Silman for taking the time to read through it and offer expert comments for improving it. Also, for encouraging me to publish this book after they had read it.

A very special thank you to my friend, Hope Wozniak, for proofreading and for drawing small graphics on pages 61 and 99 to help me publish and publicize the book. She is a wonderful artist.

I'd also like to thank my Bible College professor of Old Testament, Dr. Wilkie W. Winter (now gone to be with the Lord) for instilling in me a love for the Bible and especially the book of Ruth in both English and Hebrew.

While I'm thanking professors, I'd like to thank the professor (and boss) who got me interested in archaeology in the 1970's, Dr. Reuben Bullard (also gone to be with the Lord) who made the lands and times of the Bible come to life through archaeological research, in the classroom and at Tel Gezer in Israel.

Preface

There are many commentaries, as well as whole and partial books written on Ruth. You will find inspirational books which address one part or another of the story of Ruth. Inspirational writers seem to have a better understanding of Ruth's story than do commentary writers, but they seldom address any of the issues that pertain to the background of the book, such as when it was written, or what the period of the Judges was, or how Ruth fits into the period of the Judges.

On the other hand, it is seldom that a commentary writer will give Ruth the consideration it deserves. Usually they will lump Ruth into a volume with Judges, or with Joshua and Judges, or even with I and II Samuel, and occasionally with everything from Exodus through Ruth. For most writers, the commentary on Judges included with Ruth is perhaps enough of a look at the background times that they do not see the need to delve into Ruth's background any further. Instead they look at a few words or phrases, maybe a verse or two, give some interesting fact or supposition, and then go on. Some quote the entire book, give a few footnotes, and feel they have adequately covered anything of importance in the book, itself.

For some, the fact that Ruth is a small book of only four chapters means it has little or no significance beyond a look at everyday life during the period of the Judges within Israel. In their haste to prepare a manuscript for a volume that contains other larger Biblical books, commentators quickly skim over Ruth without really looking into it. They seek to shove it historically into one judgeship or another without any real explanation and say it is a bright spot in the dark times of the Judges within the nation of Israel's early life, before the children of Israel became a nation. Commentary writers will dwell on when the book was written, and by whom. They make a reference to agriculture and maybe a brief explanation of a custom in Judah and nothing else.

The period of Judges was no more a dark age in Israel's history, then any other period. There were dark times when the people rejected God and built alters to worship idols, after which God had to punish the Jews to bring them back to worshiping Him and Him only. Sometimes this involved famines, or attacks from neighboring countries who worshiped idols. One could easily look at these times of punishment and say these were dark despairing times for the Jews, but that would only be half of the story.

There were also bright times when the people followed God's laws and worshiped only the true God who brought them out of Egypt. At these times they prospered and had rest. Yahweh protected them from their enemies and the land brought forth plenty of food for everyone. These were times of peace and joy within Israel. If we look at the number of years the Judges ruled Israel and compare the number of good years to the number of bad years, we find there were more than twice as many good peaceful years as there were bad dark years. The good times seem to far outweigh the bad times. Perhaps that is why God kept saving the Israelites. He knew how good they could be, if they tried.

The good times and bad times seemed to run in circles. If the Jews were prosperous and had plenty to eat, they seemed to become lazy and forget who provided this time of plenty, especially after the death of a prominent Judge. At that point they allowed their sons and daughters to marry foreigners who worshiped idols, or they allowed foreigners who worshiped false gods to live among them and continue to worship their idols. Both were forbidden by God (*See Deuteronomy 7*). God knew these idol worshipers would convince the Jews to let them continue to worship their idols and false gods, instead of being converted to the worship of the one true God, Yahweh. The false gods of other nations did not mind if their followers worshipped more than one god. Why should a god that does not really exist care if you worship him as one of many gods or just him alone? **Only Yahweh had the law of worshipping Him and Him only!** This is another way of proving that Yahweh is the one true God.

Eventually the Jews would start to worship the false idols again, and Yahweh would have to bring them back to Him by allowing the land to become barren, and/or other nations to conquer the Jews. This would plunge Israel back into a dark time, but Yahweh never left them there. As soon as the people returned to God, He would immediately bless them with prosperity and help them conquer their enemies. This is much like any other period in Israel's history. Even the monarchy had its good and bad times, based on whether the nation had a king who followed the Lord or one that did not. The people followed what the King did whether it was good or bad.

In the bad times, there were those who never stopped worshipping the true God. Boaz's parents and family show us one of those families who worshiped Yahweh through good times and bad ... through famine and plenty. This is the historical background into which Ruth falls. A time when God had punished Israel for forsaking Him (so Elimelek took his family to Moab), and a time when God once again brought the Jews back into His fold and provided for them (when the famine was over and Naomi brought Ruth back to Bethlehem).

This should be only the beginning of a study of the book of Ruth. In this commentary you find much more. We will look at the historical background of the book of Ruth, and how the story fits into the background of the period of the Judges. A study of Moab will also be included. Ruth's people, the

Moabites, who were cousins of the Israelites, were also an interesting people.

> Before I go into more details on what you are going to find, let me first say that every commentary writer goes to a book of the Bible with his or her own world view, which may be considered conservative or liberal, or somewhere in between. To set the matter straight from the beginning, here is the author's view: The Bible is the word of God, inspired by God, written by persons who were guided by God to write truthfully and factually. The events within the book of Ruth is a true historical account. It is NOT historical fiction. This author believes Jesus is the Messiah foretold of in the Old Testament. He was born of a virgin. He died on the cross to be the sacrifice for all of our sins. He is risen and lives today at the right hand of God. God exists as 3 persons, the Trinity of God the Father, God the Son (Jesus), and God the Holy Spirit.

The intention of this commentary is to look at Ruth from every possible way. Besides being a true account of life in the times of the Judges in Israel and Moab, the book of Ruth has much to offer in the way of inspiration for our lives today. If examined fully, you will find many levels of help for people at any period of history, especially today. We will look at all of them throughout this book.

On first glance we see that Ruth is the account of a misplaced Moabitess who is living in a foreign country among people she did not grow up knowing. The customs are somewhat different from what she is used to. She is <u>a person out of place</u>. This is what first attracted me to Ruth. I moved from a farm to a large city to go to college. I was out of place among the "city" kids who obviously knew more about everything than I did. There are many ways to feel misplaced. Some have to do with circumstances out of our control. Others have to do with choices we make. Ruth's was a choice, but she felt just as much an outsider at first. How she deals with the situation is what makes her worthy to be included in the congregation of the Lord and the ancestry of the Messiah.

At second glance Ruth is a beautiful look at <u>LOVE</u>. The happy wife becomes a poverty-stricken widow and goes to work in the fields of a wealthy land owner only to fall in love with him. Through a series of circumstances, she becomes his wife and they live happily worshipping Yahweh. Do not read too deeply or you will find much more ... these "circumstances" were ordained by God. Be sure to notice that loving God is just as important as loving each other to this couple. This makes it an even better love story because it shows God watches over His people, even poor widows who worship Him.

Still there is more. It is really a beautiful account of <u>FAITH</u>. The faith of a couple of widows who trust God to take care of them on a difficult dangerous journey back to Him, His people, and what they see as an insecure future. Because of their faith in God, they are rewarded with a secure future.

Now do not stop there, because if you look a little more carefully you will find that if Ruth had not been loyal to Naomi and to the Lord, she would have been left in Moab like Orpah never to be heard of again. We find Ruth is also an account of <u>LOYALTY</u>. Because of her loyalty to Naomi, Ruth helped her make it back to Bethlehem. Ruth's loyalty to Yahweh also gets them food and a better life.

We also notice a theme of <u>STEADFASTNESS</u> even when times look dark and bleak. That journey for two widows must have seemed very scary once they came to the full realization of their traveling alone in the wilderness. Naomi was determined to return home to Bethlehem, and Ruth was determined to stay with Naomi no matter where it took her.

That turns it into a look at the theme of HOPELESSNESS TURNED INTO HOPE for the future as the women refuse to just give in and give up. Instead they keep looking for new ways to be a blessing. Ruth takes on menial work. Naomi takes their dwelling and makes it a comfortable home. Ruth brings home food to keep them alive in the present. Naomi plots for the future.

As if that was not enough, while doing all these things, Ruth shows us all what a VIRTUOUS WOMAN is and how she acts. This is done even before Solomon wrote those beautiful words in Proverbs 31 about the qualities of a virtuous woman. Perhaps he learned what a virtuous woman was from the stories his parents and grandparents told him about his great-great-grandmother Ruth.

Without looking very deep at all we see an account of a type of the ideal KINSMAN-REDEEMER (go'el) which points to Jesus Christ being our kinsman-redeemer. Although the kinsman-redeemer is spoken of in the law given to the Jews, the book of Ruth is the only complete example of that law in practice. As we look at Boaz as the kinsman-redeemer to take Ruth out of poverty and provide a good life for her, we will see how Jesus provided us with the redemption from our sins and provides us with a secure future though eternal life in heaven with Him.

Of course, we will look at the historical significance of the genealogy at the end of the book of Ruth. This is the first place in the Old Testament that we have a genealogy of King David's family which brings us through the period of the Judges. Lest someone think this is an incomplete genealogy, we should note that it is repeated as is within the genealogy of Jesus in Matthew 1.

There is so much to learn from the book of Ruth that it is very difficult to understand why commentators in the past have given as little as eight pages to a study of this book. This volume is organized in chapters so you can choose what most interests you for now, and then come back later to find out even more.

While I hope you will take the time to read the whole book, I understand it covers a lot of subjects you may not need right now in your walk with Christ. I have tried to create as complete a look at Ruth as I can. I hope it will be a help to you today, and in the future as your walk with the Lord develops and grows.

After you have read this work on Ruth, you may want to look at more. I have included an annotated bibliography at the end of this book which covers books about Ruth, as well as bibliographies at the end of some chapters that deal mainly with the topic of that chapter. These will give you references to help as you continue your study into the wonderful world of Ruth, Naomi, and Boaz.

Chapter One: BACKGROUND OF THE BOOK OF RUTH

Before we delve into the background of the book of Ruth, let us do an overview of the book itself. Have you read it yet? Statistically here is what you are going to find. The book of Ruth consists of the following:

CHAPTERS: Four
VERSES: 85
SHORTEST VERSES: chapter 4 verses 19-21 (8 words each – KJV; 10 words each - MEV)
LONGEST VERSE: Chapter 3 verse 13 (43 words – MEV; 64 words - KJV)
WORDS IN ENGLISH BIBLE: 2576 (KJV); 2478 (NASB)
WORDS IN HEBREW BIBLE: 1116

ORIGINAL LANGUAGE: Hebrew with some Aramaic
TRANSLATED INTO ENGLISH: Yes
TRANSLATED INTO OTHER LANGUAGES: Yes

TYPE OF WRITING: Narrative, prose
THEME: Redemption, joy, love, hope, loyalty, choices
MAIN CHARACTERS: Naomi, Ruth, and Boaz

These are facts about the book, but they tell us nothing of the background or the internal narrative. Three questions are intricately linked in trying to discover the background of the book of Ruth. Who wrote this book? When was it written? Why was it written? Looking at these three questions has caused much controversy over this small book we call Ruth. There is even controversy over whether it is properly named Ruth, as some would like to make Naomi the main character and call the book by her name. While Naomi is the only character who appears in the whole book, there is no historical or archaeological evidence that this book was ever called by any other name than Ruth.

AUTHORSHIP OF RUTH

Let us start by saying there is no absolute answer to any of these questions. The book itself does not say, "Written by...", nor does it say, "copyright XXXX". Even though the book does not say specifically who wrote it and when, there are hints within the book that can give us some clues. Let's look at the evidence and start with ... when was Ruth written?

We can look at the last verses in the book and we see David mentioned. While it does not specifically say he was King, it is obvious this is THE David who became Israel's second king after Saul's death. David was a man after God's own heart (see I Samuel 13:14). He is listed as the son of Jesse, which is proof enough that this is King David, but he is not called "king" in these verses, only David. The earliest writing of the book has to be after the birth of David. While we cannot argue specifically about the lack of the title "King" being used with David's name, it is likely Ruth was written before David became king.

Jewish tradition says Samuel wrote the books of Judges, Ruth, and I and II Samuel. We know Samuel could not have written II Samuel since he is said to have died in I Samuel 28:3. Therefore, someone other than Samuel wrote the second book of Samuel. Jewish traditions are not always the most accurate, but they do give us a place to start. Although not the author of II Samuel, Samuel is a good candidate for the authorship of Ruth. He was a prophet and a Judge of God's people. He lived at the end of the time of the Judges and the beginning of the time of the monarchy in Israel. Most importantly Samuel knew David before he became king over Israel, because Samuel was the one chosen by God to anoint David as the next king when he was still a lad (see I Samuel 16). Since Samuel died before David became king, this could account for him not calling David by that title. Samuel knew David would become King of Israel, but the people for which he was writing, did not and would not know this for several years.

If Samuel was the author of the book of Ruth, we need to ask ourselves, "Why did he write it?" As a prophet of the Lord, Samuel was familiar with the law written in Deuteronomy 23:3 which says, "No Ammonite or Moabite may enter the assembly of the LORD. Even to their tenth generation they may not enter the assembly of the LORD forever". Yet Samuel knew David was chosen by the Lord to be the future king after Saul, and he knew David's great-grandmother was a Moabitess. While Samuel understood that God had chosen David despite his background, could he be sure the Israelites would not hold this against David?

Samuel had visited with Jesse's household and, on one or more occasions, while there he was probably told the family history stories. He heard of Naomi and Ruth while sitting around a warm fire in the evening, and was probably very familiar with it. The Lord would have given him any details that might have been lost or embellished by the telling and retelling of the family story. Samuel could have written the account of Ruth to explain how the Lord had watched over this Moabitess and brought her into the congregation of Israel on purpose to meet Boaz. He may also have wanted to explain how Ruth had come to know and accept Yahweh as her God which is so eloquently stated in Ruth 1:16, "But Ruth said, 'Do not urge me

3

to leave you or to turn back from following you. For wherever you go, I will go, and wherever you stay, I will stay. Your people shall be my people and your God my God."

Perhaps by the time of Samuel, the Israelites had taken the verse in Deuteronomy out of context and provided a stricter rule to it. We must look at the whole verse and God's laws. For instance, if a Moabite converts to Judaism, is he or she still a Moabite? Or does he or she become a Jew upon conversion? Can a person be a Moabitess by birth and Jewish by religion? However, we interpret the verse in Deuteronomy, it is obvious the Lord had accepted Ruth's conversion to Judaism and now accepted her as a faithful Jew. As is often the case, God's people are less accepting of others than God is. Samuel may have originally written Ruth to show the Israelites that God had accepted Ruth's conversion into Judaism even though she was originally a Moabite. That would also explain why we see the word "Moabitess" used so often in the book of Ruth. Samuel may have been emphasizing this fact to show all of Israel that Ruth of Moab was accepted by God so they should not even think of trying to use it against David.

While Samuel fits into the time line of when the book was written, and he certainly has a motive for writing the book, there is another prolific writer who fits into the time line as well. That would be King David himself. He definitely falls into the time of "after the birth of David". We have numerous examples of David's writing in Psalms, and he certainly would have known about his family's history. Since we do not know how long Ruth lived, it is highly possible David's father, Jesse, would have personally talked with Ruth and called her "grandma". Jesse's grandmother may have even personally told him the story of how she met his grandfather and Jesse passed it on to his children, David being the youngest.

The lack of the title "King", before David's name in the genealogy at the end of the book, can be explained in a couple of ways. David may have written the story while a lad watching his father's sheep. This would have been a time when David did not think of himself as a king. Maybe he wrote it after becoming king to show the people about his parentage. Since he was writing about himself, he would not be so presumptuous as to refer to himself as King David. The people would naturally know that he was their king.

As to why King David would write the book of Ruth there are also several possibilities. The simplest would be to help him and his brothers remember their family roots … thus the genealogy at the end.

Alternatively, David may have written Ruth at a time when he was hiding from King Saul in the caves of Adullam. At this time, David took his parents to the King of Moab in Mizpah and asked the Moabite king to protect his parents. David may have written of his Moabitess ancestor to convince the Moabite king to offer his assistance and protection to his father who had Moabite blood. (See I Samuel 22:3-4) David may have had a simple reason for writing the story, but God had a better reason for preserving it in the scriptures.

If written when David was king, or while he was hiding from King Saul in the wilderness, it may have been written to answer questions about whether he was rightfully a full Israelite. Perhaps there was taunting from some of Saul's loyal soldiers about the Moabitess ancestor of David which made him unworthy to be an Israelite. David wrote the story of his Moabitess ancestor to show she was not only accepted by the people of Bethlehem, but she was part of God's plan to be among the Israelites named in the ancestry of kings and later of the Messiah.

Another possibility is that the book was written by an unknown woman. The book is written about two women primarily and from their point of view, which some would say would be difficult for a man to write. The fact that the nearest kinsman did not quickly step up to help them could be looked at as a put down of the male characters. While this is a possibility, all we have is speculation. Just because a story is written from the female point of view does not automatically rule out a male as the author, especially if the story was originally told by a woman such as Ruth herself. There could be many reasons why the nearer kinsman did not immediately come to the aid of the women. He may not have known of their return, or he may have been sick, or away on a trip. There are many other legitimate reasons that could also explain why he did not immediately come to their aid, including his being busy with the harvest of his grain fields. We should not look at his hesitance as a put down for all men in the story.[1]

Some have suggested we look in another period of Jewish history for the answer to our questions of who wrote the book and when it was written. They look for motivation for writing the book first, and find an interesting time period in the exilic to post-exilic period when Nehemiah came back to rebuild Jerusalem. He found many of the Jews who had been left in Israel, during the Babylonian and later captivity, were married to non-Jewish women from the surrounding nations. Nehemiah had ordered these Jews to divorce their wives and have nothing to do with heathens. (See Nehemiah 13:23f) Those who would like to put Ruth during this period give it as a defense of those married to foreigners, saying, "If Boaz could marry a Moabitess and their great-grandson become King of Israel, why can't we keep our foreign wives?" There are a lot of flaws in this

---

[1] Robert L Hubbard, Jr., The Book of Ruth, (Grand Rapids, MI: William B. Eerdmans Publishing Company, 1991), p. 24.

thinking. Mainly the fact that Ruth followed Yahweh even before she met Boaz, while the post-exilic foreign women continued to follow their pagan gods and lead their husbands and families away from Yahweh, the only true God. Ruth would not have been a good argument for keeping foreign _pagan_ wives, so it is unlikely that it was written at such a late period. They offer no particular name of the author, just someone wanting to provide a defense against Nehemiah's orders.[2]

While the author of the book of Ruth did not sign it, we have a pretty good case that it was either Samuel or David. Both were writers, both lived at the right time, and both had reasons to make the story public knowledge. One thing we can know for sure is the book of Ruth was inspired and blessed by God and has been protected by God to be included in the scriptures for us to gain a better knowledge of God and His plan for our salvation.

PLACE IN THE BIBLE – CANONICITY

From the beginning, the book of Ruth has always been considered canonical (belonging among the books inspired by God to be considered part of the Scriptures). Since Ruth has always been part of the Scriptures, we will look more to the placement and role of the book of Ruth in history.

HEBREW BIBLE:

Among the ancient Jews, certain books were considered holy or inspired as they were written. The books of the Law or the Pentateuch were preserved as they were finished. They were written by Moses and read by the priests to the people as

---

[2] Arthur Lewis, Judges/Ruth, (Chicago, IL: Moody Press, 1979), p. 108.

the authoritative rules from God for living. Naturally as Joshua wrote his book and others followed, they were added. As time passed more and more books were added. Before I go farther let me correct a misconception here of the word "books". We think of a book as being a rectangular bound volume with several chapters, which continue in order, or in the case of the Bible, it is a collection of smaller books bound into one volume (book). In ancient times books were actually scrolls, which were pieces of animal skin or later papyrus rolled into one scroll, or perhaps two scrolls if it was a large (or long) book. Sometimes one scroll could contain several smaller books. Saving books or rather scrolls in any particular order was next to impossible.

An example for today would be giving you several types of soda pop in cans. Now you have to put these in the refrigerator to get them cold, but you only have one shelf to put them on and the only way to get them all in there is to lay them on their sides. You start with a can of cola and place it on the shelf, next you put a can of diet cola, a can of lemon-lime soda, one of vanilla flavored cola, a cherry flavored one, etc. until you've put all flavors on the shelf. Did I mention you had to stack them two or three high to get them all in there? Here comes someone who wants a lemon lime and pulls it out of its place on the bottom. They all go rolling around and get all mixed up. Someone else takes a different one. Again, they roll a bit and some drop down from the top layer. You still know what is on that shelf but do not have a clue which one is where. In the end, it really does not matter, because a person wanting the diet cola is going to find the diet cola by moving the others around and again mixing them up more. Order is not important at this point ... only the number of different kinds. This is the way it was with the early Biblical scrolls, and this is why we find the order of the books in the Bible listed in different ways by early Jewish leaders.

Now let us say your number of soft drinks has grown to the point you cannot keep them all on one shelf or in one box or bag anymore. What do you do? You take certain ones out and put them on another shelf or in another box or bag, so you know the colas are in the first box and the lemon-lime and root beer are in the second box, and all the diet pop is in the third box.

What does this have to do with the Bible? Well, the next thing we see in the books considered sacred by the Jews is a three-fold division: The Law (Torah), the Prophets (Nevi'im), and the Writings (Kethubim). There is some disagreement on why certain books/scrolls were put into the different categories. Some say they are done chronologically, others by authors, and others by content of the scrolls. It is more likely a combination of all three.

The scrolls of the Law are the oldest. They contain the Pentateuch also called Torah, or writings of Moses that are always placed first in the Bible. The Nevi'im contains the books of the Prophets, which were books written by people who held the office of Prophet. These contained Joshua, Judges, Samuel (I and II Samuel as one book), Kings (again both I and II Kings were considered one book), Isaiah, Jeremiah, Ezekiel, and the 12 minor prophets. The twelve Minor Prophets were on one scroll. The Kethubhim contained the "Writings" or, later called in the Greek, Hagiographa. These writings are also sometimes called "wisdom" books. They included all the other books: Psalms, Proverbs, Job, the Megillot (five smaller books on one scroll), Daniel, Ezra-Nehemiah, and Chronicles.

Here again books were moved around because they were still using scrolls. Ruth is a prime example. Sometimes Ruth was included with Judges as a sort of an appendix, and sometimes even added to the same scroll. This would put Ruth among the section called the Nevi'im or Prophets. Other times it was included with the Megillot because Ruth was one of the

9

five scrolls read on a particular holy or feast day. That would put Ruth among the Kethubhim or Writings section.

Even within the Megillot Ruth was moved around, sometimes being the first of the five Megillot books, and other times being a later book. The Megillot contains the books of Ruth, Lamentations, Song of Solomon, Ecclesiastes, and Esther. These small books were read at the five main feasts of the Jewish year. In Hebrew Bibles today the five books of the Megillot are commonly arranged in the order of the feasts during which they are read. The Song of Solomon (also called Song of Songs) is read at Passover – the celebration of the Jews leaving captivity in Egypt during the Exodus.

Ruth is read at the feast of Shavuot. Shavuot was the festival celebrating the first fruits of harvest. It also commemorates the giving of the Torah to Moses on Mt. Sinai. Because it occurred 50 days after Passover, the early Christians called it Pentecost. In the Old Testament it is also called the Feast of Weeks (Exodus 34:22, Deuteronomy 16:10), Festival of Reaping (Exodus 23:16), and Day of the First Fruits (Numbers 28:26). Ruth has come to be associated with Shavuot because of the references to the wheat and barley harvest. According to Jewish tradition, Ruth is also associated with Shavuot because of her unwavering and total commitment to becoming a Jew, which means she came to love and follow the Torah. This is their way of connecting both reasons for the Shavuot feast to the book of Ruth.

Next among the Megillot books would be Lamentations, which was read on the feast known as the Ninth of Av (the destruction of the Temple). Ecclesiastes was read during the feast of Sukkoth or Tabernacles. The final feast was Purim during which Esther was read. No matter in which order the writer put the books, Ruth was always included in the Hebrew canon of the Old Testament.

DEAD SEA SCROLLS:

The next place we look for evidence that Ruth was a valued or sacred book to the Jews is among the scrolls found at Qumran. Bedouins, who then tried to sell them to antiquities dealers and others, found these scrolls between 1947 and 1956 in caves along the area of the Dead Sea near Qumran. The settlement along with many of the caves in the area have been excavated giving us many more fragments and scrolls. The scrolls were copied between 150 and 70 BC making them the oldest known copies of the Old Testament. They were mostly written in Hebrew, Aramaic, and some Greek. Besides the Old Testament many scrolls such as commentaries on Biblical books, and other non-Biblical books were found.

These scrolls are known as the Dead Sea Scrolls. Every book of the Old Testament except Esther was found in whole or in part among the scrolls and fragments of scrolls found in the caves along the Dead Sea near the settlement of Qumran where the Essenes lived. Although not all of the fragments have been translated even today, parts of four manuscripts of Ruth have been found. Two were located in Cave 2 and two in Cave 4. None of these manuscripts is complete. All are dated to the first century B.C.[3]

The largest fragment, found in Cave 2, is designated as 2QRutha. It contains the text of Ruth from the middle of chapter 2 to the beginning of chapter 4 and matches the Masoretic text. The Masoretic text is the most commonly used Old Testament Hebrew text today and dates to about AD 1000. Fragment 4QRutha contains 14 lines from the first chapter of Ruth and again shows us a Masoretic type of text with only one letter variant. Other fragments contain smaller sections of Ruth,

---

[3] Edward F. Campbell, Jr. Ruth, (Garden City, NY: Doubleday & Company, Inc.), pp. 40-41.

some only one word. Some of these do vary from the established Masoretic text, but only by a word here or there. None of these variations changes the overall meaning of the text of Ruth. What it shows us is that the book of Ruth was well known to the First Century BC Jewish sect known as the Essenes, and, in 2000 plus years since then, it is still the same book.[4]

SEPTUAGINT (Greek Language):

Next, let us look at the first translation of the Bible. The Bible is actually the first book to be translated into a different language.

Legend says Ptolemy II Philadelphus (284-247 B.C.) being a great collector of books, wanted a copy of the Hebrew law (Torah) translated into Greek for his collection in the library of Alexandria, Egypt. The Greeks were not on the best terms with the Hebrews they had conquered, so Ptolemy released 198,000 Jewish slaves and sent them to Eleazar the high priest. Along with the slaves, he also sent a request for a copy of the Torah and Jewish scholars who could translate it into Greek.

The story was told by one of Ptolemy's officers, Aristeas, in a letter he supposedly wrote to Philocrates. There is some concern among scholars that this letter, which was believed to be true for many years, is actually a fake and may have been written by someone else. Whether or not Aristeas wrote the letter, it may still contain some degree of truth, or perhaps "legend" would be a better word for what it contains. Aristeas says the High Priest Eleazar sent six rabbis from each tribe of Judaism with a copy of the Torah written in gold on scrolls made of skins. Twelve tribes times six rabbis equal 72 rabbis.

---

[4] Ibid., pp. 40-41.

Christian tradition says they were royally wined and dined and afterwards were secluded on the island of Pharos where each individually translated the Torah into Greek comparing sections as they went. After 72 days, they finished translating. This became known as the Septuagint (Seventy) or LXX (Roman Numerals for 70).[5]

The translation mentioned above was only of the Pentateuch (the first five books of the Old Testament). In reality, it took many years for rabbis to translate the whole Old Testament into Greek. The Septuagint is partly responsible for the books of the Old Testament being put into the order we see today, although it also added several books not found in the later Masoretic text of the Hebrew Bible. These books known as the "apocrypha" are of disputed origin and not considered canonical by many early church leaders. They are also rejected by the Protestant churches today.

The chart below shows the order of the books in the Septuagint (remember there are several extra books here) ...

ORDER OF THE BOOKS IN THE SEPTUAGINT:

LAW:	Ecclesiastes
Genesis	Song of Solomon
Exodus	Wisdom
Leviticus	Sirach or Ecclesiasticus
Numbers	PROPHETS:
Deuteronomy	Minor Prophets:
HISTORY:	Hosea
Joshua	Amos

---

[5] E. M. Blaiklock, "Septuagint" in Merrill C. Tenney, ed., The Zondervan Pictorial Encyclopedia of the Bible, Vol. 5, (Grand Rapids, MI: Zondervan Publishing House, 1980), p.343.

Judges	Micah
Ruth	Joel
I Samuel	Obadiah
II Samuel	Jonah
I Kings	Nahum
II Kings	Habakkuk
I Chronicles	Zephaniah
II Chronicles	Haggai
Esdras	Zechariah
Ezra-Nehemiah	Malachi
Esther with Additions	Isaiah
Judith	Jeremiah
Tobit or Tobias	Baruch
I Maccabees	Lamentations
II Maccabees	Letter of Jeremiah
III Maccabees	Ezekiel
WISDOM:	Daniel with additions
Psalms	
Psalms 151	APPENDIX:
Prayer of Manasseh	IV Maccabees
Job	
Proverbs	
The above list copied from the Wikipedia website in 2008: http://en.wikipedia.org/wiki/Septuagint	

As you can see from the chart above, we find Ruth following Judges instead of being listed with the five Megillot scrolls. In fact, the five Megillot books are not placed together at all, but are intermingled between the other books.

There are many other Greek translations of the Hebrew Old Testament in part or whole, but none gained as much acceptance nor had as much influence on other translations as the Septuagint. I should like to mention here that we do not have a complete copy of the original Septuagint translation, and the copies we have today vary slightly in the translations of some verses, passages, and books.

LATIN VULGATE:

Another translation of the Old Testament, known as the Latin Vulgate or just Vulgate, followed the same order of books as the Septuagint. The Latin Vulgate was a translation of the whole Bible, both Old and New Testaments.

Although there had been Latin translations of the Old Testament before this one, they had been translated from the Greek Septuagint. The Latin Vulgate was created at the request of Pope Damasus I in A.D. 382. Pope Damasus originally commissioned Jerome to revise the old Latin translation of the four Gospels from the best Greek texts.

In A.D. 385, Jerome was forced to leave Rome and moved to Bethlehem where he continued his work. After A.D. 390, Jerome decided to translate the rest of the Old Testament from Hebrew manuscripts instead of the Greek LXX. He did, however, keep the books in the same order as the LXX, making Ruth follow Judges. This version of the Bible in Latin became the main version used by the Roman Catholic Church and is still used today.

PESHITTA (Syriac language):

There have been many versions of the Bible translated into Syriac (a form of Aramaic) spoken in the area of Syria. The word Peshitta means "simple". Early translations of the whole Bible were begun in the first or second century after Christ, but we do not have any complete manuscripts from that period. What we have comes from the fifth through ninth centuries.

They show an influence from the Masoretic Text as well as the LXX so both were probably used for this translation. Again, we find the book of Ruth in the Peshitta version of the Old Testament.

It is believed the Peshitta was translated by Jewish Christians living in Syria. As you can see from the chart below, in the Peshitta Ruth is in a different location from the Septuagint and the Latin Vulgate, but it is there among the canonical books of the Old Testament. Down through the ages this little book of Ruth has moved around in the canon, but it has always been in the canon.

ORDER OF THE BOOKS IN THE PESHITTA:

Genesis	Cant. (Song of	Malachi
Exodus	Solomon)	Jeremiah
Leviticus	Esther	Lamentations
Numbers	Ezra	Ezekiel
Deuteronomy	Nehemiah	Daniel
Job	Isaiah	
Joshua	12 Minor	The Peshitta also
Judges	Prophets	contained
I Samuel	Hosea	most of the apocryphal
II Samuel	Amos	books and the
I Kings	Micah	Book of Syriac.
II Kings	Joel	
I Chronicles	Obadiah	------------------------------------
II Chronicles	Jonah	(Orr, James (ed.).
Psalms	Nahum	International Standard Bible
Proverbs	Habakkuk	Encyclopedia, 1915. (vol. 5)
Ecclesiastes	Zephaniah	p. 2883.)
Ruth	Haggai	
	Zechariah	

ENGLISH TRANSLATIONS:

This brings us to English translations of the Bible. The most famous English translation is the King James Version authorized by King James I of England (also called King James VI of Scotland, and King James I of Ireland). He started out as King James VI of Scotland but when he became the king of England, he became the First James to rule England and thus King James I. It was actually the Church of England that translated the Bible from the Hebrew (Old Testament) and Greek (New Testament) into English, but they could not do it without authorization from the monarch, who was also the head of the Church of England. Thus, the translation became known as the King James Version (KJV) or Authorized Version of the Bible. The translation began in 1604 and was published in 1611. It follows the same order for the books as the Septuagint and the Vulgate. That means Ruth followed Judges in the order of the books.

The King James Version was not the first translation of the Bible into English, but it was the most widely distributed one. Before and since 1611, there have been over 80 other English translations of the Bible, most of them in the last century (see chart below). All of these translations put Ruth after Judges. None of them has disputed whether Ruth should be in the canon of the Bible.

LIST OF ENGLISH TRANSLATIONS:

ENGLISH TRANSLATION	DATE		ENGLISH TRANSLATION	DATE
Wycliffe Translation	ca. 1390		God's Word	1995
Geneva Bible	1599		New International Version	1978

17

ENGLISH TRANSLATION	DATE	ENGLISH TRANSLATION	DATE
Douay-Rheims Bible	1609	Simple English Bible (Morris)	ca. 1978
King James Version	1611	The Living Torah	1981
Quaker Bible	1764	New King James Version	1982
Thomson's Translation	1808	New Jewish Publication of America Version	1985
Joseph Smith Translation	1830	New Jerusalem Bible	1985
Webster's Revision	1833	Christian Community Bible	1986
Young's Literal	1862	New Life Version (Ledyard)	1986
Julia E. Smith Parker Trans.	1876	New Revised Standard Version	1989
Revised Version	1885	Revised English Bible	1989
Darby Bible	1890	Easy-to-Read Version	1989
American Standard Version	1901	21st Century KJV	1991
Rotherham Emphasized Bible	1902	New Century Bible	1991
Ferrar Fenton Bible	1903	The Scriptures	1993
Jewish Publication Society of America Version	1917	The Clear Word	1994
New Translation (by Moffatt)	1926	Contemporary English Version	1995

ENGLISH TRANSLATION	DATE		ENGLISH TRANSLATION	DATE
Lamsa Bible (by Lamsa)	1933		New American Standard Bible (updated)	1995
An American Translation (by Smith and Goodspeed)	1935		New Living Translation	1996
Westminster Bible	1936		Stone Edition-Artscroll	1996
Confraternity Bible	1941		The Living Nach (Yaakov Elman)	1996
American Standard Version	1944		Orthodox Jewish Bible	1996
Bible in Basic English	1949		Complete Jewish Bible	1998
New World Translation	1950		Third Millennium Bible	1998
Revised Standard Version	1952		Recovery Version	1999
Knox's Translation of the Vulgate	1955		Modern KJV	1999
Berkeley Version	1958		American KJV	1999
Children's King James Version (Jay Green)	1960		King James 2000 Version	2000
Judaica Press	1963		English Standard Version	2001
Revised Standard Version (Catholic)	1965		Holy Scriptures Version	2001
Amplified Bible	1966		Easy English Bible	2001
Jerusalem Bible	1966		The Message	2002
Modern Language Bible	1969		Comfort-Able KJV	2003

ENGLISH TRANSLATION	DATE		ENGLISH TRANSLATION	DATE
New American Bible	1970		Holman Christian Standard Bible	2004
New English Bible	1970		The Apostles' Bible	2004
New American Standard Bible	1971		New English Translation	2005
The Living Bible	1971		New Cambridge Paragraph Bible	2005
King James II Version (Green)	1971		Today's New International Version	2005
The Bible in Living English	1972		World English Bible	ca. 2005
Good News Bible	1976		New Authorized Version	2006
Today's English Version	1976		New Eastern Orthodox Bible	2007
An American Translation (Beck)	1976		New English Translation of the Septuagint	2007

The Bible has also been translated into numerous other languages over the centuries and none of these has ever disputed Ruth's place within the Scriptures.

RUTH AND THE NEW TESTAMENT:

Ruth is mentioned only once in the New Testament and it is the person and not the book that is mentioned. Among the genealogy of Jesus in Matthew, we find "Boaz the father of Obed by Ruth" in chapter 1 verse 5. This is the same Boaz, Ruth, and Obed spoken of in the book of Ruth. In fact, we find the same genealogy from Perez to David in chapter 4 of Ruth as we find in Matthew 1:3-6.

We also find the genealogy of Christ in Luke chapter three. Although Luke's genealogy runs from Jesus' day backwards through time, we find the same genealogy in Luke 3:31-33 as we find in Ruth 4:18-22.

This is important as it shows us that at the time of Jesus, the Jews believed the book of Ruth was a reliable and inspired work. It also shows us the account of Ruth was believed by the writers of the New Testament as true and inspired of God.

MOAB AND SURROUNDING AREAS

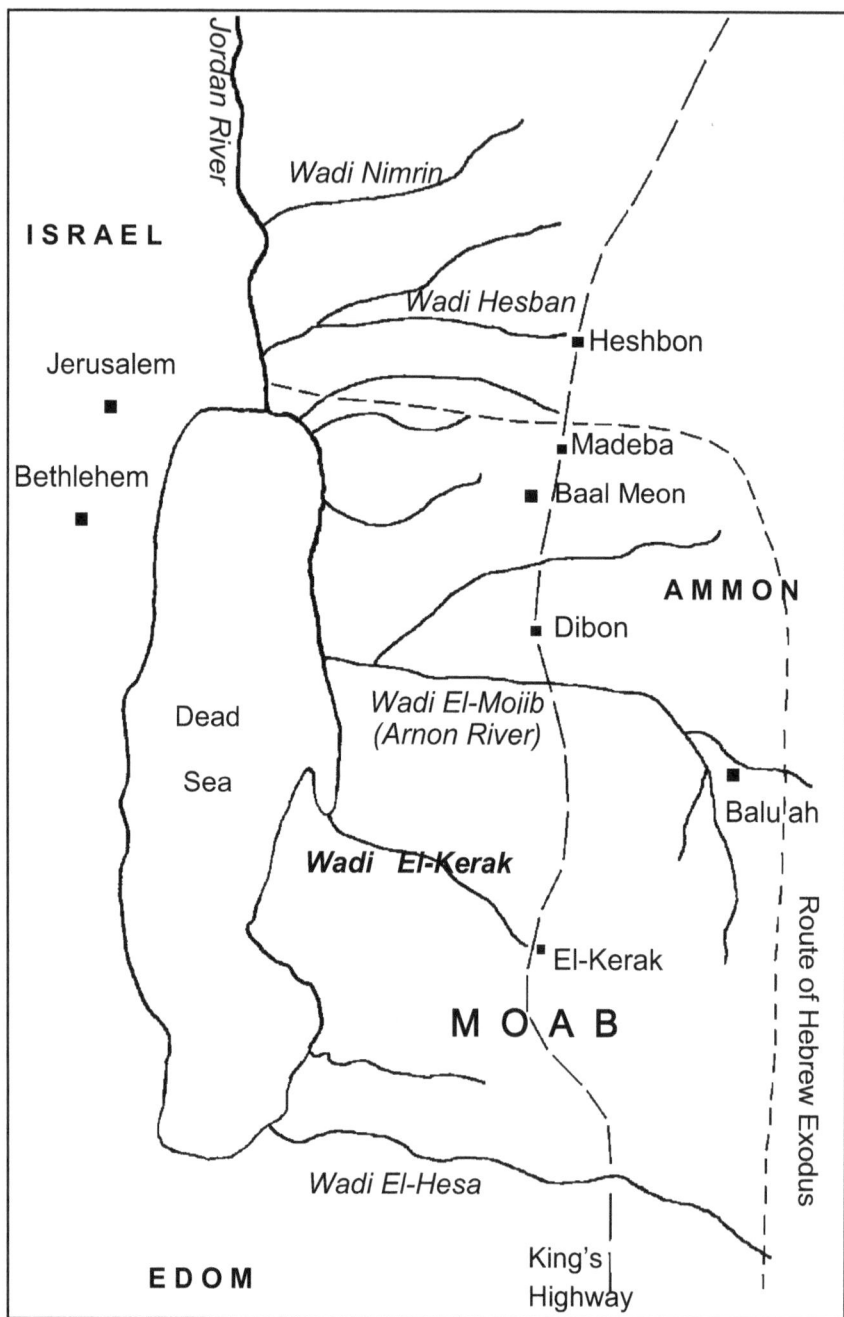

Chapter Two: HISTORY OF MOAB

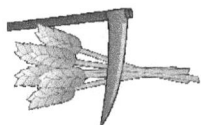

The Moabites have left us very little written evidence of their existence. To this date, only three inscriptions are known in the Moabite language: the Moabite Stone, the El-Kerak inscription, and the Balu'ah stele. The latter of these three is so worn and eroded that it cannot be read. The first two deal with the same king, Mesha, and his exploits. Since Mesha ruled Moab during the ninth century BC, he was one of the last kings of Moab. This leaves us with nothing written by the Moabites themselves that can tell of their origin or early nation. We must, therefore, rely on other sources for the information. Such sources consist of the archaeological data and written records of other countries or peoples who had dealings with the Moabites.

GEOGRAPHY:

The term Moab as used in the Bible refers more often to a group of people than to a solid location. However, the country where these Moabites settled became known as the עֲרוֹת מוֹאָב (Plains of Moab) which designated a specific geographic location. This is the region that in time came to be known as Moab. The southernmost boundary of the Moabite territory was the Wadi el Hesa or North Zered. (A Wadi is a riverbed that turns into a flowing river during the rainy season when the spring rains come, and completely dries up during the summer.) Nelson Glueck discovered a series of fortified outposts along both sides of this river, which can be dated to the Iron Age (approx. 1200 BC to 600 BC). This indicates that at least during the Iron Age this was a border between Edom and Moab.[6]

Although the northern boundary fluctuated, it extended at times as far north as the Wadi Hesban (Heshbon). At other times, the land of Moab extended only as far north as the Wadi Mujib or Arnon River.[7] There is some disagreement over the placing of the northern boundary this far south. Noth says the Moabites settled above the Arnon River from the very beginning. Part of Noth's argument comes from the Bible's description of Moses' death and burial in the land of Moab as found in Deuteronomy 34:1-8, and the description of the destruction of Heshbon in Numbers 21:27-30.[8] The evidence of surface surveys for occupation of this area during the Middle Bronze II to Late Bronze periods is almost non-existent.[9] However, because of the lack of any major excavations in this area this cannot be taken as a definite proof against occupation.

The western boundary was the Dead Sea. When Moab extended north beyond the Dead Sea, the Jordan River became the boundary. The eastern boundary was much less defined than the other three. The fertile territory east of the Dead Sea gradually thins out until it becomes desert. The Moabites probably used the land as far east as possible to graze their cattle, sheep, and goats, as did other peoples from time to time throughout the history of this land. The Moabites did not build fortified cities or even permanent dwellings in this area.

---

[6] Nelson Glueck, The Other Side of the Jordan (Cambridge, MA: American Schools of Oriental Research, 1970), p. 161.
[7] George Adam Smith, The Historical Geography of the Holy Land (London: Fontana Library, 1968), pp. 371-375.
[8] M. Noth, The History of Israel (NY: Harper, 1960), p. 83.
[9] Glueck, op. cit., p. 149.

The major occupied area of Moab was located between the Wadi Zered to and including the Wadi Arnon. The coastal regions contained fertile sections especially the southwest corner of the land and north of the Wadi Arnon. East of this coastal area was the area known as the highlands. In these highlands were fertile valleys and plateaus located north and south of the Wadi Arnon. This area was excellent for agriculture and raising animals. Raising sheep was a major occupation of the Moabites who would graze their flocks in the east during the rainy season in the spring and return to the western areas during the long hot summers.

The western section of Moab was well watered in the spring. During this rainy season the wadis flood, but during the dry season of the summer most of the wadis completely dried up. The Moabites had to depend on a few perennial springs, wells, and cisterns to get through the dry season. Irrigation was necessary for agriculture, the main crops being barley and wheat.

LANGUAGE:

We have very few examples of the Moabite language, but what we do have is very interesting. The most important example is the Moabite Stone found at Dibon in 1868. It contains thirty-four lines of writing. The only other major inscription was found at el-Kerak and contains only three lines. This inscription is fragmentary but appears to come from the same time as the Moabite stone – the ninth century BC. An inscription found at Dibon in 1951 was even more fragmentary, containing only two complete letters and four partial letters. The inscription also can be dated to the ninth century BC though it may be slightly older than the Moabite Stone.[10]

The language of the Moabite Stone and the el-Kerak inscription is very close to Biblical Hebrew. Driver says that it differs from Hebrew only as a dialect would differ from its mother language. It conforms to the style of syntax of earlier Biblical historical books.[11] The main features that Moabite and Hebrew have in common are the use of the vav-consecutive and the sign of the direct object אֵת.[12] Moabite also has some common characteristics, which link it grammatically with Ugaritic, Phoenician, Aramaic, and Arabic. However, none of these is as strong as the link with Hebrew.

The script of the Moabite language also has much in common with classical Hebrew script. The letters are written in a style that is comparable to stone inscriptions found in Old Phoenician and Aramaic that date to the eighth and ninth centuries BC.[13] The words are divided by dots. Sentences or thoughts are divided by strokes. When the inscription is translated into English, the English sentence structure does not always coincide with the Moabite sentence structure. This same use of dots between words can be seen in Hebrew in the Siloam inscription, which dates to the eighth century BC. We have no examples of Hebrew monument inscriptions or writings which date back to the ninth century BC at the present time.

---

[10] Roland E. Murphy, "A Fragment of an Early Moabite Inscription from Dibon," Bulletin of the American Schools of Oriental Research (Feb., 1952), pp. 20-23.

[11] S. R. Driver, Notes on the Hebrew Text and the Topography of the Books of Samuel (Oxford: Clarendon Press, 1913), p. xciii.

[12] John C. L. Gibson, Textbook of Semitic Inscriptions, Vol. I (Oxford: Clarendon Press, 1971), p. 74.

[13] Ibid., p. 72.

Although Moabite has some word forms in common with other Canaanite languages, the shortened vav-consecutive forms are only found in Hebrew and Moabite. The differences between Hebrew and Moabite may be due to the Moabites adopting words or idioms from other nations around them, much like some of the differences between the English spoken in the United States and in Great Britain.

RELIGION:

The Moabite religion bears many similarities to other Canaanite religions. From the names of cities in Moab, we can see the people worshipped a god called Baal locally. The city of Bamoth-baal found in Numbers 22:41 can be translated as "High place of Baal". We find a town called Beth-Baal-Meon in Joshua 13:17. The translation of the name is "house where Baal dwells" or "habitation of Baal", which showed these people worshipped Baal. The term Beth in Hebrew and in Moabite means "house", so these people considered their city to bo the house of their particular deity.

Besides these local gods worshipped during the early part of the Moabite nation, the Moabites worshipped a national god and goddess called Chemosh and Ashtar Chemosh (Moabite Stone, line 17). This god and goddess are believed to be the ones pictured on the stele (stone monument) found in the Moabite city of Balu'ah and dated to the thirteenth or twelfth century BC. Since the stele is eroded beyond any possibility of translation, we cannot be sure whether it depicts a god and goddess or King and Queen facing each other with a human worshipping them.[14] Van Zyl believes that Chemosh was the personal name of the god

---

[14] D. J. Wiseman, Peoples of Old Testament Times (Oxford: Clarendon Press, 1973), p. 244.

Baal, much the same as Yahweh is the personal name of the one true God worshipped mainly by Israelites at that time.[15]

Figurines believed to be male deities on horseback have also been found. These figurines are similar to figurines found in other parts of the Near East. They have been dated to the Iron Age. Figurines of the goddess Ashtar Chemosh found at 'Ayin Musa, el-Kerak, and other places depict a goddess of fertility holding a sacred object of fertility.[16] This is similar to the Canaanite goddess, Astarte.

Chemosh was most commonly thought of as a god of war. When he was angry with his people, they would be conquered by other nations. When he was pleased with the Moabites, they would win their battles. On the Moabite Stone King Mesha credits his victory to Chemosh's help in battle, and the previous oppression of Moab by Israel is said to have happened because Chemosh was angry with Moab (Moabite Stone, lines 4ff).

Like other Canaanite gods, Chemosh demanded sacrifices. Balak built altars and made animal sacrifices to Chemosh (Numbers 22:41, 23:1, 14, and 29). Bulls and rams were sacrificial animals. The king was the religious leader in Moab, although he was helped by priests (Numbers 23). The people of Moab participated in eating the meat of animals sacrificed to the gods (Numbers 22:40-23:2; 25:1-3; Revelation 2:14). They also indulged in sexual orgies and sacred prostitution as part of their worship ceremonies (Numbers 25:1-6).

In II Kings 3:24-27, we see that Chemosh also required human sacrifice. The king of Moab sacrificed his first-born son to appeal to Chemosh to help him win a battle. Human

---

[15] A. H. Van Zyl, The Moabites (Leiden: Brill, 1960), p. 199.
[16] R. K. Harrison, "Moab, Moabites", Merrill Tenney, ed., The Zondervan Pictorical Encyclopedia of the Bible, Vol. 4 (Grand Rapids, MI: Zondervan, 1975), p. 266.

sacrifice was not uncommon in Canaanite religions. Only in Israel was it forbidden. The Moabites also practiced a form of mass destruction of their enemies known as "herem". In this type of sacrifice, everyone captured at the fall of a city would be killed as a dedication to the god or goddess they believed had helped them defeat the city. On the Moabite Stone, King Mesha says he killed 7,000 people from the Israelite city of Nebo as a sacrifice to the goddess Ashtar Chemosh (Moabite Stone, lines 14-17). This also was a common practice among other Canaanite countries.[17]

Chemosh was worshipped at high places, as can also be seen from the Biblical descriptions and from the Moabite Stone on line 3. A high place was usually located on the acropolis of a city or just outside of a city on a high level of ground. At least one altar for sacrifices would be located there, but there could be more than one. Statues of gods and goddesses or simply a row of large standing stones was also located at the high place. High places have been found at many excavated cities, throughout Palestine. (Gezer and Hazor have two of the most noted high places in Israel. Recent excavations at Tell Dan have uncovered what appears to be a very good example of a high place there.) Solomon built a high place outside of Jerusalem where his Moabite wife could worship Chemosh (I Kings 11:7, 33; II Kings 23:13). Although no actual temple structure has been found within Moabite territory, temples were prevalent during the Iron Age among other Canaanite countries. On this basis, we can only assume that the Moabites also built temples to their gods.

Chemosh was the national god of Moab, but did not originate with the Moabite people. He existed as a deity at least 1,000 years before the Moabites became a nation. In

---

[17] For more detail on Canaanite gods and how they were worshipped, see Albright, Yahweh and the Gods of Canaan.

the third millennium BC, Chemosh was worshipped at Ebla and is mentioned in the tablets found at Tell Mardikh.[18]

ORIGIN AND PRE-MOABITE HISTORY:

The earliest recorded writings about the Moabite people come from the Biblical book of Genesis. Before the destruction of the cities of the plain, Lot and his family fled into the mountains near Zoar. While they were living in these mountains, Lot's daughters became concerned that there would be no heir to continue their father's name. They offered him wine until he was drunk and seduced him. The child born to Lot's oldest daughter was called Moab and became the father of the Moabite people. See Genesis 19:30-37 for the Biblical record of this event. The word Moab (מואב mô'âb) in Hebrew means "from her (the mother's) father". Even the name of "Moab" confirms the Biblical account of the nation's origin.

There is much discussion between archaeologists and Biblical scholars over the exact location of the five cities of the plain, which include Sodom, Gomorrah, and Zoar. They are believed to be located on the southeast side of the Dead Sea. At one time, it was speculated that the ruins of these cities were covered by the southern waters of the Dead Sea. With the drainage of some of the Jordan River in the late 1970's the Dead Sea dried up to an extent which allowed archaeologists to explore the southern area of the Dead Sea floor. With this exploration, it became evident that finding ancient cities which had been covered by the Dead Sea was highly unlikely. There was no evidence any cities had ever existed there.

---

[18] Mitchell Dahood, "Ebla and the Bible," A Lecture given at the Society of Biblical Literature Meeting, Dallas, TX, November 6, 1980.

Another more recent speculation is that Sodom was the current site of Tell el-Hammam. Tell el-Hammam is located on the eastern side of the Jordan River just north of the Dead Sea. There is no speculation as to where the other four cities of the plain are located. Tell el-Hammam is currently being excavated, so we will have to wait for those results, but at this point, it does not seem to be a city that was destroyed and

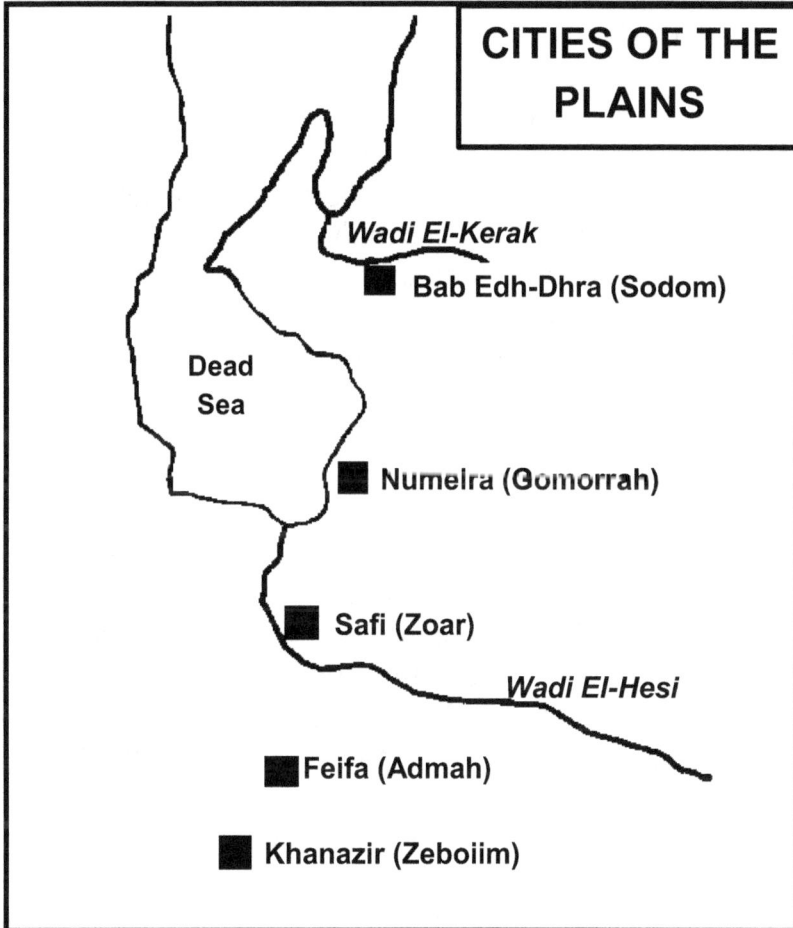

CITIES OF THE PLAINS

Wadi El-Kerak

■ Bab Edh-Dhra (Sodom)

Dead
Sea

■ Numeira (Gomorrah)

■ Safi (Zoar)

Wadi El-Hesi

■ Feifa (Admah)

■ Khanazir (Zeboiim)

never rebuilt. There is evidence of Roman ruins on the site, so it was at least rebuilt to some degree during that time frame. That in itself does not rule it out as Sodom.

Possibly a better site to look at is the ruins of a village known as Bab Edh-Dhra. The surrounding area has shown a different possibility for all five of the cities of the plain mentioned in the Bible. As can be seen from the map on page 48, the research of Walter E. Rast and R. Thomas Schaub has brought much to light about the area to the east and south of the Dead Sea region. They have found five cities all dating from the same Early to Middle Bronze period, which were destroyed and not rebuilt. Only Bab Edh-Dhra and Numeira have been excavated so far. Both show a layer of burned materials, which resulted in their total destruction.[19] It is likely from the reports on these two sites that Bab Edh-Dhra is Sodom and Numeira is Gomorrah. Safi is identified with Zoar on the ancient mosaic map located in a church in Madeba (in the area of Jordan today).

It was in the mountains of Zoar that Lot hid with his daughters after the destruction of Sodom and Gomorrah. If we can accept these five ruined cities as the Cities of the Plain mentioned in Genesis, this area where Lot's family lived is well within the boundaries of what later became the land of Moab.

According to Biblical archaeological dating, this would put Lot's lifetime within the Middle Bronze I period or about 2100 – 1850 BC. Surface surveys carried out by Nelson Glueck, Maxwell Miller, and others show that the land which later became known as Moab contained a high level of sedentary occupation during the Middle Bronze I period. At that time, the area was not known as Moab, nor were these people Moabites. They were not organized into a nation, but each large city had its own king or ruler. According to Biblical sources these peoples were known as Emim and lived in the land of Moab before it was taken over by Lot's descendants

_____

[19] "Have Sodom and Gomorrah Been Found?" Biblical Archaeology Review (Sept/Oct, 1980), pp. 26-37.

(Deuteronomy 2:9-11). The Emim were a race of giants. The Bible does not say that the descendants of Lot destroyed these giants, but only that they were destroyed before Lot's descendants became prominent in the land.

Glueck thinks this civilization, which built many unfortified cities, may have been established by the invasions of the Amorites.[20] The Amorites invaded this area coming from the east and north. This civilization has left behind the ruins of many unfortified cities, a few walled cities, many remains of houses, and much pottery. The most fascinating of objects left for the archaeologists to ponder are the *menhirs*, or *mezzeboth* (large standing stones). These stones are sometimes by themselves, sometimes arranged in rows or circles, and occasionally on platforms. Since they are occasionally accompanied by altars, it is believed they represent a high place or at least have a cultic significance.

THE MOABITE NATION:

During the Late Bronze I period (1550-1440 BC) civilization in Transjordan (the land on the eastern side of the Jordan River and Dead Sea) deteriorated sufficiently to be conquered by a new wave of semi-Bedouin tribes who developed more fortified cities and unified the country of Moab under a single king.

These people were the Moabites. The Moabites came into this land about 1550 BC. At first, they were settled into loosely united city-states. The city of Dibon is mentioned on the walls of the Karnak temple in Egypt at the time of Thutmoses III (1480 BC).[21] By the time the Israelites came to Transjordan on their way to the Promised Land in 1407 BC, the Moabite cities had developed into a united nation with one

---

[20] Glueck, op. cit., p. 143.
[21] J. Simons, Handbook for the Study of Egyptian Topographical Lists (Leiden: E. J. Brill, 1937), p. 112.

king to rule the entire country. The Israelites encountered a Moabite king named Balak, the son of Zippor (Numbers 22). The Bible does not say specifically that Zippor had also been a king of Moab, but since most thrones in Canaan were hereditary, we can assume with all probability that he did rule over Moab before his son, Balak. The Bible does say there was a king before Balak (Numbers 21:26). This makes Zippor the first Moabite king of which we have references. It is quite possible that Zippor was the first king of united Moab, but this cannot be proven at this time.

Balak was the king of Moab and their religious leader. He offered sacrifices to Baal without going through a high priest or any priest (Numbers 22:40). It is possible though that he had priests who served under him.

The northern portion of Balak's kingdom above the Arnon River had been conquered by Sihon, king of the Amorites. When the Israelites came into the land, they destroyed Sihon and took over these cities (Numbers 21). For this reason, Balak was afraid of the Israelites and sent for a prophet from Mesopotamia, Balaam, to come and curse the Israelites (Numbers 22-24). When this failed, the Moabites tried using the opposite method. They became friends with the Israelites and invited them to their sacrificial services for Baal and encouraged them to indulge in prostitution with the women of Moab (Numbers 25). The Israelites did not attack the Moabites at this time, but there was much animosity between Israel and Moab throughout the entire history of Moab because the Moabites had led the Israelites away from the worship of Yahweh into the pagan worship of Baal.

The next king of Moab we have any record of is Eglon (1319-1301 BC), who conquered at least part of the country of Israel and subjected them to pay tribute to him. An Israelite Judge named Ehud assassinated Eglon and led the Israelites in a successful revolt against the Moabites. The Moabites were then driven out of Israel back to their own territory. Even though the Israelites won the battle they did not take over any Moabite territory nor did they subjugate Moab to pay tribute to them (Judges 3).

During the time of Ramses II in the thirteenth century BC, we find Egypt came into contact with the Moabites. Moab is mentioned in the topographical list of a statue of Ramses II in front of the temple of Luxor.[22] The Balu'ah stele, from this period of Moabite history, also shows the Egyptians had much influence on the territory of Moab.

Another reference to Moab is in the Biblical book of Ruth. Ruth, a Moabite woman, had married an Israelite man whose family had moved to Moab because of a famine in Israel. After the death of her husband, father-in-law, and brother-in-law, Ruth traveled to Israel with her widowed mother-in-law, Naomi. In Israel Ruth married a close relative of her husband named Boaz. At the time of Ruth's life, there was peace between Moab and Israel. Ruth's story takes place during the approximately 300 years when the Judges ruled in Israel (from the death of Joshua about 1375 BC until the time of Samuel about 1075 BC). Only during peaceful times would a family migrate from Israel to Moab to escape a famine, and only during peaceful times would two women have been able to travel alone between the two countries.

This peace was in serious trouble during the reign of Saul in Israel. Israel's first king Saul fought against the Moabites (I Samuel 14:47). We have no record that Saul captured any Moabite territory, nor made the Moabites pay any tribute to him. It would seem the battles between Moab and Israel during Saul's reign were just border skirmishes, and did not develop into any major wars. Toward the end of Saul's reign when he was trying to find and kill David, David took his parents to the king of Moab and left

---

[22] Ibid., p. 155.

them in his care. This was done to protect them from King Saul's deep hatred of David (I Samuel 22:3).

Saul's successor, David, was more aggressive and more successful against the Moabites. David's armies defeated the Moabites and made them pay tribute to Israel (II Samuel 8). David even appointed governors to rule Moab. Joash and Saraph were two of the Israelite men who ruled Moab according to I Chronicles 4:22. They may have been the only Israelite governors of Moab. They are the only two mentioned in the Biblical records.

Since King Omri of Israel had to recapture the Moabite territory, one must assume the Moabites regained their freedom after King David's oppression. During the tenth century BC, Israel went through a period of internal tumult. The country split into two separate countries: Israel - the northern kingdom, and Judah – the southern kingdom. This would have been an opportune time for a vassal kingdom to regain its independence. While Israel was so involved with internal problems, they would not have put an enormous effort into holding on to the small vassal kingdom of Moab.

Moab was again forced to pay tribute to Israel during the reign of Omri (885-874 BC) as told in the Bible and on the Moabite Stone. II Kings 3:4 says Mesha paid 100,000 lambs and the wool of 100,000 rams to the king of Israel. On the Moabite Stone Mesha, king of Moab, says he rebelled against Israel during the reign of Omri's son which many people have taken to mean during the reign of Ahab. This is not the only possible interpretation of this phrase. Because the throne was hereditary any king that followed Omri would be thought of as his son or descendent, not just the immediate successor. This would seem to be a more reasonable explanation of what Mesha was referring to since line eight of the Moabite Stone says Omri and his son ruled over Moab forty years. Omri ruled Israel from 885 to 874 BC, a period of eleven years. Ahab ruled from 874 to 853 BC, a period of twenty-one years. If we add these together, we get only thirty-two years. Since it is not likely the first move a new king would make would be to conquer another country, we must assume that Omri spent a year or two handling domestic affairs that would normally arise as a result of a new monarch coming to power. This would leave us with only about thirty years for the oppression.

Yet, Mesha says the oppression lasted forty years (Moabite Stone, line 8). A king as proud as Mesha would not exaggerate the amount of time he was in subjection to

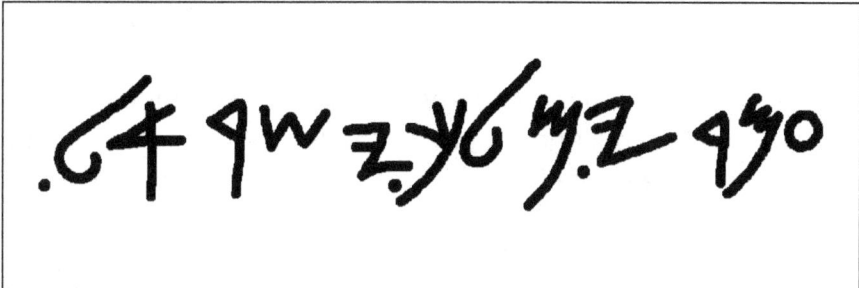

Mesha Stele (Moabite Stone): Omri, king of Israel as mentioned in the Moabite inscription (context: Omri king [of] Israel humiliated /the/ Moab [for] many days). Transliteration (modern Hebrew characters): [line 4:] עמר [line 5:] ישראל מלך י

From (2008): http://en.wikipedia.org/wiki/Image:Omri.melek.israel.gif
[I, Brave Heart, the copyright holder of this work, hereby release it into
the public domain. This applies worldwide. I grant anyone the right to
use this work for any purpose, without any conditions, unless such
conditions are required by law.]

another country. He would be more likely to reduce it or round it off to a lower number, but not to state it as more years. For this reason, we would put the rebellion of Mesha during the reign of Jehoram of Israel. The writer of the book of Kings says the rebellion of Moab took place after the death of Ahab (II Kings 1:1). It also says Jehoram rallied all of Israel to fight against Moab (II Kings 3:6). Jehoram was not the immediate successor of Ahab. Ahaziah, the older brother of Jehoram, ruled for two years before him (see I Kings 22:51).

Jehoram allied his army with the armies of Judah and Edom to attack Moab from the south. They destroyed several Moabite cities. As a last desperate measure Mesha sacrificed his oldest son to the god Chemosh on the city wall were all could see (II Kings 3:27). This rallied the Moabite people to the aid of their king and they managed to gain their independence.

According to the Moabite Stone (lines 20-31) Mesha was a great builder. He rebuilt city walls, palaces, high places, and even added cisterns in cities where water was limited. He also built and repaired roads. With all the building activity and wealth of Mesha, Moab became a prosperous nation.

After Mesha's death, Moab declined to such an extent that Shalmaneser III (king of Assyria from 859-824 BC) did not even recognize it as a nation. On a monolith of Shalmaneser III, Edom and Ammon (countries north and south of Moab) are mentioned while Moab is not. If Moab had still been a powerful nation, Shalmaneser would certainly have mentioned it in connection with its two neighbors.[23] The people were still there, but its power had dwindled to such a degree that Shalmaneser either just marched his armies through it without resistance, or they just did not think it worth conquering.

By 733 BC, Moab had regained some of its prominence, so Tiglath-Pileser III (king of Assyria) accepted tribute from Salamanu who was king of Moab.[24] Moab was never a free nation after this. While Assyria did not directly interfere with internal matters in Moab, it did expect Moab to

---

[23] Van Zyl, op. cit., p. 146, n. 1.
[24] Ibid., p. 149.

38

pay tribute annually. As long as the kings of Moab paid their tribute on time to Assyria they were allowed to carry on their usual business, even to expand their kingdom providing it did not interfere directly with Assyria's own expansion program.

Moabite laborers are listed on Prism B of Esarhaddon (king of Assyria from 681-669 BC) showing that Moab sent men to Assyria to help with building projects there.[25] The Moabites were also required to help Assyria with her battles, so Moabite men were sent to Assyria to become soldiers and fight with their armies wherever Assyria wanted them to fight. The Rassam Cylinder of Ashurbanipal (son of Esarhaddon, who reigned from 669 – ca. 631 BC or 627 BC) lists Moab among the nations that sent men to strengthen his armies (Rassam Cylinder, I, 69-74).

Moab regained power under Assyrian rule. During the reign of Ashurbanipal, the Moabite king, Kamoshalta, defeated the Arabs who were trying to take over Moabite territory. Ashurbanipal on his Cylinder B attributes the victory to the king of Moab rather than to himself. This indicates the king of Assyria had great respect for the king of Moab, and Moab had indeed regained much power.

Moab remained a vassal of Assyria until its destruction. After the battle of Carchemish in 605 BC, Nebuchadnezzar of Babylon made a trip to Palestine to establish his power over that territory. At this time, Moab as a loyal vassal paid tribute to Nebuchadnezzar. The Moabites sent armies to help Nebuchadnezzar fight Jehoiakim of Judah (II Kings 24:1-4). However, in 589 BC, Moab joined forces with the kings of Egypt, Edom, Ammon, Tyre, Sidon, and Judah to revolt against Nebuchadnezzar. The revolt was crushed by Nebuchadnezzar's army, and again Moab paid tribute to Babylon.

---

[25] Ibid., p. 152.

In 582 BC, Nebuchadnezzar's army attacked Moab and Ammon subjecting them totally to Babylonian domination.[26] Moab never regained the strength to become a threat to any country and disappeared as a nation, partially because of the Babylonian defeat and partially because the nomads raided the country after Babylon destroyed its major fortified cities. This was the end of Moab as a country.

---

[26] Josephus, <u>Antiquities of the Jews</u>, X. 9. 7.

MOABITE STONE
(MESHA STELE)

Description:

Language: Moabite
Medium: basalt stone stele
Size: 1.15 meters high by 60 to 68 centimeters wide
Lines: 34 lines of writing
Subject: Mesha, king of Moab (late 9th century BC)
Approx. Date: 830 BC
Place of discovery: Dhiban (part of Jordan today)
Date of discovery: 1868
Current Location: Louvre Museum (Paris, France)

Circa 1891 photograph of the 9th century BC Mesha Stele (also called the Moabite Stone), inscribed in the Moabite language by king Mesha of Moab. *[This media file is public domain in the United States (2008). http://en.wikipedia.org/wiki/Image:Mesha_stele.jpg]*

MOABITE STONE TRANSCRIBED INTO MODERN HEBREW CHARACTERS

1. אנכ . משע . בנ . כמש... מלכ . מאב . הד
2. יבני | אבי . מלכ . על . מאב . שלשנ . שת . ואנכ . מלכ
3. תי . אחר . אבי | ואעש . הבמת . זאת . לכמש . בקרחה | נ]בס . י[
4. ש . ע . כי . השעני . מכל . המלכנ . וכי . הראני . בכל . שנאי | עמר
5. י . מלכ . ישראל . ויענו . את . מאב . ימנ . רבן . כי . יאנפ . כמש . באר
6. צה | ויחלפה . בנה . ויאמר . גמ . הא . אעכו . את . מאב | ובימי . אמר . כ[...]
7. וארא . בה . ובבנתה . וישראל | ישראל . אבד . אבד . עלמ . וירש . עמרי . את א[ר]
8. צ . מהדבא | וישב . בה . ימה . וחצי . ימי . בנה . ארבענ . שת . וי
9. בה . כמש . בימי | ואבנ . את . בעלמענ . ואעש . בה . האשוח . ואבנ
10. את . קריתנ | ואש . גד . ישב . בארצ . עטרת . מעלמ . ויבנ . לה . מלכ . י
11. שראל . את . עטרת | ואלתחם . בקר . ואחזה | ואהרג . את . כל . העמ [מ]
12. הקר . רית . לכמש . ולמאב | ואשב . משמ . את . אראל . דורה . ואס
13. חבה . לפני . כמש . בקרית | ואשב . בה . את . אש . שרנ . ואת . אש . מ
14. מחרת | ויאמר . לי . כמש . לכ . אחז . את . נבה . על . ישראל | וא
15. הלכ . הללה . ואלתחם . בה . מבקע . השחרת . עד . הצהרמ | ואח
16. זה . ואהרג . כלה . שבעת . אלפנ . גברנ . ו]גר[נ | וגברת . וגר
17. ת . ורחמת . כי . לעשתר . כמש . החרמתה | ואקח . משמ . א]ת. כ[
18. לי . יהוה . ואסחב . המ . לפני . כמש | ומלכ . ישראל . בנה . את
19. יהצ . וישב . בה . בהלתחמה . בי | ויגרשה . כמש . מפני |
20. אקח . ממאב . מאתנ . אש . כל . רשה | ואשאה . ביהצ . ואחזה
21. לספת . על . דיבנ | אנכ . בנתי . קרחה . חמת . היערנ . וחמת
22. העפל | ואנכ . בנתי . שעריה . ואנכ . בנתי . מגדלתה | או
23. נכ . בנתי . בת . מלכ . ואנכ . עשתי . כלאי . האש[וח למ]ין . בקרב
24. הקר | ובר . אנ . בקרב . הקר . בקרחה . ואמר . לכל . העמ . עשו . ל
25. כמ . אש . בר . בביתה | ואנכ . כרתי . המכרתח . לקרחה . באסר
26. [י] . ישראל | אנכ . בנתי . ערער . ואנכ . עשתי . המסלח . בארננ
27. אנכ . בנתי . בת . במת . כי . הרס . הא | אנכ . בנתי . בצר . כי . עין
28. ----- ואנכ . בדיבנ . חמשנ . כי . כל . דיבנ . משמעת | ואנכ . מלכ
29. [ת] י] . ----- מאת . בקרנ . אשר . יספתי . על . הארצ | ואנכ . בנת
30. י. את . מה]דבא. ובת . דבלתנ | ובת . בעלמענ . ואשא . שמ . את . [...]
31. --------- צאנ . הארצ | וחורננ . ישב . בה . בה . ד
32. --------- אמר . לי . כמש . רד . הלתחמ . בחורננ | וארד
33. [וי]בה[...] כמש . בימי . ועל . ...[...] . משמ . עש
34. -------------- שת . שדק | וא

ENGLISH TRANSLATION OF THE MOABITE STONE

(Line 1) *I am Mesha, son of Kemosh[-yatti], the king of Moab, the*

(Line 2) *Dibonite. My father was king over Moab for thirty years, and I became king*

(Line 3) *after my father. And I made this high-place for Kemosh in Qarcho (or Qeriho)*

 (Line 4) *a sanctuary, because he has delivered me from all kings, and because he has made me look down on all my enemies. Omri*

(Line 5) *was the king of Israel, and he oppressed Moab for many days, for Kemosh was angry with his land.*

(Line 6) *And his son reigned in his place; and he also said, "I will oppress Moab!" In my days he said so.*

(Line 7) *But I looked down on him and on his house, and Israel has been defeated; it has been defeated forever! And Omri took possession of the whole land of*

(Line 8) *Madaba, and he lived there in his days and half the days of his son: forty years. But*

(Line 9) *Kemosh restored it in my days. And I built Baal Meon, and I built a water reservoir in it. And I built*

(Line 10) *Qiryaten. And the men of Gad lived in the land of Atarot from ancient times; and the king of*

(Line 11) *Israel built Atarot for himself, and I fought against the city and captured it. And I killed all the people of*

(Line 12) *the city as a sacrifice for Kemosh and for Moab. And I brought back the fire-hearth of his uncle from there; and I brought*

(Line 13) *it before the face of Kemosh in Qerioit, and I made the men of Sharon live there, as well as the men*

(Line 14) *of Maharit. And Kemosh said to me, "Go, take Nebo from Israel." And I*

(Line 15) *went in the night and fought against it from the daybreak until midday, and I*

(Line 16) *took it and I killed the whole population: seven thousand male subjects and aliens, and female subjects, aliens,*

(Line 17) *and servant girls. For I had put it to the ban for Ashtar Kemosh. And from there I took the vessels*

(Line 18) *of Yahweh, and I presented them before the face of Kemosh. And the king of Israel had built*

(Line 19) *Yahaz, and he stayed there throughout his campaign against me; and Kemosh drove him away before my face.*

(Line 20) *And I took two hundred men of Moab, all its division, and I led it up to Yahaz. And I have taken it*

(Line 21) *in order to add it to Dibon. I have built Qarcho, the wall of the woods and the wall*

(Line 22) *of the citadel; and I have built its gates; and I have built its towers; and*

(Line 23) *I have built the house of the king; and I have made the double reservoir for the spring in the innermost part*

(Line 24) *of the city. Now the innermost part of the city had no cistern, in Qarcho, and I said to all the people, "Each one of you shall make*

(Line 25) *a cistern in his house." And I cut the moat for Qarcho by using Israelite prisoners.*

(Line 26) *I have built Aroer, and I constructed the military road in Arnon.*

(Line 27) *I have built Beth-Bamot, for it had been destroyed. I have built Bezer, for it lay in ruins.*

(Line 28) *And the men of Dibon stood in battle formation, for all Dibon were in subjection. And I am the king*

(Line 29) *over the hundreds in the towns which I have added to the land. And I have built*

(Line 30) *Beth-Medeba and Beth-Diblaten and Beth-Baal-Meon, and I brought there . . .*

(Line 31) *flocks of the land. And Horonaim, there lived . . .*

(Line 32) *Kemosh said to me, "Go down, fight against Hauranen!" I went down*

(Line 33)............. *and Kemosh restored it in my days* ....

(Line 34) .... *So did I* ....

[Tranlation of the lines on the Moabite Stone. Taken from website: http://en.wikipedia.org/wiki/Moabite_Stone, 2008]

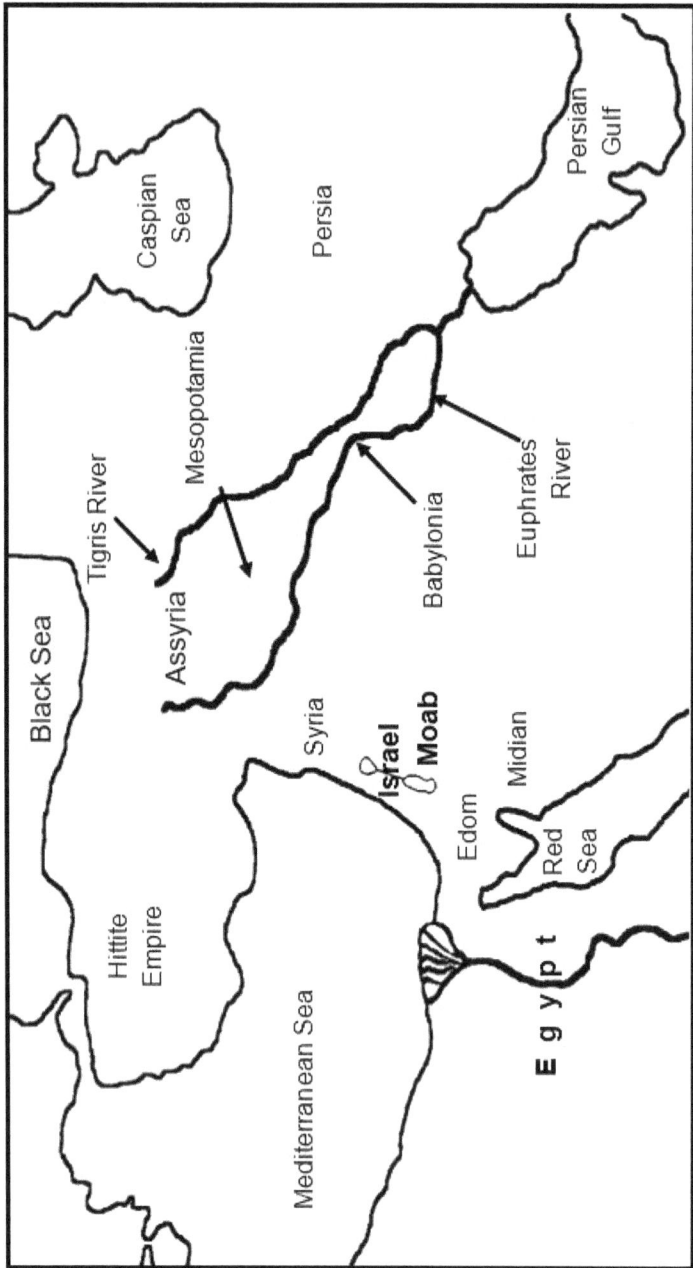

MAP OF NEAR EAST SHOWING MOAB

MOABITE HISTORY AS IT RELATES TO ISRAEL, EGYPT, ASIA MINOR AND MESOPOTAMIA:

DATE	ISRAEL	MOAB	EGYPT	MESOPOTAMIA and ASIA MINOR
1900 BC				Abraham and Lot leave Ur
	Abraham in Canaan	Birth of Lot's son, Moab[1]	XII Dynasty	First Babylonian Dynasty
1800 BC	Jacob in Egypt	Emim in control of pre-Moabite territory[2]	Hyksos Invasion	
1700 BC	Canaanite city states	Emim civilization deteriotrated[3]	Hyksos rule	Mari Age
				Hammurabi
1600 BC	Hyksos control	No major force in control of the land which was occupied by Bedouins and nomads[4]	Hyksos rule	Decline of Babylon
	Egyptian control	Moabites move into the land and take control[5]	XVIII Dynasty	Old Hittite Empire
			Ahmose (1570-1546 BC)	
1500 BC	(Moses born in Egypt)		Expulsion of Hyksos	

47

DATE	ISRAEL	MOAB	EGYPT	MESOPOTAMIA and ASIA MINOR
1400 BC	The Exodus (1447 BC) Moses; Conquest of Canaanites in Promised Land (1407 BC) Joshua	Zippor, king of Moab[6]; Dibon mentioned on Karnak Temple[7]; Sihon, king of Amorites takes Moabite territory[8]; Balak, king of Moab[9]	Thutmoses II; Amenhotep II; Thutmoses III (1480 BC)	Kingdom of Mitanni
1300 BC	Hebrews settle in Palestine (Promised Land) Judges rule Israel... Judge: Othniel Judge: Ehud		Tut-ankh-amen	New Hittite Empire; Rise of Assyria
1200 BC	Judge: Ehud (cont.); Judge: Shamgar; Judge: Deborah	Eglon, king of Moab[10]; Israel under Moabite rule[11]; Eglon assassinated by Ehud[12]; Moab mentioned on temple of Luxor in Egypt[13]; Moabites driven out of Israel[14]	XIX Dynasty; Seti I; Rameses II (1290-24 BC)	Hittite king Hattusili; Assyrian Dominance: Adad-nirari (1298-66 BC) Shalmaneser III (1265-36 BC)

DATE	ISRAEL	MOAB	EGYPT	MESOPOTAMIA and ASIA MINOR
	Judge: Gideon	Balu'ah Stele[15]	XX Dynasty	Hittites: Suppiluliuma II king
		Ruth leaves Moab with Naomi[16]	Rameses III (1175-44 BC)	Collapse of Hittites
	King: Abimelech (Shechem)			Assyrian Decline
	Judge: Tola			
	Judge: Jair			
1100 BC	Judge: Jephthah			
	Judge: Ibzan		XXI Dynasty	Assyrian Revival
	Judge: Elon			
	Judge: Abdon		Egyptian Decline	Tiglath-Pileser I (King of Assyria) 1116-1078 BC
	Judge: Samson	Saul drives Moabites out of his territory[17]		
	Judge: Eli			
	Judge: Samuel	David conquers Moab, Moabites pay tribute to Israel[18]		
	Period of Kings: (United Monarchy) King Saul			
	King David	Joash and Saraph are governors of Moab[19]		
1000 BC				

49

DATE	ISRAEL	MOAB	EGYPT	MESOPOTAMIA and ASIA MINOR
	King Solomon Divided Monarchy: Judah: Rehoboam to Asa Israel: Jeroboam to Nadab	Moab regains independence[20]	XXII Dynasty Shishak (935-14 BC)	Assyrian Decline Adad-nirari II (king of Assyria)
900 BC				
	Judah: Jehoshaphat to Johoash Israel: Baasha to Ahab (874) to Jehoahaz	Chemosh-vat, king of Moab[21] Omri forced Moab to pay tribute to Israel[22] Mesha frees Moab from Israel[23] (Moabite Stone erected)	XXIII Dynasty Egypt weakens	Syria: Ben-Hadad I and II Assyrian Revival: Shalmaneser III (859-25 BC) Adad-nirari III (811-784 BC) Battle of Karkar
800 BC				

DATE	ISRAEL	MOAB	EGYPT	MESOPOTAMIA and ASIA MINOR
700 BC	Judah: Amaziah to Hezekiah Israel: Joash to Hoshea Conquest of Israel by Assyria	Decline of Moab[24] Salamanu, king of Moab, pays tribute to Assyria[25]	XXIV Dynasty Egyptian decline	Assyria: Shalmaneser IV Tiglath-Pileser III (745-28 BC) Shalmaneser V Sargon II Syria: Ben-hadad II Rezin
600 BC	Judah: Manasseh to Jehoiakim	Kammusunadbi, King of Moab, pays tribute to Assyria[28] Moab regains strength while under Assyrian rule[27] King Kamoshalta drives Arabs out[28] Moab is a vassal to Babylon[29]	XXV Dynasty	Assyria: Sennachrib Assur-Banipal Battle of Carchemish (605 BC) Fall of Nineveh and the Assyrian Empire (612 BC)

DATE	ISRAEL	MOAB	EGYPT	MESOPOTAMIA and ASIA MINOR
	Judah: Zedekiah	Moab helps Nebuchadnezzar defeat Judah[30]	Pharaoh Hophra	Babylon: Nebuchadnezzar II (605-561 BC)
	Judah conquered by Babylon	Moab, Egypt, Edom, Ammon, Tyre, and Sidon unite in unsuccessful revolt against Nebuchadnezzar[31]	Conquest of Assyria	
	Judah in exile	Nebuchadnezzar destroys Moab[32] Exiled, never to be heard from again[33]	XXVI Dynasty	Nabonidus
			Pharaoh Necho (609-594 BC	Fall of Babylon (539 BC)
500 BC				

52

NOTES FOR CHART OF MOABITE HISTORY:

[1]Genesis 19:30-37

[2]Deuteronomy 2:10-11

[3]Glueck, Nelson, The Other Side of the Jordan (Cambridge, MA: American Schools of Oriental Research, 1970), p. 143.

[4]No mention of this territory in the Armana tablets.

[5]We have no exact date for this. Since Moab was well settled and unified under a king when the Israelites first encountered them during the exodus near the end of the fifteenth century BC, we can assume they entered the land about a century earlier.

[6]Numbers 22; Joshua 24.

[7]Simons, J., Handbook for the Study of Egyptian Topographical Lists Relating to Western Asia (Leiden: Brill, 1937), p. 112.

[8]Numbers 21.

[9]Numbers 22; Joshua 24.

[10]Judges 3.

[11]Judges3.

[12]Judges 3.

[13]Simons, op.cit., p. 155.

[14]Judges 3.

[15]Glueck, op.cit., p. 158.

[16]Ruth 1

[17]I Samuel 14:47.

[18]II Samuel 8.

[19]I Chronicles 4:22.

[20]This time of tumult during the dividing of Israel into two countries was a perfect time for Moab to regain its independence.

[21]Moabite Stone, line 1. El-Kerak inscription, line 1.

[22]Moabite Stone and II Kings 3.

[23]Moabite Stone and II Kings 3.

[24]Both Edom and Ammon are mentioned by Shalmaneser III but Moab is not. Therefore, Moab must have been insignificant as a power during this time.

[25]Van Zyl. A. H., The Moabites (Leiden: Brill, 1960), pp. 37-38; 149. Nimrud Tablet, lines 7-13.

[26]Ibid., p. 151.

[27]Ibid., pp. 150-153.

[28]Cylinder B of Ashurbanipal, col. VIII, lines 31-44.

[29]II Kings 24:2.

[30]II Kings 24:1-4.

[31]Jeremiah 27.

[32]Josephus, <u>Antiquities of the Jews</u>, X. 9. 7.

[33]Jeremiah 48:7.

BIBLIOGRAPHY FOR MOAB:

Books:

Albright, William F. The Archaeology of Palestine. Baltimore: Penguin, 1960.

_____. From Stone Age to Christianity. Garden City, NY: Doubleday, 1957.

Albright, W. F. Yahweh and the Gods of Canaan. London: The Athlone Press, 1968.

Burrows, Millar. What Mean These Stones? New York: Meridian Books, 1957.

Donner, Herbert. Neue Quellen zur Geshichte des Staates Moab in der Zweiten Halfte des 8 Jahrh. V Chr. Berlin: Akademie-Verlag, 1957.

Driver, S. R. Notes on the Hebrew Text and the Topography of the Books of Samuel. Oxford: Clarendon Press, 1913.

Gibson, John C. L. Textbook of Semitic Inscriptions. (vol. I) Oxford: Clarendon Press, 1971.

Glueck, Nelson. The Other Side of the Jordan. Cambridge, MA: American Schools of Oriental Research, 1970.

Harding, G. Lankester. The Antiquities of Jordan. New York: Frederick A. Praeger, 1967.

Josephus, Flavius. Antiquities of the Jews. (William Whiston, trans.). New York: A. L. Burt Company, Publishers, n.d.

Keller, Werner. The Bible as History. New York: Wm. Morrow and Company, 1956.

Kittel, Rudolf, ed. Biblia Hebraica. Stuttgart: Wurttembergesche Bibelanstalt, 1937.

Noth. M. The History of Israel (Stanley Godman, trans.). New York: Harper, 1960.

Pfeiffer, Charles F., ed. The Biblical World. Grand Rapids, MI: Baker, 1966.

Pritchard, James B., ed. Ancient Near Eastern Texts. Princeton, NJ: Princeton University Press, 1969.

Sayce, A. H. Fresh Light from the Ancient Monuments. London: Religious Tract Society, n.d.

Schoville, Keith N. Biblical Archaeology in Focus. Grand Rapids, MI: Baker, 1978.

Simons, J. Handbook for the Study of Egyptian Topographical Lists. Leiden: J. J. Brill, 1937.

Smith, George Adam. The Historical Geography of the Holy Land. London: Fontana Library, 1968.

Tenney, Merrill, ed. The Zondervan Pictorial Encyclopedia of the Bible. Grand Rapids, MI: Zondervan, 1975.

Thomas, D. W., ed. Documents from Old Testament Times. New York: T. Nelson, 1958.

Van Zyl, A. H. The Moabites. Leiden: Brill, 1960.

Wiseman, D. J. Peoples of Old Testament Times. Oxford: Clarendon Press, 1973.

Periodicals:

Bartlett, J. R. "The Historical Reference of Numbers XXI. 27-30." Palestine Exploration Quarterly (July-Dec., 1969), 94-100.

Glueck, Nelson. "Some Ancient Towns in the Plains of Moab," Bulletin of the American Schools of Oriental Research (Oct., 1943), 7-26.

"Have Sodom and Gomorrah Been Found?" Biblical Archaeology Review, vol. VI, No. 5 (Sept/Oct, 1980), 26-37.

Liver, J. "The Wars of Mesha, King of Moab," Palestine Exploration Quarterly (Jan-June, 1967), 14-31.

Miller, J. "Archaeological Survey of Central Moab: 1978," Bulletin of the American Schools of Oriental Research 234 (1979), 43-52.

Miller, Max. "The Moabite Stone as a Memorial Stela." Palestine Exploration Quarterly (Jan-June, 1974), 1-18.

Murphy, Roland E. "A Fragment of an Early Moabite Inscription from Dibon," Bulletin of the American Schools of Oriental Research (Feb, 1952), 20-23.

_____. "Israel and Moab in the Ninth Century B.C." The Catholic Biblical Quarterly, (Oct, 1953), 409-417.

Tushingham, A. Douglas. "Excavations at Dibon in Moab, 1952-1953," Bulletin of the American Schools of Oriental Research (Feb, 1954), 6-25.

Winnett, F. V. "Excavations at Dibon in Moab, 1950-51," Bulletin of the American Schools of Oriental Research (Feb, 1952), 7-70.

Yamauchi, Edwin M. "Documents from Old and Recent Discoveries," Westminster Theological Journal. (Fall, 1978), 1-32.

Zadok, Ran. "Phoenicians, Philistines, and Moabites in Mesopotamia," Bulletin of the American Schools of Oriental Research (April, 1978), 57ff.

Other:

Dahood, Mitchell. "Ebla and the Bible," A Lecture given at the Society of Biblical Literature Meeting. Dallas, Texas, November 6, 1980.

Mare, Harold. "The Archaeological Survey of Central Moab," Newsletter of the Near East Archaeological Society (Winter, 1980).

Websites:

http://www.abu.nb.ca/ecm/topics/arch5.htm

http://www.christiananswers.net/q-abr/abr-a007.html

Chapter Three: THE PERIOD OF THE JUDGES

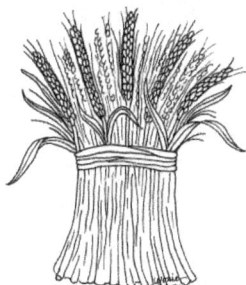

The book of Ruth starts by telling us an approximate time when the events took place, "In the days when the judges ruled ..." (Ruth 1:1) This was the time in Israel's history right after the Jews entered the Promised Land, and before the people of Israel had kings to rule over them. During this time, there were many people who served as judges over people in their local geographical areas, but there were several judges who held major roles in helping the people serve the Lord and Him only. Yahweh was the actual ruler/judge over the people of Israel, and he chose the Judges to be His voice to lead His people out of times of trouble. These Judges judged over a much larger portion of Israel, not just in one small geographical area.

The time in Israelite history when Judges ruled the people has come to be referred to as the "Period of Judges". It is not that judges did not exist in other periods, they did. In Exodus 18, we see that Moses was growing weary from trying to deal with the troubles and problems of over 400,000 Israelites in the wilderness. His father-in-law Jethro spoke to him about it and suggested he set judges over thousands, hundreds, fifties and tens. Small matters were brought to the judges of tens, larger matters to the judges of fifties, and so on until only the gravest disputes were brought to Moses. Also, in Deuteronomy 16:18 the Israelites were told to have judges and officers at every city gate in every village. These judges continued to judge the people even during the time of the monarchy in Israel. During the period of the Judges, one main judge actually ruled all the people, because there was no ruler (king or other) in the land. The Period of Judges lasted over 300 years from the death of Joshua until the time when Saul became king.

There were sixteen Judges during this time period. The entire period went something like this … The Israelites would worship God and Him only. They would have peace, prosperity, and rest. As time passed, they would forget that God was giving them this peace and protecting them from their enemies, and they would forget to worship God and Him only. Instead, they would look at the pagan nations around them and become curious about their false gods. They would start thinking, "These pagans look like they're having fun. I think I'll try it."

It is a lot like we do when a fellow worker says, "Hey, we're going to the bar after work to have a few drinks and relax. Want to come along?" At first, we say, "No thanks. I don't drink." Then we start thinking, "You know it sounds like they are having a lot of fun. I guess it would not hurt to go with them once in a while. After all I don't have to drink." The next thing you know, you are getting home late, and missing dinner with the family. Then one day you oversleep and get to work late with a hangover. Now your boss tells you if you keep it up, you will be fired. You have to do something. This cannot go on, but what? How do you stop? You need help. Where can you go? You appeal to the Lord for help. This is just what Israel did … appeal to the Lord for help from their punishment.

When the Israelites would forget about Yahweh and start worshipping false idols or otherwise ignoring God's laws,

God would punish them by allowing the land to stop producing food (famines), or allowing enemy nations to conquer Israel and subjugate them. After a time, the Israelites would realize why they were being punished and appeal to Yahweh for help. At these times, Yahweh would send a Judge to lead the Israelites both spiritually and physically to fight off their enemies.

It was during a time of famine when the Israelites were not following Yahweh's laws, that Elimelek took his family to Moab. When the Israelites had returned to worshipping Yahweh, He ended the famine and Naomi brought her daughter-in-law Ruth back to Bethlehem. The book of Ruth does not tell us specifically which judge was ruling Israel when they came back, so we need to look at all the Judges and see which are likely candidates. We have four clues in Ruth as to when the events of the book took place: (1) the period of the Judges, (2) the famine, (3) Elimelek's family was in Moab 10 years, and (4) the genealogy at the end of the book which shows two generations between the entrance of the Israelites into the Promised Land and Boaz. It also shows three generations between Boaz and King David. First, let us look at the Judges individually and see what the Bible tells us about each.

Note here that Judges in Israel were not like judges in a courtroom in the USA today. While they did handle disputes between two people, or between two groups of people, they did not have a jury, lawyers, or courtroom. They did much more than just decide which person was right and which was wrong. It might be easier to think of a Judge of this period as a cross between a Prophet and a King. They ruled the nation and they spoke for Yahweh to the people and for the people to Yahweh.

OTHNIEL (Judges 3:5-11):

After Joshua's death, the Israelites turned away from Yahweh's laws. They allowed their sons to marry pagan women who corrupted them. They allowed their daughters to marry foreign men who in turn began to worship the foreign false gods. This displeased God so He allowed a foreign power to conquer Israel. This foreign power was Cushan-Rishathaim, King of Mesopotamia. Mesopotamia was to the east of Israel and while it usually refers to the land between the Tigris and Euphrates Rivers, it does extend outward from that area, depending on the strength of the king controlling it. King Cushan-Rishathaim was obviously a powerful ruler in Mesopotamia at this time, because he extended his kingdom westward into Israel. He controlled Israel for eight years. During this time the people cried out to God to help them.

Othniel was sent by God to do just that ... help Israel out of their troubles. With the Lord's help, Othniel led the men of Israel to battle against Cushan-Rishathaim and they defeated him. Not only did they defeat him, but they drove him completely out of Israel and back to Mesopotamia.

Who was Othniel? He was from the tribe of Judah. He was the younger brother of Caleb. Caleb was one of the original twelve spies Moses sent to check out the Promised Land. He and Joshua were the only two who reported back to the people, that with the Lord's help, they could conquer the peoples living in the Promised Land. Obviously, Othniel came from a family who was serious about worshipping God.

You can read more about Othniel in Joshua 15 and Judges 1, where it tells of how Caleb promised his daughter Achsah to the man who would conquer the city of Kirjath-Sepher for him. Kirjath was in the territory given to Caleb for his inheritance in the Promised Land and he was busy conquering other cities in his territory, so he challenged others to conquer that city for him. Othniel took Caleb up on his offer, conquered Kirjath-Sepher, and presented it to Caleb. Caleb being an honest man gave Achsah to Othniel and they were married.

Therefore, we know that Othniel was a righteous man, a man of valor, and a leader of men. God chose a man to lead or judge the people who had already proven he was a righteous leader. He judged Israel for 40 years during which the people of Israel followed God's laws and had peace and prosperity. After his death, things changed again. There is no mention of a famine during Othniel's judgeship, and it is too close to the time of Joshua's death for Ruth to fit into the time of this Judge.

EHUD (Judges 3:12-30):

The people of Israel again began to forget about God and all He had done for them. They worshipped the pagan gods and forgot Yahweh. Moabite King Eglon joined forces with the Ammonites and the Amalekites to fight against Israel. Apparently, Moab was the strongest of these nations, because the Bible says King Eglon of Moab ruled Israel. It says nothing about the Ammonites and the Amalekites after Israel was conquered. They probably took animals and property from the conquered Israelites and went home to their country.

King Eglon was ruler over Israel for 18 years, during which the Israelites paid tribute to him. This tribute was brought to him on a regular basis. We are not told how often that was, but it was at least annually, because they would take a percentage of the harvest as part of the tribute. Apparently Eglon was present when the tribute was brought and accepted it personally, probably so he could gloat over the conquered people who brought it, and remind them that he allowed them to live to serve him.

Again, the Israelites cried out to God to help them, and He did. Ehud was the son of Gera. He was from the tribe of Benjamin. The most unusual thing about him was that he was left-handed. In those days being left-handed was as rare as it is today (maybe even more rare), so it is worth noting for its rarity as well as how Ehud used it to fool King Eglon's guards.

The Bible tells us Ehud made a dagger. I am sure he could have bought one, but remember he was left-handed. Daggers as well as other weapons and tools were made primarily for right-handed people. After all, that is what the majority of people are and were ... right-handed. Being a left-handed person myself, I understand well how that works. Ehud made his own dagger, so it would be easy for him, a left-handed person, to use it. This dagger was 18 inches long and double-edged. It fit quite nicely under his clothing strapped to the inside of his right thigh. This too, was done because he was left-handed and could get the dagger more quickly if it was on his right thigh than he could have if it was on his left, as the majority of the people would do. We can also figure that Ehud must have been a tall man to have an inside thigh length that was longer than 18 inches. He had to be well over six feet tall. He was a man that stood out among men.

With that dagger strapped to the inside of his right thigh, he took the tribute to King Eglon. It was not just Ehud alone. He had others who helped with the load as it would have been a pretty good size load that Eglon demanded. Ehud and his group took the tribute to the Moabite king. Naturally, when they came into the court of the king, they were searched. This searching was done by right-handed men, who never gave a thought to anyone being anything but right-handed. They searched the Hebrews, but only searched the inside of their left thigh to see if a weapon was hidden there. After all, no right-handed man would strap a weapon to the inside of his right thigh. It would be too awkward to get to when it was needed.

After the Hebrews presented their tribute to King Eglon, Ehud sent his fellow Hebrews away, perhaps to give them a head start home. Judges chapter 3 verse 19 in the King James Version of the Bible, says he then turned away from the "quarries". The Hebrew word here actually means "carved images". The Modern English Version says "stone idols". King Eglon tried to further demoralize the conquered Hebrews by making them leave their tribute at the feet of the carved images of the Moabite gods.

Now that Ehud had left the tribute and sent his men away, he turned to Eglon and told him he had a secret message for him. Eglon was immediately intrigued so he sent his servants away, and led Ehud to an upper chamber of his private quarters. There alone with Eglon, Ehud made his move. It was not difficult for Ehud to be faster moving than Eglon. Eglon is described as fat and that is indeed an understatement. Eglon was so fat, Ehud's whole dagger (all 18 inches plus the hilt) went into him and the fat came out and concealed it, even the handle.

Ehud then locked the doors to the King's chambers and made his way out the window, over the porch and away from the city. King Eglon's servants came up to check on him but noticed the doors locked and figured he was in the bathroom, or what served as a bathroom in those days, so they did not bother him. Meanwhile he lay on the floor dying. By the time, his servants realized it had been too long for him to be finished, he was dead, and Ehud was long gone.

When Ehud got to the town of Seirah, he blew a trumpet which was the signal for the Ephraimites to join him in attacking the Moabites. They completely ran the Moabites out of Israel's territory all the way to the Jordan River, but stopped there. During the battle they killed 10,000 Moabite men.

Ehud's time as judge of Israel totaled 80 years. The Bible does not say Ehud lived for 80 years, but just that the land had peace for 80 years which indicates that Ehud judged Israel for that long. He actually lived longer … perhaps to be over 100 years old.

Although many writers like to put Ruth during Ehud's judgeship there are two reasons why Ehud was not the judge of Ruth's time. First, it is unlikely a Hebrew family would have been welcomed in Moab at a time when Moab had conquered Israel. They would have been ridiculed and made into servants or slaves if they had moved to Moab during a time like this. Even after Ehud drove the Moabites out of Israel, the Moabites would have hated the Israelites even more for defeating them. This definitely would not have been a time when any Israelite family could have easily moved from Israel to Moab. The second reason Ehud could not be the judge of Ruth is that there is no mention of a famine during Ehud's time. In fact, it seems to be just the opposite of a famine. King Eglon wanted the Israelites to have prosperous crops, so they would have to give more to him as tribute. Both of these reasons make it unlikely Ruth lived within Ehud's judgeship.

SHAMGAR (Judges 3:31 and Judges 5:6):

There are only two verses in Judges about Shamgar and he is not mentioned anywhere else in the Bible. We do get a nice picture of Shamgar from the first verse though. He was a strong man, a hard worker, and he followed God. The verse simply says he was a son of Anath (who we also know nothing about); that he slew 600 Philistines; and he delivered Israel. We assume the enemy he delivered Israel from was the Philistines, since that is the only enemy nation listed in Judges 3:31.

We can infer from the description of his battle with the 600 Philistines that Shamgar was a strong man. He used an ox goad to slay them. An ox goad was a tool used by farmers. It was about eight feet long with a spike of iron on one end (used to urge the oxen on when plowing), and an iron scraper or spade on the other end (used to clean dirt off the plow). Use of this goad as a weapon needed a lot of strength physically, but for one who knew how to use it, it was a formidable weapon.

Considering Shamgar took on 600 Philistines in battle, shows his total faith in God's ability to give him the strength and ability to become victorious. He was able to show the Israelites that God does care for them and rally them to victory over the Philistines.

There is no mention of the Philistines holding Israel in subjugation. In addition, there is no mention of how long Shamgar judged the nation. It is possible the Philistines never actually conquered Israel, but simply kept Israel's western border busy with constant border skirmishes until Shamgar killed the 600 Philistines. That act by Shamgar may have been enough to stop them from bothering Israel. This could mean Israel had not been conquered by any nation and therefore did not need to defeat a more powerful nation. Shamgar may have merely followed Ehud as the next Judge or more probably, he was judging Israel at the same time as Ehud was ending his career as Judge. Shamgar's rule is joined with that of Ehud, totaling the 80 years that Israel had rest as stated in verse 30. He is the only judge, until Samuel's time, that is not given a specific number of years for his rule. Adding to that the wording at the end of Ehud's judgeship is very general, and since the next chapter starts with "And the children of Israel again did evil in the sight of the LORD when Ehud was dead", it is plausible that Shamgar's judgeship overlapped both Ehud's and Deborah's judgeships. In Judges 5:6 in the Song of Deborah it says, "In the days of Shamgar the son of Anath, in the days of Jael ..." which would put Shamgar alive in the time of Jael, the woman who killed

Sisera in the time of Deborah's judgeship. If Shamgar's judgeship overlapped the end of Ehud's and the beginning of Deborah's this would explain why we have no mention of a certain number of years for Shamgar's rule.

Yet again we have no mention of famines. Given the time frame purposed by the genealogy at the end of Ruth, we cannot put the book of Ruth during this Judgeship either.

DEBORAH (Judges 4-5):

Deborah was many things other judges were not. She was the only woman judge, thus showing the Lord does not regard women as inferior to men. She was a prophetess. She was the wife of Lapidoth (who we know nothing else about). As she was judging a local area of Israel, the Israelites as a whole again sank into evil ways, and God sent Jabin, the king of the Canaanites to conquer Israel. Jabin set up his headquarters in Hazor in northern Israel. He was a mighty king having 900 iron chariots. That is a lot of chariots, and since they were made of iron, rather than wood, they could withstand more attacks from the enemy. Jabin's army commander was Sisera. Together they oppressed Israel for 20 years.

Deborah called Barak from Kedesh in Naphtali and told him God was ordering him to take 10,000 men from the tribes of Naphtali and Zebulun and attack Jabin. Barak was willing to do this, only if Deborah would go with him. She did, but told him since he would not go on his own; he would not have the victory over Sisera himself. That victory would go to a woman, and she was not talking about herself! (Note that Barak was not a judge, but was the leader of the army.)

They went into battle and won, but Sisera escaped to the tent of Jael who invited him in to rest. She waited until he fell asleep, then used a tent peg and drove it through his head. The rest of the Canaanites, along with Jabin, were driven out of the land. After that Israel had rest for 40 years.

Deborah's time still does not seem right for Ruth's story to fit. There is no mention of famine or of the people being hungry, although famine is always a possibility during an oppression. Deborah could fit into a good time period for Ruth, because she ruled about 145 years from the time the Israelites entered Canaan. We could put two generations into 145 years easily. However, it seems unlikely that she was Judge during the time of Ruth, because she does not fit the other criteria. Although it is probable that Boaz was alive during Deborah's judgeship, not one commentary writer chooses her as the Judge of Ruth's time.

GIDEON (Judges 6-8):

After Deborah's judgeship ended, Israel again did evil in the sight of the Lord. For this, the Lord allowed Midian to conquer Israel and oppress it for 7 years. During this time the Israelites made caves, dens, and strongholds in the mountains to hide their food and other valuables from the Midianites. The Midianites would wait for the Israelites to plant their crops and cultivate them. At harvest time the Midianites would come along and steal the crops, or destroy them. They also took their own camels, sheep, and cattle into Palestine and allowed them to eat up all the grass in the fields, leaving nothing for the Hebrews' cattle and sheep to graze on. The Midianites lived east and south of the Jordan River and Dead Sea, in much the same area as Ammon, Moab, and Edom, though perhaps farther east and south than these three at times.

The Midianites were joined by the Amalekites and people of the east, during their raids into Israelite fields. These people of the east may have included Ammon, Moab, and Edom.

At this time, the Angel of the Lord appeared to Gideon in a winepress. Gideon was threshing what little wheat he had managed to grow, and he was doing it in the family winepress. The Midianites apparently would not think to look in the winepress for wheat. If they couldn't find it, they couldn't steal the wheat. It was a very unlikely place to be threshing wheat, unless you were trying to hide what you were doing, which was exactly what Gideon hoped to do.

Gideon was the son of Joash the Abiezrite from the tribe of Manasseh. He tore down the high place near his village and destroyed the images of Baal. He used the wood from this high place and images to create an altar to the Lord. This made the people of the village angry, so he told them to let Baal plead for himself, which of course he knew could not happen since Baal does not really exist. However, the people started calling him Jerubbaal which means "let Baal plead".

God used Gideon and an army of 300 Israelites to drive the Midianites out of Israel. Afterward the Israelites wanted to make Gideon king of Israel. He refused, telling them God rules over them, not Gideon. Unfortunately, his son, Abimelech did not feel the same way. After 40 years Gideon died and his son Abimelech set himself up as King over Israel in Shechem (see Judges 9 for an account of this King). He was an evil king. His last act before becoming king was to murder 69 of his 70 brothers. He would have murdered all of them, but the youngest hid and got away without him knowing it. He ruled for 3 years, and was killed in battle when a woman dropped part of a millstone on his head.

Right before Gideon's time, we have a period of famine when the Israelites were being oppressed by the Midianites and people of the east. During this time their crops were being destroyed before they could harvest them. Their animals (sheep, and cattle) had little or no grazing land. Judges says the famine (oppression) lasted for 7 years. Naomi and her family were in Moab for about 10 years before she heard the famine was over. This does not mean the famine lasted all of the 10 years, but that Naomi did not hear it was over until a few years after it ended. Most famines are caused by a lack of rainfall, but if lack of rain had caused a famine in Bethlehem, it would surely have affected Moab as well. If the famine in Israel was caused by raiders taking and destroying the crops, it would not necessarily have affected Moab. In addition, if Moab was a country unaffected by these raiders, it would have made it a very inviting place for Elimelek to take his family until the famine was over.

Again, allowing for seven years of oppression (famine) by the Midianites and their friends, and then giving a year or two for the Israelites to drive them out and plant new crops, as well as allow the pasture lands to re-grow grass, gives us nine years of famine. Naomi probably heard from a passing caravan that the famine was over in Israel. They did not have the internet back then, and every caravan that passed through Moab did not necessarily pass through Israel, so a one- or two-year span (or even three years) for the knowledge of the end of the famine in Bethlehem, to get to Naomi in Moab, was not unusual at all.

Given this information it is quite likely Ruth takes place right before and during the judgeship of Gideon. We also find that Gideon could fit into the timeline of the genealogy at the end of the book of Ruth. Since we do not have specific ages for the people in the genealogy, we cannot place the story in a particular year. Many commentators think Gideon was the likely judge at the time Ruth and Naomi came back to Bethlehem, but there is by no means a consensus of this opinion as we will see as we continue to look at the judges of Israel.

TOLA (Judges 10:1-2):

We know very little about Tola. We have his background, genealogical information but nothing else. He was the son of Puah and grandson of Dodo. He was from the tribe of Issachar and he judged Israel for 23 years. Nothing is said about any foreign oppression during his judgeship, so we can assume these were peaceful years for Israel. When he died, he was buried in Shamir. Shamir is believed to be a town in Mount Ephraim, but its exact location is unknown.

This is not likely the time of Ruth, because of the lack of oppression and no mention of Israel turning away from Yahweh to serve pagan gods.

JAIR (Judges 10:2-5):

Jair was a Gileadite but we have nothing about his family background. We do know he was wealthy. He had 30 sons who rode on colts of donkeys, and he had 30 towns called by his name. "Havoth Jair" means "villages of Jair". When he died, he was buried in Camon which was probably a family tomb.

There is no mention of the Israelites worshipping foreign gods, or forgetting to obey God's laws during his 22-year judgeship. We can safely assume the people and land were at peace and prosperous while he was judging them. Again, this judge does not fit the information we have in Ruth to consider him for the time period of Ruth and Naomi.

JEPHTHAH (Judges 10:6-12:7):

Between the time of Jair and Jephthah there is a period of 18 years when the people of Israel turned to pagan foreign gods to worship. They forgot about worshipping the Lord, and lived in their own sinful ways. The Lord gave them up to oppression from the Ammonites and Philistines. The Ammonites came from the east to conquer Israel and the Philistines came from the west. It was a difficult time for the Hebrews living under the oppression of these two nations. Apparently, the Ammonites were the worse.

The people cried out to Yahweh to help them but this time Yahweh said, "No". Yahweh explained to the Israelites that they had plenty of time to worship Him but they refused and He was not going to help them unless they gave up ALL pagan worship and turned to Yahweh only. Yahweh told them to cry out to the gods of Moab, or Ammon, or whatever nation they wanted for help, because He was through helping them unless they gave up ALL the other gods and only worshipped Him.

During these 18 years of oppression there was no judge in the land. Only after the people realized God was right, did they turn away from the foreign idols and turn back to worshipping the God of Israel only. At that time the people called to Jephthah to lead them. Jephthah is described as a mighty man of valor. His parentage was somewhat less valiant. His father apparently visited a prostitute and the result was the birth of Jephthah. Although he seemed to be raised by his father Gilead, his brothers (legitimate sons of Gilead and his wife) were selfish. They drove Jephthah away so he could not inherit anything of his father's. Yet Jephthah is still described as a "mighty man of valor". Even though an outcast from his family, everyone else knew he was not just a righteous person, but someone to be praised for his actions.

When the Ammonites made war against Israel again, they called Jephthah to lead them. One of the first things he did was send messengers to the Ammonites asking them why they wanted to attack Israel.   Their response was, "because when Israel came out of Egypt, they attacked Ammon and took their land." Now they wanted it back. Jephthah again sent messengers to the Ammonites, but this time he explained that Israel did not attack the Ammonites; the Ammonites attacked Israel when they were entering the Promised Land. He also said very plainly that it had been 300 years ago, and asked why it had taken them so long to want to get revenge.

The Ammonites would not listen but attacked instead. Jephthah's strategy of trying to talk with the Ammonites had given him enough time to gather an army of Israelites to fight. Before going into battle, Jephthah made a vow to the Lord saying if God would give him this victory over the Ammonites, Jephthah would give the Lord whatever came out of his house to meet him when he returned home and he would offer sacrifice to the Lord. The victory was won and Jephthah returned home to be met by his only child, a daughter coming out of the house to meet him. Jephthah kept his vow and dedicated his daughter to the Lord for the rest of her life.

Jephthah judged Israel for six years, during which time the Israelites worshipped only Yahweh. Jephthah's time could have fit the time of famine in Israel. Although the Bible does not mention a famine, it is possible the Ammonites and Philistines destroyed crops and took food from the people. This could have resulted in famine, but this is just conjecture. If that was the case, the famine would have lasted too long to fit the famine in Ruth, making it unlikely this is the time for the book of Ruth to take place.

IBZAN (Judges 12:8-10):

Ibzan is another judge we know little about. He was from Bethlehem and he had 30 sons and 30 daughters, all of which were married. He judged Israel for seven years and was buried in Bethlehem. He was probably pretty old when he judged Israel, since he had 60 married children by the time he started judging, and he only judged for seven years. There is no mention of any oppression during, before, or immediately after his judgeship, so we can easily understand that Israel was at peace with the surrounding nations when he was judging. We can reasonably say he died of natural causes, since how he died was not interesting enough to mention.

There were two towns called Bethlehem in Israel. One was located within the territory of the tribe of Judah in southern Israel and one within the tribe of Zebulon in northern Israel. The Bible does not tell us which one this was, so some commentators speculate it was one and some think it was the other. In Ruth 1:1 we see that Elimelek and his family were from Bethlehem in Judah, meaning it was the Bethlehem located within the tribe of Judah or southern Bethlehem. Most Jewish commentaries use the fact that Ibzan was from Bethlehem to say this was the judge of the book of Ruth. They will go even farther to say Ibzan was actually another name for Boaz and thus putting Ruth's life into this time period.

Other commentators will say this was the Bethlehem in Zebulon because the next Judge after Ibzan was from the tribe of Zebulon. Using the logic that one Judge followed another in his area, this could be right. However, we have no other evidence that God chose men or women as Judges based on the location of the previous Judge. In fact, the opposite is found more often. Saying Ibzan was from Bethlehem in Zebulon means he could not possibly be Boaz nor could Ruth fit into this time period. We just cannot say for sure if Ibzan was from Bethlehem in Judah or Bethlehem in Zebulon.

While it is true Ibzan is the only judge listed as being from Bethlehem, the Scriptures do not tell us which Bethlehem. There is also no reference in the book of Ruth to make us think that Boaz was a judge of Israel, nor to equate him with Ibzan if he was. Also, the time frame for Boaz to fit into this period would make him more than an old man ... he would have had to be very very very old to fit this judge's time period.

ELON (Judges 12:11-12):

We know even less about Elon than we did about Ibzan. We do know that he was from the tribe of Zebulon. He ruled Israel for ten years. After he died, he was buried in Aijalon in the territory of the tribe of Zebulon. Again, we are not told of any oppression or attacks on Israel during his time as Judge, so we can surmise Israel was worshipping Yahweh which resulted in peace and prosperity during the ten years of his rule.

ABDON (Judges 12:13-15):

Abdon's father was Hillel the Pirathonite from the tribe of Ephraim. He had 40 sons and 30 grandsons (note: KJV says "nephews", but could also be translated "son's sons" or "grandsons). All 70 rode on donkey colts. This would indicate that his family was wealthy as they owned 70 young donkeys. Now if they owned 70 donkeys, chances are they owned lots of other cattle (cows and sheep) as well as lots of land. It is reasonable to say this man was rich.

Having 40 grown sons who were married and many of them having sons of their own, means Abdon was also pretty old when he judged Israel. He judged for only eight years. Again, since there is no mention of wars in Israel or accidents, it appears he died of natural causes. He was buried near his home town of Pirathon in the land of Ephraim.

SAMSON (Judges 13-16):

The Hebrews again fell away from worshipping the true God, and instead did evil things like worshipping foreign idols, building graven images, and participating in the cultic practices of the nations around them. God allowed the Philistines to conquer and rule over Israel for 40 years. During this time Samson was born. Samson's father was Manoah. Manoah's wife was barren until the angel of the Lord appeared to her and told her she would conceive and have a child.

This child would be a Nazirite from the time of his birth. A Nazirite was not a tribe or associated with a location as in Nazareth. A Nazirite was one who had taken a vow to do three things:

1. Abstain from any form of wine, grapes, or even raisins.
2. Would not use a razor (on his face or head).
3. Never touch a dead body.

All this was vowed, that the person might serve the Lord. It could be for any amount of time from 30 days to a lifetime. Samson was a Nazirite from his birth. It was another way of showing his parents had concentrated him to the Lord's service. However, since the vow was made by his parents and not by Samson himself, we see that he did not take it as seriously as he should have.

Samson fell in love with a Philistine woman (a pagan) and got his father to arrange a marriage with her. On their wedding day she deceived him into telling her the answer to a riddle he had proposed to her friends. Then she told her friends so they won a bet against Samson. When Samson found out, he was angry. He had told them he would provide 30 changes of clothing for them, but since they cheated, he went out, killed 30 Philistines, and took their clothing to pay off the bet. He then left his wife, and her father gave her to another man to marry without telling Samson.

After that, Samson married a Philistine woman named Delilah (another idol worshipper). She also deceived him. Her deception was to get him to tell her how he got to be so strong. He in turn deceived her by lying to her two times, until at last she convinced him to tell her the truth … that if his hair was cut his strength would leave him. Delilah told her friends and they cut his hair while he was sleeping. After that Samson was taken prisoner by the Philistines. They blinded him and as a prisoner made him work as slave labor.

One day during a feast or holiday of the Philistines they brought Samson to the temple of their false god to show off to the people and leaders how they had captured the mighty Hebrew strongman. While everyone was being merry and enjoying the day's activities, Samson asked to be able to lean against the pillars that held up the temple. When he was led to the pillars, he prayed to God to give him the strength he had before his hair was cut, just one more time. God answered his prayer and Samson pushed the pillars until they fell. When the pillars fell, so did the whole temple, killing thousands of Philistines as well as Samson.

Samson judged Israel for 20 years, during which the Philistines were not driven out of Israel. They continued to subjugate and harass the Israelites for some time after Samson had died.

ELI (I Samuel 1 – 4:18):

Eli is the first judge of this period mentioned outside the book of Judges in the Bible. While some only count the Judges of Israel as the ones mentioned in the book of Judges, it is obvious that Israel continued to have Judges after the book of Judges ended. I Samuel 4:18 says Eli judged Israel for 40 years. It is likely he was judging Israel when Samson was born, so Samson's 20 years actually fall totally within Eli's judgeship.

We really do not know much about Eli except as he relates to stories about others. The first of these is the story of Hannah, who was barren and wanted a baby so badly she went to the tabernacle and prayed earnestly for God to give her a child. Eli was also a priest serving at the tabernacle. The priest Eli saw Hannah praying, but he did not understand what was going on with her since he could see her mouth move but did not hear any speech coming out. He assumed wrongly that she was drunk and rebuked her. When she explained what she was praying for, he offered her a blessing instead.

The child Hannah gave birth to was a boy and she named him Samuel which means "heard of God". The next time we read about Eli is when Hannah brings Samuel to Eli to dedicate Samuel to the Lord's work. Eli took him in and trained him to follow the Lord. You can read more about Samuel in the next section since he was a Judge also.

We find during Eli's time, the Philistines were harassing and fighting with Israel still. This is further proof that Samson's victory at the destruction of their temple did not completely drive them out of Israel. Instead, the Israelites were continuing to fight with them, and loosing miserably. (The Philistine menace lasted into the time of the Monarchy in Israel.) The Israelite army asked Eli to bring the Ark of the Covenant to the battle so the Lord could go before them. Eli was 98 years old and had grown fat by this time, so his sons, Hophni and Phinehas, went to the battle front and took the ark with them. Hophni and Phinehas died in the battle and the ark was taken by the Philistines. When Eli heard the ark had been taken, he fell off his seat resulting in a broken neck and his death.

SAMUEL (I Samuel 1-28:20):

As we see in I Samuel 7:15, Samuel was more than a Judge. Like Deborah, he was also a prophet. The Bible tells us more about Samuel than any other Judge. Circumstances of his birth are told along with his mother's visit to the tabernacle to pray that the Lord would give her a child. When Samuel was weaned, Hannah took him to Eli at the tabernacle to turn him over to the Lord. Every year she would return to the tabernacle and take him a new coat.

The Lord called Samuel in the night when he was still young. Samuel thought it was Eli who was calling him and kept waking Eli to find out what he wanted. Finally, Eli realized it was the Lord calling Samuel and told him to stay where he was the next time he heard his name, and say "Here am I, Lord". The Lord revealed to Samuel that Samuel would take Eli's place and that Eli and his sons would die soon. They did die in the battle with the Philistines as mentioned in the previous section.

The Philistines continued to battle against Israel during Samuel's time, until King Saul defeated them. Samuel anointed Saul king of Israel both privately and publicly. Samuel also continued to work with Saul, speak the words of God to him, and confront him about things done right or wrong for the Lord, until Samuel died ... actually even after he died.

Saul wanted to find out if the Lord would be with him in a battle so he went to the witch of Endor. Witches were forbidden in Israel, and consulting them was also forbidden by God. That is why Saul had to disguise himself when he went to see her. When she asked who he wanted to see from beyond the grave, he said "Samuel." To her surprise the Lord allowed Samuel to appear to Saul and tell him that he would not only lose the battle, but he and his sons would die in it.

Before Samuel died, he already knew the Lord had rejected Saul and his family from ruling Israel. At the command of the Lord, Samuel went to Jesse's home and anointed his youngest son, David to be the next king after Saul. This is the same Jesse and David who are mentioned in the genealogy at the end of the book of Ruth ... Ruth's grandson and great-grandson.

JOEL AND ABIAH (I Samuel 8:1-3):

Joel and Abiah were the sons of Samuel. Samuel (not God) appointed them Judges when he was getting older and felt he needed to pass the office on to someone else. We have no other records of anyone passing the judgeship on to a son, although Gideon's son certainly tried to become a king of Israel after Gideon died. We do not really know much about Joel and Abiah except they were evil. They accepted bribes and perverted judgment. They were the reason the Israelites asked Samuel to give them a king like the other nations.

As seen on the chart and map at the end of this chapter, the Judges came from many tribes within Israel. Yet the Bible says they ruled over ALL of Israel. Over and over when the Judges are spoken of it says, they judged Israel, or Israel went up to be judged, etc. It does not say only one tribe or only one section was judged by a specific Judge. The Bible does tell us what tribe most of the Judges were from, but when they judged, they judged all of the Israelites. God did not give one tribe rule over another.

The oppressors of Israel also came from a variety of places. God did not give one pagan nation the right to punish Israel. Instead He used all the alien nations left in the area to punish Israel's evil ways. He also did not allow any of the pagan nations to continue to punish Israel once Israel returned to worship the Lord.

WHERE DOES RUTH FIT INTO THIS PERIOD?

While there is much speculation about where Ruth fits into the period of the Judges, the truth is, we do not really know for sure, but as stated in the beginning of this chapter, we do have clues to guide us. Ruth 1:1 says "It came to pass in the days when the judges ruled ..." We have looked at the time when the judges ruled and it covers over 300 years, so we need to narrow it down.

The second clue is also in Ruth 1:1 which tells us there was a famine in the land of Israel, especially around and including Bethlehem. In Gideon's time there was famine in Israel, because the Midianites came from the east and took the crops as they ripened or destroyed them in the fields. They also took their own camels and other cattle into Israel allowing them to eat up all the grass.   The grazing lands were barren leaving nothing for the Israelite cattle and sheep.

Ruth 1:4 says Elimelek's family dwelled in Moab about ten years. Looking at Gideon again, we see the Midianites oppressed Israel for seven years. Allowing at least a year or two for the land to produce a good harvest again would make eight or nine years. Considering news traveling from one country to another took quite a bit of time, it is certainly acceptable for there to be a one- or two-year gap between the end of the famine and the news traveling from Israel to Moab. That would make ten years fit into this time frame. If Elimelek left Bethlehem at the beginning of the oppression, and allowing for news to travel by caravan to Moab, it could allow for about 10 years to pass before the news reached Naomi in Moab. That does not mean there was only one caravan that passed through during those two years, but that Naomi did not hear the news until that time. Most people in Moab would not be interested in what news came out of Bethlehem or even Israel.

The last clue comes from two places. Ruth 4:21 says, "Salmon begat Boaz and Boaz begat Obed." That allows for two generations from Salmon to Obed. We know from Matthew 1:5 that Salmon was married to Rachab (Rahab). Joshua 2 and 6:25 tells us the story of Rahab who was a prostitute in Jericho at the time the Israelites crossed the Jordan River. She helped hide the spies Joshua had sent out to secretly look over the city of Jericho. Therefore, we have a time period here that goes from the time of the Israelites entering the Promised Land under Joshua's leadership to the time of Obed's birth. Two complete generations fall within this time period. Our only problem is we do not know how long each generation was. We are not told how old Salmon was when Boaz was born. Nor are we told how old Boaz was when Obed was born.

We know from Ruth 3:10 that Boaz was not a young man when he married Ruth, but we do not know exactly how old he was. Looking at the chart of the Judges at the end of this chapter we see the time from Joshua to the tenth year of Gideon's judgeship would total 195 years. That would make approximately 100 years per generation. I say "approximately", because we do not know how old Salmon was when he followed Joshua into the Promised Land, or how old Rahab was when she helped the spies. Assuming they were both young adults could mean they were both in their middle teens or early twenties. Therefore, if we add 25 years to those 195 years, we have 220 years and that makes the generations between the birth of Salmon and the birth of Obed about 110 years each. If we assume, they were only 15 years old (which is very possible) and add 15 to 195 years we get 210 years, making the generations only 105 years each. From this we can safely say the generations between the entry into the Promised Land and the time of Obed averaged between 105 and 110 years each. Again, I say "averaged" because Salmon could have lived to be 125 years or older and Boaz be only 85 or younger.

Is this possible? Of course, it is, since all things are possible with the Lord, but we do not have any records of any life, within this time period, being supernaturally prolonged. Let us now look at other people mentioned in the Old Testament around this time period to see if it is likely. We have the following information from this time period and later ...

Moses lived to be 120 years when he died, and his eyes were not dimmed, nor his energy slowed (see Deuteronomy 34:7). God chose the time for Moses to die because of Moses' sin which prevented him from entering the Promised Land. Otherwise, he might have lived much longer.

Aaron was 123 years old when he died (see Numbers 33:39). Again, this was another situation where he died because he was not allowed to enter the Promised Land, so he too might have lived a lot longer.

Caleb, one of the spies who urged the Hebrews to follow God and enter the Promise Land as God had told them to, lived to be more than 85 years old. In Joshua 14:10 it tells us Caleb was 85 when he entered the Promised Land and was still fighting to drive the pagan nations out of his land. It does not say how long he lived after that, but apparently, he was still a very healthy fighting man at 85 years.

Joshua lived to be 110 years old (Joshua 24:29-30; Judges 2:8-9). He was the leader of the Israelites who led them into the Promised Land. The period of the Judges started right after his death.

We are not told how long any of the actual Judges lived, only how long they judged. From what we know of the Israelites before entering the Promised Land, an age of well over 100 years was pretty normal, barring any accidental or battle related deaths. In addition, people of that age group were just as strong as much younger men or women. If Boaz was a child of Salmon's old age, and Obed was a child of Boaz's old age the two generations could easily fit into the 215 years between the entrance into the Promised Land and the time of the tenth year of Gideon's judgeship.

With all this evidence in mind, Gideon is a prime candidate for the time period of the events surrounding Ruth. He is the only Judge that fits every clue found in the book of Ruth. Naturally, we cannot be positive about the ages of Salmon and Boaz. However, it is possible they fit into the 215-year time period without any intervention from God to prolong their lives.

Do not totally rule out God's intervention either. God could very well have prolonged Salmon, Rahab, or Boaz's lives so Boaz would be in the right place to meet Ruth at the right time. We should never under estimate God's providential hand.

THE JUDGES OF ISRAEL CHART

BIBLE	JUDGE'S NAME	TRIBE (see map on the next page)	OPPRESSOR OF ISRAEL
Judges 3:5-11	Othniel	Judah	Mesopotamia
Judges 3:12-30	Ehud	Benjamin	Moab with Ammon and Amalek
Judges 3:31 and 5:6	Shamgar	(not given)	Philistines
Judges 4-5	Deborah	Ephraim (Based on the area she judged)	Canaanites
Judges 6-8	Gideon	Manasseh	Midian and Amalekites
Judges 10:1-2	Tola	Issachar	None
Judges 10:2-5	Jair	Manasseh (Gileadites = Manasseh tribe)	None
Judges 10:6-12:7	Jephthah	Manasseh	Ammonites and Philistines
Judges 12:8-10	Ibzan	Judah	None
Judges 12:11-12	Elon	Zebulon	None
Judges 12:13-15	Abdon	Ephraim	None
Judges 13-16	Samson	Dan	Philistines
I Samuel 1-4:18	Eli	Levi	Philistines
I Samuel 1-28:20	Samuel	Ephraim	Philistines
I Samuel 8:1-3	Joel and Abiah	Ephraim	Philistines

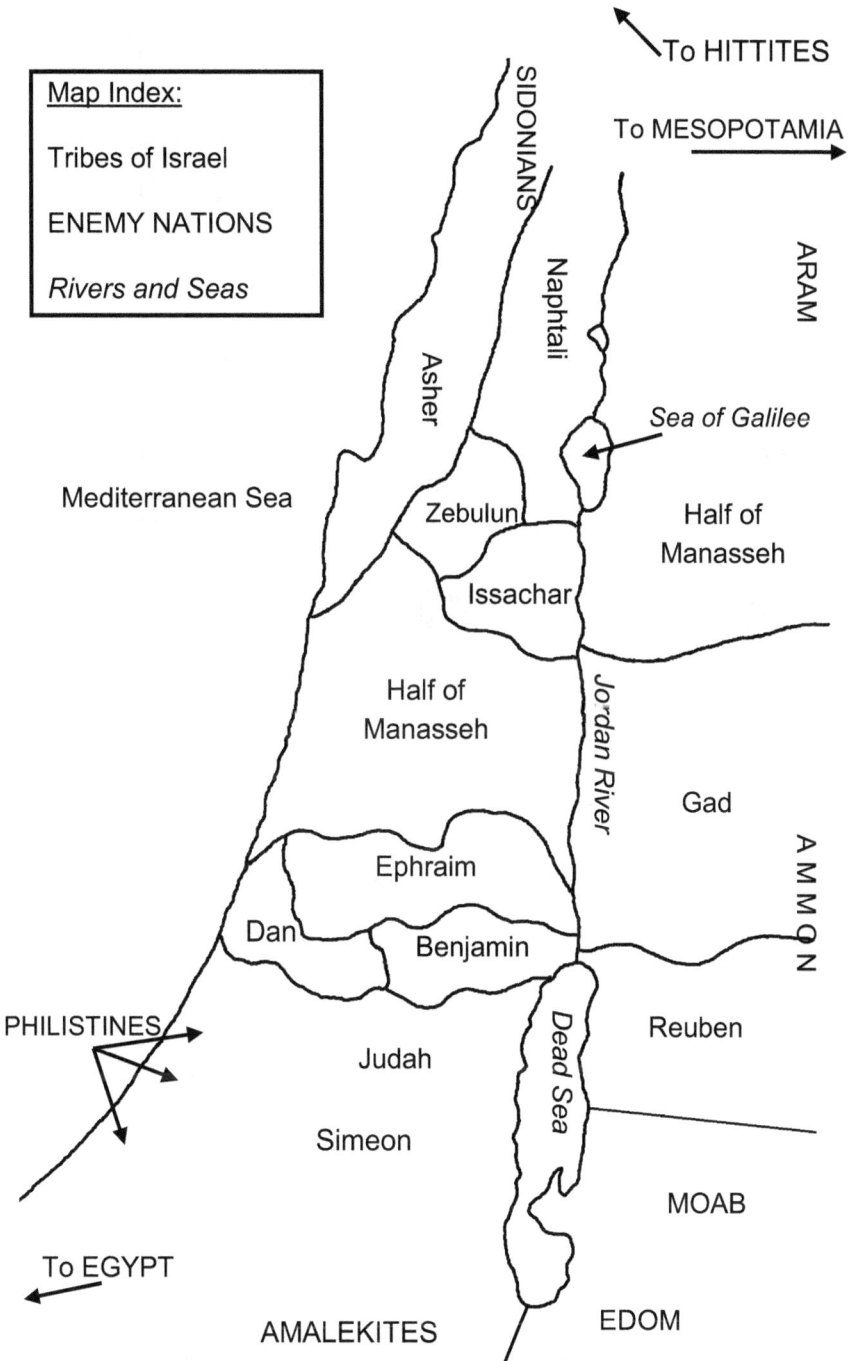

ISRAEL - THE TIME OF THE JUDGES

To HITTITES

To MESOPOTAMIA

Map Index:

Tribes of Israel

ENEMY NATIONS

Rivers and Seas

SIDONIANS

Naphtali

ARAM

Asher

Sea of Galilee

Mediterranean Sea

Zebulun

Half of
Manasseh

Issachar

Half of
Manasseh

Jordan River

Gad

Ephraim

AMMON

Dan

Benjamin

PHILISTINES

Dead Sea

Reuben

Judah

Simeon

MOAB

To EGYPT

AMALEKITES

EDOM

PERIOD OF THE JUDGES IN ISRAEL

Othniel judges Israel 40 years		Ehud judges Israel		Deborah judges Israel	
			Shamgar judges Israel		
Cushan-Rishathaim of Mesopotamia oppression 8 years	REST	Moabite oppression 18 years	REST	Jabin Canaanite Oppression 8 years	REST
Joshua – 25 +/- years					

Gideon judges Israel 40 years	King Abimelech 3 years	Tola judges Israel 23 years	Jair judges Israel 22 years	The Israelites deserted God and He left them alone.	Jephthah judges Israel 6 years
REST / Midianite oppression 7 yrs.		REST	REST	Ammonite oppression 18 years	REST

Ibzan judges Israel	Elon judges Israel	Abdon judges Israel	Samson judges Israel – 20 yrs.			
			Eli judges Israel – 40 years			
				Samuel judges Israel -- ? years		King Saul
					Joel & Abiah ??? years	
7 years	10 years	6 years	Philistine oppression			*The period of the Judges ends with the beginning of Saul's kingship.*
	REST		40 years			

NOTES ON THE PREVIOUS CHART
"PERIOD OF THE JUDGES IN ISRAEL"

1. We do not know exactly how long Joshua ruled Israel, but most estimate it to be between 25 and 30 years after entering the Promised Land. This is based on the number of battles fought with the pagan peoples living in the Promised Land at the time, and time lines that deal with these battles.
2. Othniel (Judges 3:5-11)
3. Ehud (Judges 3:12-30)
4. Shamgar (Judges 3:31; 5:6)
5. Deborah (Judges 4-5)
6. Gideon (Judges 6-8)
7. King Abimelech (Judges 9)
8. Tola (Judges 10:1-2)
9. Jair (Judges 10:2-5)
10. Jephthah (Judges 10:6-12:7)
11. Ibzan (Judges 12:8-10)
12. Elon (Judges 12:11-12)
13. Abdon (Judges 12:13-15)
14. Samson (Judges 13-16)
15. Eli (I Samuel 1-4:18)
16. Samuel (I Samuel 1-28:20)
17. Joel and Abiah (I Samuel 8:1-3)
18. King Saul (I Samuel 9-31)

Notes on the chart as a whole:

This chart was created by the author, using only the Bible as the guide. Most commentaries try to put the Judges right after each other with the periods of oppression between the judgeships; or they try to make a lot of them overlap. We are not told exactly which is correct, and maybe the better example is a combination of the two. Again, we have clues throughout the Bible to help us decide on this. Below are the clues and how this chart fits into them.

1. Judges 11:26 says there were 300 years between the entrance to the Promised Land when the Ammonites were first conquered by the Hebrews and the time of Jephthah who made the statement. If we assume Jephthah rounded the number off, it fits with the chart. It adds up like this …

   25 years for Joshua after they enter the Promised Land
   +266 years for the time of the Judges from Othniel to the beginning of Jephthah's rule as Judge
   ----
   = 291 years. That rounds off to 300 years quite nicely.

2. I Kings 6:1 says it was 480 years from the Exodus out of Egypt until the beginning of the building of the Temple in Jerusalem, and that the Temple building was started in the fourth year of Solomon's reign. We can work out the time of the Judges like this …

   480 years (the starting point for I Kings 6:1)
   - 4 years of Solomon's reign = 476 years (I Kings 6:1)
   - 40 years of King David's reign = 436 years (I Kings 2:11)
   - 40 years of King Saul's reign = 396 years (Acts 13:21)
   - 40 years of wandering in the wilderness = 356 years
   - 25 years of Joshua's life after entering the Promised Land
   ----
   = 331 years

That makes approximately 331 years for the time of the Judges. The chart shows 297 years for the judgeships from Othniel through Abdon.

We know that Samson, Eli, Samuel, and Samuel's sons overlapped a lot, and we know that Saul's reign as King (which ended the period of Judges) overlapped Samuel's judgeship. We know Eli judged Israel for 40 years. It is possible that Eli's Judgeship overlapped Samson's completely, since the oppression of the Philistines is mentioned during both, and it appears Samson did not drive the Philistines out of Israel. He only crippled them for a time.

We may also assume that Samuel's judgeship overlapped Eli's towards the end. This is because Eli raised Samuel and they worked closely at first.

We know the last Judges judged Israel for at least twenty-nine years before Saul became king, and Samuel continued to judge Israel until his death, which was about a year before Saul's death. Most scholars end the period of the Judges at the beginning of Saul's reign as King. We don't know how old Samuel was when he died, or how old he was when he started his Judgeship, so there is no way to tell exactly how long he judged Israel after Elli's death or before Saul become King.

We can't say with certainty that the number 480 wasn't rounded off to some extent. At most this might have been rounded off 4-5 years +/-). In addition, other Judges may have overlapped slightly.

Adding 40 years for Eli's judgeship (since that is the only number we are given for certain) to the 297 years from Othniel to Abdon gives us 337 years. Again assuming at least some of the dates in the Bible were rounded off, this brings the chart close enough to agree with the I Kings passage.

3. Looking into the New Testament we see in Acts 13:20 it says the time that God gave Israel judges was 450 years. After reading the entire passage from verse 17 to 20 and looking at the Greek, it becomes more obvious that this should be interpreted as 450 years from the time of the Exodus through the time of Samuel.
    We would add it like this …

    297 years = Time from Othniel through Abdon
    +40 years = wandering in the wilderness after the
        exodus
    +25 years = Joshua's time as leader of Israel (we do
        not know the exact number of years here, so this
        could vary +/- a few years.)
    ----

    362 years = time from exodus until the end of Abdon's
        judgeship
    +80 years = time of Eli, Samson and Samuel (Note:
        Samuel died a little over a year before King Saul.
        We do not know the exact number of
        years for this time period, so following it to the end
        of Samuel's life instead of to the beginning of
        Saul's reign, we get approximately 80 years. This
        could vary +/- a few years.)

    = 442 years (which rounds off to 450 years easily)

In all of these examples there are variables we just do not know for sure. This chart seems to come closer than any other I have seen for putting everything together with the other scriptures on the period of the Judges. We do not have exact numbers on things like Joshua's time from the entrance into the Promised Land to the time of Joshua's death, or the length of time Samuel judged Israel before Saul became king. Nor do we know whether the numbers were rounded off or how much they were rounded off. Therefore, it is impossible to come to exact numbers on a chart like this.

Chapter Four: COMMENTARY AND LESSONS FROM RUTH

NAOMI AND ELIMELEK (Ruth 1:1-3)

Ruth 1:1 "In the days when the judges ruled, there was a famine in the land. And a man from Bethlehem in Judah went to live in the land of Moab, he and his wife and his two sons."

In this introductory verse, we see the time frame into which this story fits. The time is "when the judges ruled". The Hebrew here actually says, "when the Judges judged". This refers to the time between Joshua's death and the kingship of Saul. (Reading the books of Judges and I Samuel will give you an overview of the time.) The country of Israel was ruled by men and one woman who explained what God wanted the people to do, by explaining or interpreting God's laws. The people would bring disagreements to a Judge, he or she would make a decision based on the Law and explain it to the people. These Judges would also lead the people in their fight against enemies or instruct the people where, when, and who God wanted them to fight. God also spoke to the Judges and they, of course, spoke directly to God.

The Judge who ruled Israel was more than someone who sat in front of a court room and listened to cases all day. This Judge was a cross between a ruler and a prophet. He/she spoke God's words to the people and they settled disputes between the people. These disputes might be between two individuals, or it might be between two groups of people, even between two tribes within Israel. And sometimes the people of Israel (either in part or as a whole) would go to the Judge to ask what they should do when an outside nation attacked them. The Judges led the people to follow God's plan for them and for the nation of Israel.

There were times during the period of the Judges when the people ignored their Judges. They worshipped pagan false gods and also ignored God's laws. At these times, God allowed other nations to conquer Israel and oppress them. It's interesting that when the children of Israel worshipped the gods of pagan nations, God allowed those pagan nations to make the Israelites lives miserable. It is like God was saying, "Look! If you want to worship useless gods, see if they make your life better than I can?" He allowed them to be miserable in their own sin. Instead of their lives being better, they became worse.

In the 28th chapter of Deuteronomy we see God telling the Israelites if they will follow God and do His commandments, He will bless them with blessings beyond their wildest dreams. They will prosper. "The LORD will make you overflow in prosperity, in the offspring of your body, in the offspring of your livestock, and in the produce of your ground, in the land which the LORD swore to your fathers to give you" (Deuteronomy 28:11).

However, if the Israelites do not worship God and follow His commandments the last part of chapter 28 tells what will happen and it is not pretty. The people and all they have will be cursed by God. Nothing will survive these curses including the land. "A nation that you do not know will consume the produce of your land and all your labors, and you will be nothing but oppressed and crushed all the time" (Deuteronomy 28:33).

Only after the Israelites realized the idols they worshipped could not save them did they finally return to God and Him only. Then God would go with them to drive out their oppressors and restore peace and happiness to the people and the land.

This time of ignoring the Judge and God's laws is what brought the famine to the land, and drove Elimelek to take his family to Moab. It was to be a temporary move. The Hebrew word (לגור) in this verse is better translated as "sojourn". Unfortunately, sojourn is a word not used much anymore. It means to stay in a place only for a short while ... not to emigrate permanently. It is a temporary move for the family. Elimelek only meant to live in Moab until the famine was over in Bethlehem, and then move his family back to the Promised Land.

> *Ruth 1:2 "The name of the man was Elimelek, the name of his wife Naomi, and the names of his two sons were Mahlon and Kilion. They were Ephrathites from Bethlehem in Judah. And they went to Moab and lived there."*

There is some question about the use of the word "Ephrathites" in relation to this family. Most commentaries and Bible dictionaries consider *Ephrath* or *Ephrathah* to be just another name for Bethlehem. It is perhaps an older name for the town, before the Israelites came into the Promised Land and changed the name. Ephrath (אפרת אפרתה *'ephrâth 'ephrâthâh*) means "fruitful land". That is even more interesting when you look at the name Bethlehem (בית לחם *bêyth lechem*) which comes from two Hebrew words: *bêyth* which means "house" and *lechem* which means "bread", making the whole name of Bethlehem mean "house of bread". For centuries this village has been called fruitful land and house of bread. It must have been a place of rich soil, which produced abundant crops, vineyards, and olive groves. A famine in this area had to be devastating to the people who lived there after knowing all that abundance.

It still seems odd that the writer would use the term *"Ephrathites"* to describe this family from Bethlehem. Why not "Bethlehemites"? If we assume the writer was using Ephrathites to mean Bethlehemites, it seems like he was being redundant for saying Bethlehemites from Bethlehem. Where else would Bethlehemites be from but Bethlehem? For some time now English translations of the Bible have assumed the Hebrew word (which is Ephrathi) translated as Ephrathites was related to Ephrath and Ephrathah and therefore refers to Bethlehamites. It has also been confused with the word Ephraim, but a closer look shows there is no "m" in Ephrathi (Ephrathites) in Hebrew or in English. The word Ephrathi (Ephrathites) only occurs in five verses in the Old Testament. We will look at these five verses more closely later.

Jewish tradition says "Ephrathite" refers to the old families of the village – the nobles, princes, or aristocrats. These were the respected, wealthy families. If Elimelek's family was one of these wealthy aristocratic families, this would explain how Elimelek had the money to move his family from Israel to Moab on the other side of the Dead Sea and settle in that area temporarily during a famine. Although in Hebrew the words for Ephrath and Ephrathites are very similar, they are actually two different words, possibly coming from two different root words in Hebrew. This makes Ephrath or Ephrathah refer to the city of

Bethlehem, while the other word Ephrathites refers to family members of the aristocrats, noblemen, or just the leaders.

We know from Numbers 1 that Nashon (the son of Amminadab) and other specific men were called "princes" (KJV) or "leaders" (MEV) or "heads" of the tribes of Israel. Then we find in Matthew chapter 1 that Nashon was the father of Salmon, and Salmon was the father of Boaz. We know from Ruth that Boaz was a near kinsman of Elimelek, perhaps even a brother. This would make him among the leaders or noble family of Bethlehem.

Since the Bible is the best interpreter of the Bible, let us examine the use of the Hebrew words for Ephrath/Ephrathah (אפרתה) and Ephrathites (אפרתי) as used in the Bible.

We find the following uses of both words …

Ephrath/Ephrathah (אפרתה)	Ephrathite (אפרתי)
Gen 35:16 "They journeyed from Bethel, and when they were still some distance from **Ephrath**, Rachel went into labor, and she had a difficult labor." [The Hebrew word used here refers to a location near or in Bethlehem.]	*Judges 12:5* "Gilead captured the fords of the Jordan River leading to Ephraim. Whenever an Ephraimite fugitive would say, 'Let me cross,' the Gileadite men would say to him, 'Are you an **Ephraimite**?'" [Above we see the Hebrew word Ephrathite

	(translated here as Ephraimite) referring to a group of people, not a location. [Note: The Hebrew word translated as Ephraimite earlier in this verse is a different word. The last word translated as Ephraimite might have been an oversight of the translator, since it does not have a "M" (the Hebrew letter is actually a "Mem") in it like the former two words translated as Ephraim or Ephraimite in this verse.]
	The Gileadites were trying to identify the Ephraimites who had a speech impediment. This cannot refer to people from Bethlehem in the tribe of Judah as Judah was two tribes south of Ephraim.
	Since it talks of a speech problem these people had, and speech problems can run in families or family groups,

	this could very well refer to a family group (clan) of people who all share this speech problem. This family group may have been the aristocrats or leaders of the tribe of Ephraim who were from this area. It could also have referred to the whole tribe of Ephraim.]
Genesis 48:7 *"As for me, when I came from Paddan, Rachel died beside me in the land of Canaan on the way, when there was still some distance to get to* **Ephrath**, *and I buried her there on the way to* **Ephrath** *(that is, Bethlehem."* [As the scripture says here, the Hebrew word for *Ephrath* refers to Bethlehem.]	**1 Samuel 1:1** *"Now there was a certain man of Ramathaimzophim, of mount Ephraim, and his name was Elkanah, the son of Jeroham, the son of Elihu, the son of Tohu, the son of Zuph, an* **Ephrathite**:" (KJV) [*Ehprathite* here could refer to Zuph's standing among men in his tribe. He was an *Ephrathite* or nobleman from the hill country of Ephraim (as translated in the KJV, ESV, and other versions). However, some versions (MEV, NIV, NASV and

	others) translate it Ephraimites, but again there is no "M" (nor "Mem") in the word Ephraimites. Either way it does not refer to Bethlehem.]
Ruth 4:11 *"Then all the people who were at the gate, along with the elders, said, 'We are witnesses. May the LORD make the woman who is coming to your house like Rachel and Leah, who together built up the house of Israel. May you do well in* **Ephrathah** *and be famous in Bethlehem!'"* [In this instance the Hebrew word obviously refers to a place and it is Bethlehem.]	**1 Kings 11:26** *"Jeroboam the son of Nebat, an* **Ephraimite** *of Zeredah, who was Solomon's servant and whose mother's name was Zeruah, a widow woman, even he lifted up his hand against the king."* [Here again *Ephrathite* is translated as Ephraimite and could refer to a person from Ephraim (as translated by the MEV), or a nobleman (*Ephrathite* as translated in the KJV) from Zereda which is located in Ephraim. Looking at the context of this verse, it makes more

| | sense to have a nobleman rise up against the King. Listing a common servant, no matter which tribe he was from, as opposing the King would have little effect on the people.

However, saying a nobleman who was serving the King had risen up against the King meant others might follow this nobleman in this uprising. After all, he was a leader of his tribe, not an average person.

Either way it does not refer to Bethlehem.] |
|---|---|
| *Micah 5:2* *"But you Bethlehem **Ephrathah**, although you are small among the tribes of Judah, from you will come forth for Me one who will be ruler over Israel. His origins are from of old, from ancient days."* | *1 Samuel 17:12* "Now David was the son of that **Ephrathite** of Bethlehem in Judah whose name was Jesse, who had eight sons."

[Here Ephrathite does refer to a person from Bethlehem in Judah. As in other passages it is |

[Again, we see *Ephrathah* being used as part of the name of Bethlehem. Perhaps the author was trying to be more specific or more formal in getting his message across.]	used as a description, not as a place. Jesse was more than just a person from Bethlehem – he was an "Ephrathite" from Bethlehem. That is, an aristocrat or nobleman from Bethlehem in Judah.]
	Ruth 1:2 "The name of the man was Elimelek, the name of his wife was Naomi, and the names of his two sons were Mahlon and Kilion. They were **Ephrathites** *from Bethlehem in Judah..."* [Like the passage in I Samuel, here in Ruth we see that Elimelek and his sons were from Bethlehem in Judah. However, they were more than just citizens of Bethlehem. They were "Ephrathites" or noblemen or aristocrats (leaders of the people). We know that an ancestor of Elimilek's, Nahshon, was described

	as a "prince" or "leader" of the tribe of Judah in several places in the Old Testament. I Chronicles 2:10 is one of those places. It's possible that Elimelek's family were considered the nobility of the tribe of Judah.]
CONCLUSION: In cases where the Hebrew word for Ephrath (although spelled in different ways in English) is used, it does refer to a place and specifically to Bethlehem or near Bethlehem.	**CONCLUSION:** In cases where the Hebrew word for Ephrathite(s) is used, it does not refer to Bethlehem or to a specific place. This can be seen by the use of names of different cities after Ephrathite. It is therefore this author's conclusion that the Hebrew word for Ephrathite(s) means "nobleman, aristocrat or a leader" and can refer to any city or tribe within Israel.

This second sentence in the second verse of chapter 1 of Ruth could be better understood if translated as *"They were aristocrats (or nobles) from Bethlehem in Judah."*

Ruth 1:3 "Now Elimelek, the husband of Naomi, died, so she was left alone with her two sons."

Who were Elimelek and Naomi? The obvious is they were Israelites from Bethlehem in Judah. Looking at the meanings of names in the Bible is very interesting. If we were to translate them instead of transliterating (change the Hebrew letters into English letters only) them, I often wonder if we would think differently about them. The name Elimelek (אלימלך) is actually a combination of two Hebrew words. *Eli* which means "my God", and *melek* which means "king". Putting them together we get "My God is king". Imagine calling him MY GOD IS KING, instead of Elimelek. You see him coming down the road and wave at him and say, "Hi, MY GOD IS KING! How are you doing today?" What a great reminder that Yahweh is King of everything.

Naomi (נעמי) means "PLEASANT". So now we have MY GOD IS KING married to PLEASANT. Now imagine MY GOD IS KING coming home and saying, "Hi, PLEASANT how was your day?" She answers, "Hi, MY GOD IS KING, I had the most wonderful day. You should have seen what the boys did today." During this time people gave their children names that meant something. It could be something they hoped the child's personality would develop into, such as "Pleasant", or it could be something to remind them of an important thing in their life, such as "My God is King", or it might be something that happened that wasn't good, such as Rachel naming her second son Ben-oni (בן־אוני) which means "Son of My Sorrow" just before she died, and then Jacob changing his name to

Benjamin (בנימין) which means "Son of My Right Hand" (Genesis 35:18). If Jacob had not changed his name, Benoni would have forever been reminded that his mother died giving birth to him, whenever anyone called out his name. Instead he was reminded that his father loved him and considered him important.

MY GOD IS KING (Elimelek) and PLEASANT (Naomi) were from the tribe of Judah. They were from the village of Bethlehem. Most of us know Bethlehem as the city in Israel where Jesus (the Messiah) was born. It was a small town about five miles southwest of Jerusalem. There is not much there today. I remember it taking about 2.5 hours to walk from Jerusalem to Bethlehem back in the 1970's when I was there. It was a pleasant walk early in the morning. The trees were green, the people along the way friendly, and it was a beautiful day. There is nothing there to remind us of Elimelek and Naomi, except shepherd's fields and grain fields outside the city. Inside the city are lots of souvenir shops hoping to sell their wares to tourists coming to see the Church of the Nativity where Jesus is supposed to have been born. In Elimelek's day, it was a beautiful village with homes, fields, families, and friends … most of the time.

Except in the beginning of our story we find those fields barren and the people starving for lack of food. As shown in the preceding chapter of this book, this famine was probably caused by raids from the Midianites. The Midianites waited until the Israelites had done all the work of planting and cultivating their crops. Then they came into the land to steal or destroy those crops before they could be harvested and stored by the Israelites. This was indeed a bleak time for any family living in Israel.

Elimelek and Naomi had two sons. Their names were Mahlon and Kilion. Mahlon means "sick", or "weakly". Kilion means "pining". We have to wonder why Naomi and Elimelek would give their sons such defeatist type names. Did they not want their sons to become strong responsible men? Even though they did, it is possible that Mahlon was a sickly baby. He was given the name to remind him when he became a strong adult that he started out as a sickly child. Perhaps knowing that would give him more incentive to work towards being healthy and strong.

Kilion may have also been a fragile infant. If this was the case and the children continued to be delicate and sickly as they grew, we can see a reason why Elimelek and Naomi chose to leave the suffering land and friends they loved to travel into a foreign country where food was plentiful. The lack of food would have had a detrimental effect on these weak sickly children making them more physically ill. Elimelek took his family to Moab in an effort to save his sons' lives.

Some would like to say Elimelek was cowardly and evil because he took his family and moved to a foreign land where there was food, during a famine in Israel. Whether it was a sin for him to move his family during a time of crisis or not, it definitely showed a lack of faith in God on Elimelek's part. He left others who were also suffering, so his family could have plenty, instead of staying and helping them fight off their attackers. It has even been suggested that Elimelek did not worship Yahweh, but was worshipping idols like the Moabites and Yahweh punished him by making him die in a foreign land. Maybe he was just trying to keep his sons from dying because of the lack of food. He could not stand to see them suffer. It is bad enough to have to watch friends suffer and die, but to see your children die when there is nothing you can do about it is worse. Elimelek did the only thing he thought he could do to save his family … he moved them to Moab where there was no famine.

They planned to live in Moab temporarily. The King James Version (KJV) of the Bible says they *sojourned*. Other translations say they went to Moab to *live* there. While sojourned is a word not used much today, it is a better translation of the Hebrew word here, since it means they moved to Moab temporarily. They never meant to stay permanently in Moab. They probably figured a few years would be plenty of time for the Lord to drive the Midianites out of the Promised Land. Then they would return and help their neighbors rebuilt their farms and grow new crops. Unfortunately, it did not work out that way. Elimelek died and Naomi was left to care for her two sons. We do not know how long they were in Moab before Elimelek died, but apparently it was long enough to get comfortably settled into the Moabite community.

Mahlon and Kilion were old enough by now to provide for their mother. They had now grown up in a foreign land, and had no interest in traveling back to Bethlehem even if the famine had ended, which it had not, or at least they had not heard about it, if it had. Their interest in marrying pagan Moabite girls showed they wanted to stay in Moab.

At a time when Moab and Israel were at peace with each other, living in Moab would not have been terribly difficult for a Hebrew family, except for the religious aspect. The Moabites worshipped several gods, but the chief was Chemosh who required infant sacrifice among other things. That aspect of Moabite life would have been very distasteful for the Hebrew family of Elimelek who worshipped the one true God, Yahweh. As for language, the Moabites spoke a dialect of Hebrew and even used the same alphabet to write it, so there would not be much difference when it came to speaking to them or reading scrolls in Moabite. The Moabites were actually relatives of the Hebrews, having been born of Abraham's nephew, Lot.

Throughout history there were good times when the Israelites and Moabites existed peacefully with each other, and bad times when one conquered the other. During Elimelek's time Moab and Israel were at peace.

Even though the Moabites and Israelites were not fighting each other, they still did not like each other as a whole. Individually, though, it was another story. Elimelek's family probably settled in an area near a small town where they could farm or work on a farm owned by a Moabite. The Bible does not specifically tell us what Elimelek's occupation was, but since he owned a field back in Bethlehem it is likely he was a farmer. Moab had much the same climate and land type as Israel, so it would be easy for Elimelek to settle into an area where he could farm, or work for a Moabite who owned land. All this would present no more of a problem for the Jewish family than it would for someone in the USA today to move from one state to a neighboring state.

While the move would not have been difficult for the family to adapt to, the culture would have caused a few problems at first. The Moabites would have heard of the famine in Israel and knowing the Jews were weakened by the attacks of the Midianites would not have feared Jews moving into their territory. Since they were not buying land or houses, it was obvious to the Moabites these newcomers were not looking to take over. Elimelek probably rented a vacant house and worked for the landowner. Mahlon and Kilion probably worked for him as well.

Things were going along very well for this Hebrew family at first. The family settled into the comfort of a new lifestyle knowing it was only to be temporary and looking forward to a time in the near future when they would pack up again and go back to Bethlehem ... back home. The important thing was that they were together as a family and the boys had plenty of food to eat to get and keep them healthy.

Then disaster struck. Elimelek died. Did he have a heart attack? Did he die from an accident while working in the field? Did he get sick and suffer a long time? We just do not know. It is not as important what he died from as it is that he died and left Naomi alone with their two sons in a foreign land. The boys were growing up now, and there still was not any relief from the famine in Israel, so Naomi could not take them and return to their home in Bethlehem. The boys were sure to be old enough to work in the fields, and that would be enough to keep them going for now. The longer they stayed, the more the boys learned about the Moabite people and society.

For Naomi this must have seemed like a hopeless situation. Here she was trying to raise her sons to be good Jewish men, and the only example of a Jewish man in the area had died. She was left without a husband. How could she go on? She had to go on for her sons' sake, and she did go on. She continued to make a proper Jewish home for her sons in a foreign land. Naomi was a very strong woman even though she did not admit it to herself. She could have just given up, said, "Woe is me! What will I do?", and sunk into nothingness. She did not. She continued to raise her sons and watch over them. She trusted Yahweh to guide her along the right path even though she did not know what that was ... yet! We need to take Naomi as a role model when bad things happen ... Pray and trust the Lord!

INSPIRATIONAL LESSON:

By naming him Elimelek (My God is King), his parents showed an understanding of God's place in Israel that many Jews at that time did not. Judges 21:25 says "*In those days there was no king in Israel."* This was near the end of the period of the Judges and it shows how the people had forgotten about the Lord. This is also seen in I Samuel where the people ask Samuel to give them a king. Samuel does not want to do this because they should have recognized God as king over them. Finally, Samuel admonishes them with, *"But you have today rejected your God, who saves you from all your troubles and your distresses. And you have said to Him, 'No, but set a king over us.'"* (I Samuel 10:19) We need to be sure we keep God as king of our lives always. It is sometimes easy for us to set other things (people or items) ahead of God. That shiny new car gets more attention from us then God does. We spend more time surfing the internet for a new game or other information then reading the Bible. Who or what is King in your life?

MAHLON AND KILION MARRY (Ruth 1:4-5)

> *Ruth 1:4 "They took Moabite wives for themselves; the name of one was Orpah and the name of the other Ruth. They lived there about ten years."*

> *Ruth 1:5 "Then Mahlon and Kilion also died, and Naomi was left without her two sons and her husband."*

It is not clear in the previous verses which woman married which son. Normally the first mentioned son would be the oldest, so since Mahlon is mentioned first, he appears to be the first born. It naturally follows that the woman mentioned first would be the wife of the first son mentioned. Since Orpah is mentioned first, it would appear she was the wife of Mahlon. This would make Ruth the wife of Kilion. Yet in Ruth 4:10, Boaz says Ruth was the wife of Mahlon indicating he was the oldest as his is the name to be preserved by the child of Ruth and Boaz.

It is quite possible that Ruth was the original wife of Kilion. We are not told which son died first. Perhaps Kilion died first, and Mahlon took Ruth into his home as his second wife to raise up children to Kilion's name. This is called a levirate marriage and is still practiced among Arabs in the Near East today.

INSPIRATIONAL LESSON:

Naomi kept a proper Jewish home for her sons, but they were indeed growing up. They noticed the women of Moab were as beautiful as the women they remember from Israel, and they knew it was time for them to think of starting families of their own. Naomi probably objected to their interest in the women of Moab, but there were no other choices. Here we see that the migration from Israel during this famine was not widespread. Only this one family left Bethlehem and moved to Moab. If others had left, they would have traveled together, settled in the same area, and Naomi would have looked to them to find wives for her sons, but she had no choice. They were too far from Bethlehem and it was too dangerous a journey to send the boys back to Israel to find proper Jewish wives.

Elimelek's family must have been accepted into the Moabite society. Even though he was dead, the people of Moab allowed his sons to marry their daughters. Without being accepted in their new homeland, any marriage would have made the wives outcasts, and could have made the whole family of the girls' outcasts. This does not seem to be the case here, as we see later; the wives would have been welcomed back to their mother's houses and could marry other Moabite men after their Jewish husbands died.

Still it was a hopeless situation for Naomi to go through. The Moabite women were pagans who worshipped not just one pagan god, but many gods. They might even convince their husbands (her sons) to begin worshipping these pagan gods. At least one of these gods required the sacrifice of babies and children to appease him. What if one of her sons was having a rough time and his wife convinced him to sacrifice their child … her grandchild … to this idol!?! What a horrible thought for a widow who was too old to remarry and have more children herself. As a woman she was looking forward to a time when she would hold her grandchildren and teach them about Yahweh. What a hopeless time for her.

Again, Naomi does not give in to hopelessness. She accepts the Moabite wives of her sons and teaches them about Yahweh, instead of letting them teach her sons to be pagans. She also teaches the women to be good Jewish wives. She teaches them so well that they cannot imagine a time when they would ever want to leave her or Yahweh. Although their nationality will always be Moabite, they do become children of Yahweh and abandon the worship of Moabite gods. They come to think of Naomi as their mother too, which is another way of saying they were accepted into the Jewish family and faith.

This is how we should look at our daughters-in-law or sons-in-law. It would be great if our sons or daughters chose good Christian spouses but sometimes, they do not. That does not mean the person they have chosen is a bad person. We still need to welcome them into our family and pray for them. We also need to set a good example for them and teach them about God as Naomi did with her daughters-in-law. Remember we are all sinners in need of God's grace and forgiveness.

NAOMI AND HER DAUGHTERS-IN-LAW
(Ruth 1:6-15)

> Ruth 1:6 *"So she got up with her daughters-in-law to return from the land of Moab, for in the land of Moab, she had heard that the LORD had visited His people by giving them food."*

How had Naomi heard in Moab that the famine was over in Israel? There was no e-mail, and no phone service. It was very unlikely that a friend or relative from Bethlehem would be traveling over to Moab for a visit. The only way for her to hear news from far away, was through traveling caravans who might pass through the area where she was living. This gives us an idea that Elimelek took his family to an area near a city or at least along a trade route. A caravan would travel along a certain route which would take it to cities where they could stop, trade their goods, get food and water, and relax for a time before continuing on to the next city. Naomi had been trading goods with people from the caravan and learned it had come through the southern part of Israel. She would eagerly pump them for news from the area. "Had they been in Bethlehem?" "Who did they deal with there?" "How are the people?" "Is the famine still as bad as it was?" "What?" "The famine is over?" "The crops have been good?" "Hallelujah! I am going home!!!"

> Ruth 1:7 *"She set out from the place where she had been, with her two daughters-in-law, and they went on their way to return to the land of Judah."*

Naomi was suddenly so happy, that Orpah and Ruth could not help noticing it. She had been so sad and miserable since her sons died. They thought she would never come out of it, but here she was happy again. They encouraged her and packed, planning to stay with her wherever she went.

> *Ruth 1:8 "Then Naomi said to her two daughters-in-law, 'Go, return each to her mother's house. May the LORD deal kindly with you as you have dealt with your deceased husbands and with me.'"*

Even though Naomi is sending Orpah and Ruth back to their parents' homes, she asks God to bless them. There is a definite bond between these three women. Obviously, Ruth and Orpah have come to accept Yahweh as their God, or as one of their gods, or Naomi's blessing on them would not mean anything to them. It is interesting that the only true God will not allow His people to worship other gods, but pagan gods (who really do not exist) do allow their people to worship any other gods as long as they keep worshipping the pagan gods. It is another proof that pagan gods do not really exist, because if they did, they would also want to be the only god their people worshipped. That is further proof that Yahweh is the only one true God of the universe, because He wants His people to worship only Him.

> *Ruth 1:9 "'May the LORD grant that you each find rest in the house of another husband.' Then she kissed them, and they raised their voices and wept aloud."*

> *Ruth 1:10 "They said to her, 'We will return with you to your people.'"*

This was a sad time for all three women. Ruth and Orpah had not given much thought to whether or not they would go with Naomi. They just expected to go. Now Naomi gave them the choice and all they could do was cry at the thought of their lives without her. What a wonderful relationship existed between these young women and their mother-in-law.

> *Ruth 1:11 "But Naomi said, 'Turn back, my daughters. Why would you go with me? Are there sons in my womb, who could become your husbands?'"*

> *Ruth 1:12 "'Turn back, my daughters! Go, for I am too old to have a husband. Even if I thought that there was still hope for me, that I could have a husband tonight and give birth to sons,"*

> *Ruth 1:13 "would you wait until they were grown? Would you refrain from getting married? No, my daughters. It is much more bitter for me than for you for the hand of the LORD has turned against me.'"*

Naomi had thought long and hard about this. Family was the most important thing to Naomi. She could not think of any other reason for Orpah and Ruth to want to travel with her to a foreign land. She missed her home and if she got back safely, she planned to never leave it again. Living in Moab had brought misery to her. How could she subject these young women to the same misery of missing their friends and family from Moab? Whether she was right or wrong, her love for Ruth and Orpah made her determined to save them from the agony of missing their homeland. She did not realize how much of an affect being married to Mahlon and Kilion had had on them and their idea of God. They (at least Ruth) had obviously learned a great deal, from their husbands and from Naomi, about being part of God's people, as we will see later.

> *Ruth 1:14 "Then they raised their voices and wept aloud once more. Orpah kissed her mother-in-law, but Ruth clung to her."*

121

Ruth 1:15 *"Naomi said, 'Look, your sister-in-law has returned to her people and her gods. Return with her!'"*

If Orpah was Mahlon's first wife and Ruth married him after her husband Kilion died, it was even more interesting that Orpah did not accompany Naomi back to Bethlehem. If she had she would have been the widow who Boaz would have needed to redeem to raise up children to the family of Elimelek. Of course, Naomi did not know that at the time, and she actually thought no Israelite man would want to marry either of them because they were from Moab. She had given up all hope of having grandchildren, or even of having a family again. She would be alone the rest of her life, but it would be better for her to be alone in her home town of Bethlehem where she had lifelong friends who shared her faith in Yahweh.

Naomi also loved her daughters-in-law, and would have loved to have them near her. Because of this love for them, she chose to send them back to their parents' homes. Naomi did not want her sons' wives to share a fate like hers. No matter how much these young Moabite women loved Naomi, Naomi only saw a hopeless situation for them. They would be living in a foreign land. Naomi knew what that was like. She moved to Moab with her husband and sons with the idea it would only be for a short time and it had turned into 10 years or more. If Ruth and Orpah returned to Bethlehem with her, it would be for the rest of their lives. She could not do that to them unless there was hope for them to have a husband and children there.

Naomi had been gone from Bethlehem for so long, she did not know who of her friends and relatives would still be alive and who would have died during the famine. It was not enough to imagine some of her male relatives might be alive, but would they be single? If they were married would they be willing to take on another wife to raise up children to her sons' names. If they were willing to do that, would they want to marry a foreigner, and a Moabitess at that? Because of their treatment of the Hebrews when they were traveling from Egypt to the Promised Land, the Moabites were forbidden to enter the congregation of Israel (Deuteronomy 23:3). These were all pretty big "ifs" for Naomi to overcome. She had just buried her only sons, and the grief was too great for her to think about the God who had protected her this long. She decided it would be a better life for her loved daughters-in-law to return to their mothers. She would return to Bethlehem alone. It was hopeless for her.

All she had left to do was tell Ruth and Orpah to go home to their parents. Maybe she would not have to tell them? Maybe they would not want to go with her? Maybe they would just stay? Naomi announced she would return to Bethlehem. To her surprise both Ruth and Orpah were willing to go with her. They all packed. Ruth and Orpah would need to pack anyway if they returned to their parents' home, so Naomi did not say anything yet. Naomi would allow them to walk a little way with her as sort of a sendoff. Just maybe on the way, Naomi would change her mind and let them come.

The three of them walked a bit. Ruth and Orpah tried to keep Naomi's spirits up by talking about the trip, or making mention of the pretty wildflowers along the road. Orpah would hesitate a little and fall behind while Ruth walked with Naomi chatting about the weather or whatever came to mind. Orpah would catch up and she and Ruth would start talking about something not realizing Naomi was ahead of them. Then they would catch up with Naomi who only partially listened to their chatter.

All the time Naomi was trying to decide what to do. Her thoughts argued with themselves. If she allowed the girls to go all the way to Bethlehem with her, they would be a great comfort to her. Maybe they could do some weaving or dress making to earn some money to buy food. It would certainly be better to have three women working than just one. On the other hand, that would not be fair to the girls. They would be better off going back to their mothers who would find new husbands for them. They might even have children and be happy. On the other hand, they would be going back to worshipping Chemosh and other pagan idols because that would be what their husbands worshipped. If they went with her, they could continue to worship the true living God they had learned to worship while married to her sons. In her grief over the loss of her own sons and no grandchildren, she did not see that God had protected her family. Maybe it would be better for them to have a living family than to have none and worship Yahweh. She thought that was not right either, but the grief of losing her husband and sons had her confused. It was a royal battle going on in her head, and she needed to make a decision.

When would she tell them? That was bound to be more sorrow for Naomi. Finally, she realized they had been walking for nearly half a day. The sun was just about overhead. Naomi would need to make a decision now if she was going to send them back. Waiting any longer would mean they would not make it back to their mothers' houses before dark and young women traveling alone after dark would not be safe.

She stopped and turned around to face them. This was going to be difficult but it had to be done for their futures. With tears streaming down her cheeks, she told them to go back. They were surprised. They had intended to go all the way to Bethlehem with her. They objected to being sent away. Perhaps Naomi just didn't understand, so they told her, "We will go with you all the way to Bethlehem."

"No, you must go back", she tells them. Now they are crying also. It must have been heart breaking for Naomi, but she was a strong woman. Orpah is finally convinced and kisses Naomi before she leaves, but Ruth will not be persuaded. Orpah gives in to the easy path. Ruth takes the hard path but the one she knows is right. She stays with Naomi and with God.

INSPIRATIONAL LESSON

It's often difficult when faced with a decision to know what to do. We feel obligated to do one thing, but another thing looks easier or more fun. Naomi was faced with a decision: take Ruth and Orpah with her (which would have been better for her) or send them back to their mothers (which she thought would be better for them).

This was especially difficult for her since the likelihood of her making it back to Bethlehem alone was almost impossible. It would still have been difficult but her chances of arriving in Bethlehem were much better with Ruth and Orpah with her. She chooses to put Orpah's and Ruth's welfare before hers and send them back to stay safe in Moab. If she died on the journey by herself, at least she would be with Elimelek, Mahlon, and Kilion. Hopefully, she would make it to Israel if not all the way to Bethlehem before she died. Considering how much she wanted to see her friends back in Bethlehem this decision to send her daughters-in-law back was an extremely difficult one. She chose love over safety.

Ruth and Orpah also had difficult decisions to make. They could do as Naomi urged them and go home to their mothers, get married again, have children and maybe live good lives ... or ... they could go on with Naomi and see that she got back to Bethlehem safely and lived a comfortable life until she died. It would mean no husband, no children, never to see their families or homeland again.

If we compare them to people Jesus mentioned in the New Testament, we see a very interesting illustration. Orpah had decided to go with Naomi, but when Naomi explained everything she would face, Orpah turned back to what she thought was the safe thing to do. In Luke 9:62 Jesus said, "No man, having put his hand to the plough, and looking back, is fit for the kingdom of God." Orpah looked back and turned back to what she really wanted, and it was not God.

Ruth chose to stay with Naomi. As we will see in the next section, Ruth chose to follow God no matter what it cost her! Ruth put her hand to the plough and never looked back. She trusted God to help her and Naomi reach Bethlehem and prepare a future for them there.

NAOMI AND RUTH TRAVEL TO BETHLEHEM (Ruth 1:16-18)

Ruth 1:16 "But Ruth said, 'Do not urge me to leave you or to turn back from following you. For wherever you go, I will go, and wherever you stay, I will stay. Your people shall be my people and your God my God.'"

Ruth 1:17 "'Where you die, I will die, and there I will be buried. May the LORD do thus to me, and worse, if anything but death separates you and me!'"

Ruth 1:18 "When Naomi saw that she was determined to go with her, she said no more to her."

Ruth tells Naomi not to speak of her leaving Naomi anymore, because she simply will not go. No amount of persuasion will change her mind. If she has to be single and never have children, then that is the way it will be. Naomi has hope again. She will not be alone nor will she be a lonely old woman.

How many mothers of sons can say they have a relationship with their daughter-in-law like that? Unfortunately, in America today, the mother-in-law has become the joke of many comedians and movies. She is the hated member of any family, and the wife quickly learns to avoid her at all costs. Naomi is an excellent example of what a mother-in-law should be. She cares for her daughters-in-law. She puts their welfare before hers. She teaches them about the true God and how to worship Him. She wants them to have happy lives, happy families, and the right to choose how to live. She laughs with them when they are happy, and she cries with them when they are sad. Possibly best of all, she allows them to disagree with her. She listens to them and even allows them to change her mind when she sees that is what is right. In short, she loves them like her own daughters.

How many daughters-in-law can say they have a mother-in-law that is all those things? As a daughter-in-law, we should do everything we can to show our mother-in-law that we appreciate how they raised their son to be the man with whom we fell in love. If she could do that, then we should strive to learn directly from her, how she did it, so we can raise our sons and daughters to be the kind of people others will admire and want to marry. If we can do that, we will be helping to have a good relationship with our mothers-in-law. It is not just the mother who needs to put forth the effort, but the wife must make a home where her mother-in-law feels comfortable to visit. We should strive with all we can to change this warped idea of the evil mother-in-law.

Let us not lose sight of the daughter-in-law's place in this ideal family either. If you notice, both Orpah and Ruth loved their mother-in-law. They were both willing to go to Bethlehem with her, just to see her happy again. They had both lost husbands, but they put their own grief aside to see that Naomi would be happy. They set out on the journey with Naomi, even though they knew it would be a dangerous trip. Three women traveling alone or even with a caravan could meet with all types of danger … robbery, kidnapping, even death from evil people or from wild animals. Yet, Orpah and Ruth did not hesitate to go with Naomi. They could have argued with her. They could have tried to convince her that they would find new husbands in Moab that would be willing to take care of her too. Naomi had heard the famine was over in Israel and they knew how much she longed to go home to Bethlehem, so they all packed and started on the journey.

They made it half way through the first day when Naomi put a road block in their way. Her love for them was so overwhelming she had to send them back. Orpah and Ruth both struggled with doing what Naomi told them to do. Should they insist on going along? It would be even more dangerous for Naomi to travel alone. Should they risk upsetting Naomi more by ignoring her wishes for them to go back? Would Naomi be angry with them and hold it against them if they insisted they go with her? Did Naomi really mean to hurt them by insisting they were going with her only to find new husbands? Orpah decided to give in to her mother-in-law's wishes and go back. After all, if it made Naomi angry with her for leaving, at least she would not know it. It must have been extremely hard for her to turn around and go back to the pagan gods of Moab after knowing the love of Yahweh. It would be extremely difficult for her to continue to worship Yahweh when all around her were worshipping pagan gods, but she did go back. That is the last we hear of her.

Ruth risked making her mother-in-law angry by insisting she would go with Naomi. Not only insisting she continue on the journey, but insist that Naomi stop trying to persuade her to go back. She risked having Naomi angry with her for the rest of her life, too. That would have been a miserable life. Living in a foreign land and the only person you know is just angry all the time. Ruth knew her mother-in-law too well; she knew that if Naomi got angry at her for disobeying, she would not stay angry. Naomi was a good woman and a great mother-in-law who loved her daughters-in-law. How could she be angry if Ruth explained why she was going to disobey?

Here we have one of the most beautiful passages of love in the whole Bible. There are few expressions of love today that do not include the sexual aspect of "love making".
This passage has nothing to do with sex. Although it is often used at weddings to express the love of a woman for the man who is becoming her husband, that is not how it is used here. I have also seen this passage used to validate homosexual love of two women, but that is a perversion of the text. There is nothing of a homosexual nature here. This statement of "where you go ..." is simply and beautifully set apart as the pure love of one person for another. In today's society the word love has become a synonym used for sexual activities. It has lost the basic meaning of a bond between two people. Funk and Wagnalls Standard Desk Dictionary defines love first as "a deep devotion or affection for another person or persons". This defines Ruth's statement to Naomi. It is a devotion to the woman she thinks of as mother and friend. She cannot bear the thought of leaving Naomi because of her devotion to Naomi and to Naomi's God. Giving up security and a future family in Moab is a small sacrifice for staying with such a friend.

POSSIBLE PATHS OF RUTH AND NAOMI

→ Northern Path ·········▶ Southern Path

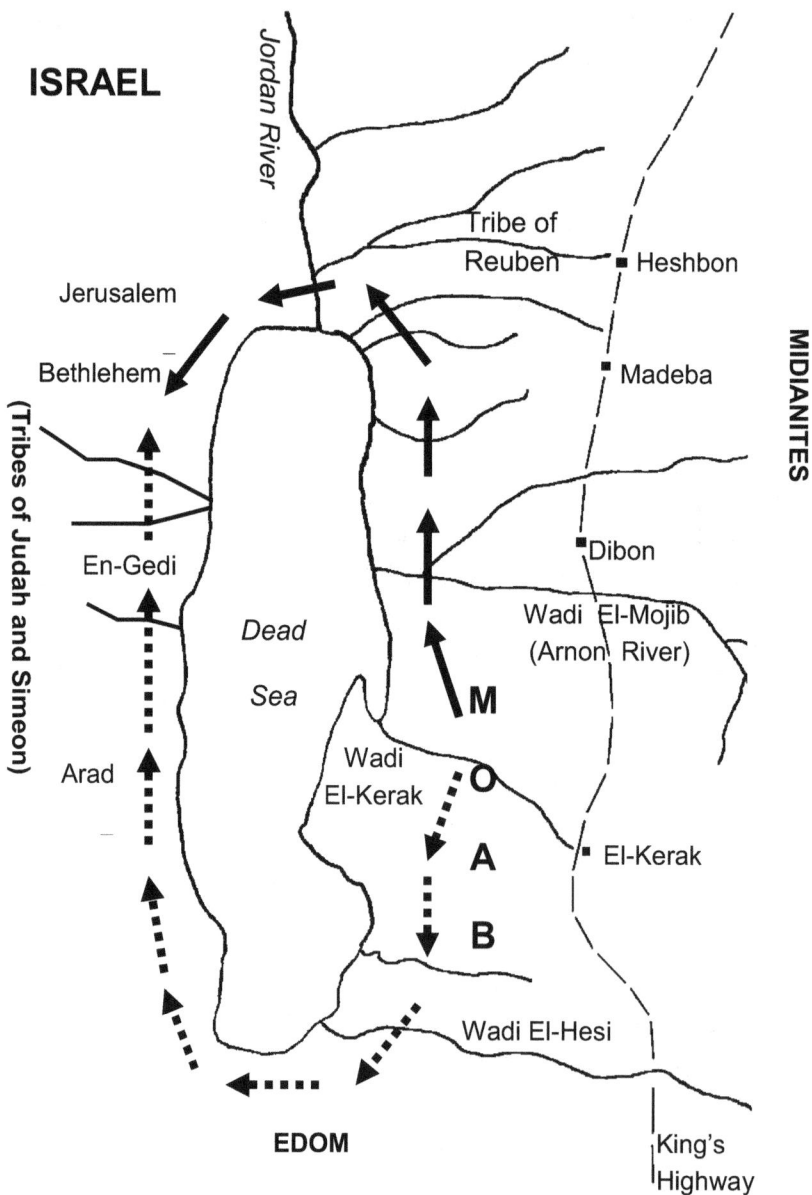

ISRAEL

Jordan River

Jerusalem

Bethlehem

En-Gedi

Arad

Dead
Sea

(Tribes of Judah and Simeon)

Tribe of
Reuben

Heshbon

Madeba

MIDIANITES

Dibon

Wadi El-Mojib
(Arnon River)

M

Wadi
El-Kerak

O

A

B

El-Kerak

Wadi El-Hesi

EDOM

King's
Highway

130

This type of love and devotion is also spoken of in I Corinthians 13, and more importantly in John 3:16-17, "For God so loved the world, that he gave his only begotten Son, that whosoever believeth in him should not perish, but have everlasting life. For God sent not his Son into the world to condemn the world; but that the world through him might be saved." God loves us and is devoted to us even more than Ruth loved Naomi, and He proved it by sending His only son to save us. WOW! What a love! Nothing we can come up with can rival this type of love.

The journey for Naomi and Ruth took at least three days on foot … more depending on how many stops they took to rest. Since nothing is said about them joining a caravan, we can only assume they walked by themselves. The caravan that brought the news from Bethlehem, had come from that area a few days before, and was now traveling away from Israel and Moab, so there was no way for it to help Naomi and Ruth get to Bethlehem. They had to travel alone or wait until a caravan came through their area headed in the other direction. That could take months. Naomi was not willing to wait. She wanted to go home to Bethlehem, and she wanted to go now. She wanted to see old friends and hear what news they had from the past ten years. It would have been about the same distance if they had gone north on the east side of the Dead Sea and crossed the Jordan River just above where it goes into the Dead Sea, or if they had walked around the southern end of the Dead Sea and northward on the western side of the Dead Sea. Since we do not know exactly where they were in Moab, we really cannot speculate on which way they went. The southern route would have been hotter and drier, with fewer towns to pass by or through, but they would not have had to worry about crossing the Jordan River. Either way they would have had to be on watch for bandits and wild animals. Food along the way would have consisted of whatever they could carry or barter for at any settlement or town they passed through. Their main food would have been unleavened bread as it could be kept for several days without going bad. Perhaps a few figs or other fruits that were ripening early could have been picked along the way, or some of the barley grain that was ripening in the fields. Jewish law allowed a traveler to enter any field or vineyard and pick what they needed to eat at that time. They were not allowed to pick extra to save for another day. The famine was over in Israel, so the fields were full of grain to be harvested.

The terrain would have been difficult as well. They would have traveled on hard dirt paths during the hot days and slept on the hard ground during the cold nights. Sometimes the way would be flat and hard, other times it would be steep and jagged. Finding shelter for the cold nights would also be a necessity. There are caves along the Dead Sea in some areas, or they might use tree or bush branches to make a sort of lean-to shelter. They may have gone out of their way a little to spend the night in a village along the way. They may have actually stayed in a village for a day or so to work for someone in exchange for food needed to continue the journey.

While walking they would have stayed near the Dead Sea although not on the same level of ground. There is a plateau on the eastern side of the Dead Sea that would have been better for traveling as the climate is very hot the nearer you get to the Dead Sea. On the western side of the Dead Sea the hilly terrain may have caused them to stay nearer the Sea to find flatter land. By the time they arrived in Bethlehem, both women would have been exhausted and worn out from the constant walking. Even with frequent stops to rest, the journey was long and difficult for the two women traveling alone. It must have seemed like a hopeless journey for them, but they made it. They arrived in Bethlehem in time for the Barley harvest in early spring. This was the first grain to be harvested during the year and it was an exciting time for the people. In fact, it was a very hopeful time. It meant there would be food for the community. Considering Naomi left Bethlehem during a famine and had only recently learned the famine was over, she would have seen the barley fields as a sign of hope for the future. It must have been a wonderfully beautiful site to her as she walked into Bethlehem.

INSPIRATIONAL LESSON:

Ruth's love shown in "Do not urge me to leave you … wherever you stay, I will stay … your God my God …" can be seen in Jesus's love for us. Jesus loves us so much he begs us not to send Him away. He came to earth where we dwell to live where we live, to die where we die, to save us and to redeem us.

After doing all that, we can see His love for us by changing the words of Ruth slightly. Just close your eyes and hear the savior saying to you … "I will not leave you ("I am with you always, even to the end of the age" Matthew 28:20), for where I go you will go and where I stay you will stay ("In My Father's house are many dwelling places. If it were not so, I would have told you. I am going to prepare a place for you," John 14:2). He is waiting for us now. "My people will be your people." ("For whoever does the will of My Father who is in heaven is My brother, and sister, and mother," Matthew 12:50). We have become part of the family of Jesus. He is our brother and God is our father. We are His people. "Where I die you will die … but death will not part you and me." ("For He is not the God of the dead, but of the living. For to Him all live," Luke 20:38.)

Christ died on earth to redeem us from our sins, so we will not stay dead, just as He did not stay dead. He has given us everlasting life with Him in heaven.

RUTH AND NAOMI IN BETHLEHEM (Ruth 1:19-22)

Ruth 1:19 "So they both went on until they came to Bethlehem. When they came to Bethlehem, the whole town was stirred because of them, and the women asked, 'Is this Naomi?'"

Ruth 1:20 "But she said to them, 'Do not call me Naomi. Call me Mara, because the Almighty has brought great bitterness to me.'"

Ruth 1:21 "'I was full when I left, but the LORD has caused me to return empty. Why should you call me Naomi when the LORD has opposed me? The Almighty has brought misfortune upon me!'"

Ruth 1:22 "So Naomi returned from the land of Moab with Ruth the Moabite, her daughter-in-law. They came to Bethlehem at the start of the spring barley harvest."

When Naomi arrived in Bethlehem all the hopelessness came flooding back in. The people of Bethlehem still remembered Naomi, but they barely recognized her. "Is this Naomi?" they ask surprised to see her. Why were they surprised? There are a number of reasons. She had been gone for ten years. After all that time many felt she and her family would never come back. Elimelek and Naomi had been well off financially when they left, but this woman comes back looking like a pauper. She had lost weight from the journey as well as lack of food along the way. Naomi had two sons when she left, but this woman comes back with only a young girl who is obviously too old to have been born to Naomi while she was away. Although Ruth may have been trying to care for Naomi, she did not look or act like a servant. It is understandable the people of Bethlehem would ask each other, and Naomi, "Is this Naomi?"

If Naomi looked so differently why did they even think this was Naomi. Because Naomi had gone to Moab, and they could tell by her clothes that the young girl with Naomi was from Moab. Maybe Naomi's clothes looked somewhat Moabite-ish also. After ten years she would surely have adopted some of the styles or used some of the same cloth the Moabites used to make her clothes.

Also, many of these women had been young girls when Naomi and her family left. They remembered her from the point of view of a young child, but now were looking at her through the eyes of a woman with a husband and children of their own. This woman they were looking at, resembled the adult woman who had children they had played with, but was now much older with hair of grey and wrinkles. Where was her former smile and cheerful voice?

Yes, the woman looked a little like the Naomi they remembered, or perhaps she looked like her mother had when she was Naomi's age and they recognized the family resemblance. Whatever it was, they did recognize her, but she was so different they had to ask to be sure … "Is this Naomi?" Naomi was understandably depressed. She had been longing to go home for so long; she had given little thought to how much everything and everyone would have changed … or even to how much she herself had changed. For Naomi, time had stood still in Bethlehem. She still remembered the Bethlehem she had left 10 years before. For the people of Bethlehem time had moved on. Now the reality of 10 years away came flooding in to Naomi.

She had to ask herself, "Am I the Naomi that left Bethlehem ten years ago?" Her answer was "ABSOLUTELY NOT", so she responded to the people of the town with that answer. "Don't call me PLEASANT (Naomi), because MY GOD IS KING (Elimelek) is dead!" How could she ever be pleasant or happy again? Her life was "full" when she left Bethlehem. She had a family ... a husband who obviously loved her, and two sons. They were happy together. Now, not only her husband, but also her only two sons (the reason they had left Bethlehem in the first place) were dead! This was just more than she could bear for the moment. All those feelings of loss, and helplessness came flooding in. She was bitter. Here she had traveled the long difficult journey back to her home and all she felt was hopelessness. "Call me BITTER (Mara)!" she complained, and then she began to tell them all the bitterness that had happened to her.

It is interesting here that Naomi declares that Almighty (God) had afflicted her. Why would she think God had done all this to her? Did she feel guilty for leaving Bethlehem -- the land God had promised to His people? Did she not know God had allowed the famine to cause them to go hungry because of their sins? Did she really think she was the only one to suffer over the last ten years?

We have all known people like that ... people who think they are the only ones who have had anything bad happen to them. After a while (weeks, months, or however long we allow it) of listening to them, we start to think they may just be seeking attention, and we start staying away from them. This was not the case with Naomi.

Naomi was normally a very pleasant, happy person. Even though she tried to persuade Ruth not to go with her because of possible bad things, she probably did everything she could along the journey to keep Ruth's spirits up. Now she arrived in Bethlehem where she felt her friends were, and the realization of ten years of change in her and the people of Bethlehem suddenly came crashing down around her. She just let it all out at once. No doubt the people had mixed reactions to her outburst. Many continued to ask "can this really be Naomi?" She would never act like that before. Then they moved away from her. Others did the opposite. They moved closer to her. They asked her to explain. They probably asked who this girl was traveling with her, too. Others brought her and Ruth some food to give them strength while Naomi told her story of the past ten years. When it was all over, someone may have told Naomi that her old house was still empty and they could probably live there if they cleaned it up a bit, which they gladly agreed to do. Maybe some of the friends and neighbors even helped, or sent their sons and daughters over to help.

You may think I am just assuming things here ... maybe being optimistic about the situation, but I do not think so. Why? The next chapter shows Ruth and Naomi living somewhat comfortably in a home that is implied to be Naomi's. Although the chapter ends leaving us on a somewhat hopeless note, if we keep in mind that chapter divisions were not in the original text, we can continue to notice that what seemed hopeless, actually turns out to be hopeful for the women newly arrived in Bethlehem. That Naomi did not stay in this state of hopelessness is also implied in the fact that no one ever actually called her Mara (bitter).

INSPIRATIONAL LESSON:

We can learn a lot from Naomi's outburst. How many times have you felt depressed over something real or imaginary and you just kept it to yourself? You just sit around feeling bad, and the more you sit around thinking about the situation, the worse it seems to get. You think there is no one who cares about what happened, or about how you feel about it. This goes on for a long time and you begin to think you cannot even pray about it, because it is just so awful. All you can say, is "Lord, please help me."

Then you see an old friend who says, "How are you doing?" For some reason you just blurt out everything that happened and how miserable you feel, etc. Then you think, "Oh no, why did I tell him or her all of that?" To your surprise your friend puts his/her arm around you and says, "Let's see if I can help you with this." WOW! A burden has been lifted off your shoulders. Maybe it is not as bad as you thought. Maybe there is a way to make things better.   Maybe there is hope! Maybe this person was the answer to your prayer?

There is always hope where God is concerned. He does not give up on any of us, just as He did not give up on Naomi. He will send someone to help us through the bad times as well as through the good times. We just need to trust Him and His people … our Christian friends. Satan wants us to think something is so bad we cannot tell anyone else about it, not even God. That just is not true. God already knows about it. A burden shared is a much lighter load to carry and soon the burden is gone all together.

RUTH IS A VIRTUOUS WOMAN (Ruth 2:1-3)

Ruth 2:1 "Now Naomi had a relative of her husband, a man of prominence and means from the clan of Elimelek. His name was Boaz."

We are not told in this verse exactly what Boaz's relation was to Elimelek, but it is likely he was a brother, since Ruth uses the levirate marriage law to ask him to marry her and raise up a child to Mahlon and by extension to Elimelek. Naomi was too old to bear any more children as she mentioned in chapter one. In addition, she did not qualify for a levirate marriage because she had had children with her husband even though they were now dead. Ruth was the person who qualified for a levirate marriage, but there were no brothers of her husband left to marry. A brother of her father-in-law was the closest relative, but he was not bound by the law, unless he wanted to be. There is no law that speaks of anyone performing the duty of a levirate marriage except a brother of the dead man.

The Hebrew word translated "prominence" (חיל Chayil) here actually refers to more than just a man of means. He could be a valiant man or a man of riches, virtue or strength. It is obvious Boaz was a man looked up to by the people around him. He had money as seen by the fact that he had people who worked for him, and not just workers, but workers who were overseers of other workers. He was also a man of virtue as we see by his greeting to his workers later in this chapter, and by the way he treats a stranger in his fields.

The meaning of the name Boaz (בֹּעַז bô'az) is not known for sure. Commentators are divided on its meaning. Some say it means "strength" or "in him is strength", while others say it means "fleetness" or "quickness". It is only found in the Bible referring to two things ... the Boaz we see here, and the name of the left of two pillars in front of Solomon's temple (See I Kings 7:21 and 2 Chronicles 3:17). Since it was used for a pillar of the temple, it makes more sense that it would mean "strength" rather than "quickness". One would suppose the pillar would be named for an attribute of the temple and of God ... we know we have a strong God who watches over us.

Ruth 2:2 "Ruth the Moabitess said to Naomi, 'Please let me go into the field and glean among the heads of grain behind anyone in whose eyes I may find favor.' Naomi said to her, 'Go, my daughter.'"

Ruth was not totally familiar with the customs of Israel, so she consults her mother-in-law to be sure she understands her rights here. If she had misunderstood the custom, Naomi would have said, "No, don't go" and would have explained why. Since Naomi says to go, Ruth knows she has understood correctly. Also, notice that Ruth does not just say, "Let me go glean anywhere." She specifically says; let me glean "behind anyone in whose eyes I may find favor." She knew she was a widow and a foreigner in this land, and these qualified her to glean in the fields. She did not want to force herself on anyone. That would not be a good way to be accepted in her new country. Instead she assured Naomi she would only glean in the field of someone who approved of her being there. She would ask first and then glean only when she had permission. Naomi approved of this decision. At this point she was not looking for a husband, but only to find food for herself and her mother-in-law. If she and Naomi were to make it through the year, they would need to have food for now and for the winter. That would mean she needed to get started as soon as she could.

We are not told how long it was between the time Ruth and Naomi arrived in Bethlehem and when Ruth volunteered to go to the fields to glean, but it was probably only a day or two at most. While friends and family may have brought some food for the two women, they could not expect to live only on food provided by others. Ruth had talked with other women when she went to the well to get water, and learned about the right of widows, orphans, and foreigners to glean in the fields during the harvest. This was a law among the Jews. It is recorded in

Leviticus 19:9-10; 23:22; and Deuteronomy 24:19-21 that when a farmer harvests his fields or vineyards, he should not clean the grain all the way to the corners, and he should not go back a second time to pick up anything he had missed or dropped. These grains left were to be untouched by the farmer or his servants. They were to be left to the widowed, orphaned, or stranger. The stranger would refer to people from other lands Jewish or not.

Naomi may not have told Ruth about this law because she was afraid Ruth would insist on going to the fields to glean and that could be dangerous. In ancient times farms were very different than they are today. Good farm fields, while owned by an individual or family, were mostly all located in the same area outside the city. The fields were separated by stones setup every few yards to indicate the extent of the field owned by a specific person, or in many cases the owners just knew which fields were theirs and there might be a small strip of land left without grain between them.

At harvest time, the farmers and their workers would go out into their field(s) and pick the grain. Young men would use sickles to cut the grain (stem and all) near the ground. Young ladies would come behind them and bundle the stalks of grain into bunches, which would then be gathered by the men and loaded onto donkeys, oxen, or carts pulled by oxen, and taken to the threshing floor. Harvesting the grain was difficult work. Bending, cutting, bundling and carrying all took a strong body. Harvesting all the fields would take several weeks.

It is interesting how artists depict scenes of Ruth and other women working in the grain fields. They almost always show them barefooted. From my years growing up on a farm I can tell you that walking barefoot over the stubble left from cut grain (whether cut by machine or hand) is something no one wants to do. The stems left in the ground are sharp enough to cut right through flesh. You would not want to walk through a cut grain field without wearing sandals or shoes unless you wanted painful bleeding feet. You can be sure Ruth and the other workers wore at least sandals with strong leather soles or other types of covering on their feet while harvesting or gleaning in the fields.

All the farmers knew about God's laws to allow the widow to glean, but as we have seen before, not all Jews followed God's laws completely. When Naomi left Bethlehem to move to Moab with her family, Israel was not following God's laws. She may have known of men who chased gleaners away, or treated them harshly, or even raped widows who had no one to protect them. Naomi may have feared some of these same things might happen to Ruth if she went alone to the fields. Naomi did not realize all the people had returned to worshipping Yahweh and following His laws and that is what led to the end of the famine. Any major breach of the law would certainly have brought the elders of the city down on the man who dared to ignore these laws.

Naomi had land that could be planted, and she and Ruth would have certainly done their best to raise food for themselves, but it was harvest time now … not planting time. Even if they started to plant that very day, it would be months before their field would produce any food for them. They had to do something now to keep from starving. Ruth knew Naomi was older and the strain of working all day in the fields might be too much for her. Ruth was young and she could certainly work in the fields if it was permitted. She was a foreigner and a widow, so she was allowed, if she understood the law she had heard correctly. Instead of just going out to the field though, she asked Naomi about it. Naomi knew God's laws, and she would guide Ruth. Ruth was the newcomer so she did not want to take a chance of doing something wrong and embarrassing both Naomi and herself.

We should note here that in the King James Version of this verse it says "corn" (בַּשִׁבֳּלִים be-shib-bo'-lem), the Hebrew word used here actually refers to any type of grain. In old English the word "corn" also referred to any type of grain, so that is why King James' translators used it. Today "corn" refers to a specific type of vegetable that is yellow and sweet to eat. We know from the last verse of chapter one, the grain that was being harvested at this time was actually barley.

Barley was a grain planted in the Fall about the time of the first rains. It then stayed in the ground over the winter and came up in the Spring. It would be harvested during March and April. It was a highly nutritious grain, having lots of fiber, potassium, folate, and vitamin B6. In addition, there is little to no cholesterol in Barley. This makes it good for the heart. It was used for bread, although the low amount of gluten made it better for flat breads rather than breads that need to rise (wheat was better for those breads). It was also used in soups, porridge, and stews. In ancient Israel, it was also a popular feed for cattle.

> Ruth 2:3 *"So she went to glean in the field behind the harvesters. She happened to come to a part of the field belonging to Boaz, who was from the clan of Elimelek."*

Ruth did not hesitate to work for her food. She did not sit around and cry about having little or no food. She did not blame Naomi or expect Naomi to provide for her. Instead she looked for ways to earn food. The Israelite law allowing widows, orphans, and foreigners to glean in the fields or harvest vineyards or olive groves, was God's welfare plan for Israel. No one got by without working. They did not go down to the

Bethlehem Office of Human Resources and sign up for a weekly package of grain and fruit. Instead everyone worked. It was no disgrace to be poor in Israel. It was a disgrace not to provide for your family. God had made provision for everyone, even the poor, to provide for their family, but they had to work for it. They had to go to the field and pick up fallen grain, or pick the grain from the corners of the fields. Then they had to beat it out and take it home and cook their own food.

While it could be said the farmer supported the poor, the farmer did NOT do the work for the poor. The farmer did NOT harvest his own grain, winnow it, load it into a sack or basket, and deliver it to the poor families' door. NO, just the opposite, the farm owner did nothing to get the food to his poor neighbor. He just left it in the field, so the poor person could feel good about gathering his own harvest from the leftovers. Of course, it all came from God, but by providing for the land owner, God also provided for the poor.

It would be great if our welfare system worked like that today. Instead of giving healthy people a check every month, we give them a place to harvest their own food. Instead of giving out food stamps, we say, "Well, farmer Brown is harvesting his corn this week; you can go down to his farm and pick the corn that's left after his workers get finished. You will probably get enough to make cornmeal and keep your family fed for a week. Then farmer Smith will be harvesting his tomatoes, you can get the tomatoes that are left when he finishes. Some of them may still be green but they will ripen in your kitchen. Ruth skipped the welfare office and with Naomi's consent she went straight to the fields.

The beginning of this verse is interesting and translated several ways, which ultimately mean the same thing. The MEV simplifies this verse by starting it with "So she went to glean in the field ..." The KJV translates it that Ruth "went and came", while the ESV says, "So she set out and went and gleaned in the field...". Some have said this shows she was unfamiliar with the area so she went a little way, came back to Naomi's home, and then went out a little farther, etc. Obviously, the people who say this did not grow up where I did. This was how we talked when I was growing up on a farm in Kentucky. We went and came to school, or we went and came to grandma's house, etc. For those who do not understand this, perhaps a better way to translate it would be she "went until she came" to a field which happened to be the field of Boaz. Ruth would have known where to go even though she was new in the area. If she did not know, she only needed to ask Naomi before she left home. Naomi grew up there and knew exactly where the grain fields were. If Ruth had gone out a little way and then back to Naomi's home and repeated this many times until she was familiar with the land, the day would have been mostly over before she reached the fields. The MEV and ESV translations give a much easier to understand translation of the beginning of the verse.

Notice also, Ruth happened on the field of Boaz. This was no coincidence. God was guiding her quietly to the field He wanted her to go into. She may have stopped at other fields along the way and met with resistance when she asked if she could glean, or Boaz's field may have been the first one a person would come to when traveling from Bethlehem. We do not know which was the case, but we do know God was watching out for her.

INSPIRATIONAL LESSON:

Ruth's new life in Bethlehem must have been a bit overwhelming at first. There were lots of people that Naomi knew but none Ruth knew, except Naomi. The area was also new to her. Ruth knew where the well was and went every day to draw water for their needs. Other than that, she knew only what Naomi and Naomi's friends told her. It must have seemed pretty hopeless at first for her. They had food for today, but none for tomorrow and today's food may have been sparse. She could have given up and just sit in the yard thinking of her father's house back in Moab where there was plenty of food, but she did not. Instead she took what she had learned about gleaning and went to work. With the Lord's help she found a good field to glean in so she and Naomi had food to last for a while.

What do we know about Ruth's qualities? We know she was a listener. She listened to Naomi who taught her how to be a good wife to Naomi's son. She stood up for what she knew was right even if it meant making someone angry with her, because she stood up to Naomi when she wanted Ruth to go back to Moab. Ruth knew it would be wrong to leave Naomi, and Ruth knew it would be wrong to go back to the Moabite idols. She was a hard worker. She gleaned in the field which was hot, hard work. She did not complain. I imagine that first night she came home from the fields with aches and pains in places she did not know she had places. Yet she went back the next morning and the next and the next for weeks to do it all over again. This was a brave woman who knew when to speak up and when to bow down; when to go to work and when to stay at home.

Looking at the description of a virtuous women in Proverbs 31, we find in several verses that she "works willingly with her hands", "brings her food from afar", "strengthens her arms", "strength and honor are her clothing; and she will rejoice in time to come", "She looks well to the ways of her household, and does not eat the bread of idleness", "a woman that fears the LORD", and "let her own works praise her in the gates". We see all these things in Ruth and there is more to come. Already we know she truly was a virtuous woman. We should try to follow her example.

RUTH AND BOAZ (Ruth 2:4-16)

> Ruth 2:4 *"Just then Boaz came from Bethlehem and said to the harvesters, 'May the LORD be with you!'"*

What a wonderful way to greet people. Imagine how much better the world would be if everyone you met greeted you with "May the LORD be with you." Boaz obviously liked the people who worked for him and they obviously liked him. There was mutual respect here and it showed. There was also a love of the Lord here and that showed, too.

> Ruth 2:5 *"Then Boaz said to his servant who was in charge of his harvesters, 'Whose young woman is this?'"*

Boaz was an observant man. He knew his employees. When he looked over his fields, he immediately noticed a strange woman. She could have been a new employee his overseer hired that morning, but Boaz probably knew all the people in and around Bethlehem, and he did not recognize this young lady. There was also something different about her. Being a Moabite, it might have been that her clothing was different, or it might have been that she was awkward in the way she worked. Ruth was not used to gleaning and may have been getting used to the back-breaking work, so instead of a steady movement like the usual women who worked in Boaz's fields, Ruth's movements were somewhat jerky, or uneven as she tried to take it easy on her sore muscles that were becoming more sore each time she stooped to pick up grain. Whatever it was, it immediately caught Boaz's attention.

> *Ruth 2:6 "So the servant who was in charge of his harvesters answered, 'She is the young Moabitess woman who came back with Naomi from the land of Moab.'"*

The overseer tries to explain why this woman is unfamiliar to Boaz and why she is in his field all at the same time. The story of Naomi's return had by now spread all over Bethlehem and the surrounding areas. Gossip travels fast. The servant could explain with only a few words: the young woman who came from Moab with Naomi. The servant knew Naomi's husband Elimelek and Boaz were brothers. His explanation led Boaz to understand immediately who she was.

> *Ruth 2:7 "She said, 'Please let me glean and gather grain among the bundles behind the harvesters.' So she came and has remained from morning until now, though she rested a little while in the house.'"*

The servant may not have known if all the gossip about Ruth and Naomi had reached the boss's ear, so he went on to explain that she was indeed a hard worker. She has been working from early morning and only stopped for a short time to go into the house. The house he referred to was probably more of a shed without walls. Something similar to a permanent canopy. It was built to provide shade for the workers, so they could get out of the sun for a while to rest during mealtime and breaks. It was not a house in the sense that someone lived there all the time.

Ruth 2:8 "Then Boaz said to Ruth, 'Listen, my daughter. Do not go to glean in another field and leave this one. Stay close to my young women."

Ruth 2:9 "Keep your eyes on the field in which they reap and follow after them. I have commanded the men not to touch you. When you are thirsty, go to the vessels and drink from what the young men have drawn."

Boaz realized Ruth was the widow of a close relative. As such he had an obligation to her. He should guide her in her work, and he should let his employees know she is welcome in his fields. He does both with one effort. He walks right over to her and talks to her. The employees notice she has his attention, so they should not harass her. Then he says to her, listen to me, daughter? He could have said, listen to me child or woman, but by using the word daughter he shows he realizes she is family. Ruth herself may not have understood this yet. Naomi does not tell her about their relationship with Boaz until Ruth gets home that evening. Boaz goes on to tell Ruth to stay in his fields until the harvest is over. Do not go to other people's fields, but stay in his. He is taking care of her needs without embarrassing her. Then he notices she did not bring a water jar or food, so he tells her to drink from the jars of water his employees bring from the well every day. This was a privilege reserved for workers and family members, but not for gleaners. Here again, Boaz shows he realizes Ruth is a relative. It does not matter to him that she is a Moabitess. What matters is she was married to a member of his family and that makes her family.

Another reason Boaz may have been more lenient with Ruth even though she was a relative is because his own mother was not originally a Jew. We learn in Matthew 1:5, Boaz's father was Salman and his mother was Rahab. Why is that name familiar? Because she was the harlot who saved the spies Joshua sent out to Jericho (see Joshua 2). Rahab sent the men of Jericho out to the wilderness to look for the Jewish spies while all the time she had them hidden on her roof. Her only request was that the Israelites spare her and her family when they destroyed Jericho. She believed in the true God Yahweh from the beginning even though she was not a Jew. The spies told her to hang a scarlet cord out her window and everyone in her house would be spared (See Joshua 6:23 and 25). Boaz knew from stories his mother told him, what it was like for a foreign woman to come to be a believer in Yahweh, and what it was like when she was finally accepted by the people of Yahweh.

> *Ruth 2:10 "So she fell on her face, bowed down to the ground, and said to him, 'Why have I found favor in your eyes, that you should acknowledge me, a foreigner?'"*

Ruth humbled herself before Boaz. She did not know that he was a near relative and even if she had, it probably would not have made any difference in her response to his kindness. All she knew was that he was the owner of the field she was working in and he was going out of his way to be nice to her. On the other hand, Boaz knew she was a relative. He had heard the stories going around Bethlehem about Naomi's return and that she had brought her widowed daughter-in-law with her. Being a wealthy man of high esteem in the village, he was probably kept appraised of everything that went on in Bethlehem, so he knew Ruth was a good person who cared for Naomi.

She did not know that he knew. All she could think of was, "Why is this obviously wealthy man paying attention to me?" Her curiosity got the best of her and she could not help asking the question, but she did not blurt it out in an unkind manner. Instead she humbled herself in front of him bowing to the ground, and while in this position she asked, "Why are you being so nice to me since I am obviously a stranger?" We do not know what sort of answer Ruth expected, or if she even expected one at all. It is doubtful she expected Boaz to have heard about Naomi and her. If she had known Boaz was a relative, she might not have asked the question, but would have assumed he was being nice to her because she was a relative, or at least because she was taking care of his relative.

Ruth 2:11 *"Boaz answered and said to her, 'I have been told all that you have done for your mother-in-law after the death of your husband, and how you left your father and mother and your homeland and came to a people you did not know before.'"*

Boaz was known in the village to be an honorable man. His workers would not think twice about him talking to a gleaner. They also already knew that Naomi (and Ruth) were relatives of Boaz. Boaz's actions did not cause a stir among the workers. They saw how he immediately took notice of Ruth, but then she was a beautiful girl. She was also young enough to be his daughter, maybe even his granddaughter. Boaz does not tell Ruth that he is a relative, but he lets her know he knows who she is. He has heard not only that she came back to Bethlehem with Naomi, but that she is a Moabitess and has left her parents to stay with her mother-in-law. These are important facts, because they told Boaz what type of woman she is. Now that he has met her, he sees that she is indeed an honorable woman.

Ruth 2:12 "'May the LORD reward your deeds. May you have a full reward from the LORD, the God of Israel, under whose wings you have come to take refuge.'"

Not only does Boaz tell Ruth that he knows who she is, but he seeks a blessing for her from the Lord. He knows she has not only left her homeland, but the false gods of Moab as well. This blessing is especially interesting when we look at the word used for "wings" in this passage. The Hebrew word כָּנָף (kânâph) used here refers to a covering. It can be translated "wings", or can be used for a corner of a blanket, skirt, or garment. This is the same word used later at the threshing floor when Ruth asks Boaz to spread his cloak over her. Boaz's blessing for Ruth will come back to him to fulfill. The important thing here, though, is that Boaz recognized that Ruth had already accepted Yahweh as her Lord. She was already an Israelite in her heart.

Ruth 2:13 "Then she said, 'May I find favor in your eyes, my lord, for you have comforted me and have spoken kindly to your servant, though I am not like one of your servant girls.'"

Ruth continues to be humbled by Boaz's speech to her. She is attracted to him because he is kind to her, and tells him that he has comforted her by being kind, but she reminds him that she is not like the other women in the village. She is a foreigner and she has no qualms about not being allowed to do the things the other women do. Much to her surprise, Boaz not only allows her to do all those things, but provides more for her.

Ruth 2:14 "At mealtime Boaz said to her, 'Come over here, and eat some bread, and dip your piece in the vinegar.'

So she sat down beside the harvesters, and he passed
her some roasted grain. She ate and was full and had
some left over."

When mealtime comes, Boaz calls Ruth over to the table
where he is eating with his hired workers. Verse 14 does not
follow verse 13 immediately. Boaz had gone back to consulting
his overseer and helping with the work. When mealtime arrived,
Boaz called to Ruth to come sit with the workers and eat of the
food that had been prepared for him and his workers.

Ruth must have been very surprised at this invitation, but
she sits beside the workers, not Boaz – a show of humility.
Boaz does not stop with just an invitation. He hands her
parched grain. Parched grain was a treat. It was made from
grain that was not quite ripe. The grain was harvested and
roasted over a fire and then eaten dry. We could compare it to
popcorn, except barley grain does not pop up as big as
popcorn. Parched grain was available only during the beginning
of the harvest time, so it was a treat for the people who had the
time to roast it.

Since Boaz obviously sat at the head of the table or even
at a different table from his workers, it is quite possible he had
to get up and take the parched grain over to Ruth to offer it to
her. He may have poured a large portion into a bowl and
passed it down the line of workers to her showing them all that
she was favored by him. She would not have assumed the
grain was available to her if Boaz had not offered it. Even
though it was a large portion, and more than she could eat, she
did not dare leave any behind when she was full for fear of
looking as if she did not appreciate his enormous generosity.
She also did not want to eat so much that it would make her
sluggish for working in the field during the afternoon. Boaz had
given her so much she could not eat it all, so she wrapped up

153

what was left and took it to her mother-in-law in the evening. Perhaps Boaz was testing her to see what she would do with more food than a person would normally eat. Would she waste it, or gorge herself, or save some for later, or even take it home to her mother-in-law? If it was a test, Ruth obviously passed with flying colors.

> Ruth 2:15 *"When she got up to glean, Boaz commanded his young men, 'Let her glean even among the bundles, and do not harm her.'"*

> Ruth 2:16 *"'Also pull out some grain for her from the bundles and leave it so that she may glean it, and do not rebuke her.'"*

Boaz must have been really impressed with Ruth. After she goes back to work which seems to be before the workers go back to the fields, Boaz takes the opportunity to tell his workers to let her glean among the already bundled grain. Normally a gleaner would stay behind the workers some distance and only pick up what was dropped or left behind as they cut the grain and bundled it into sheaves. The sheaves were then gathered up and piled at the side of the field to be loaded on wagons or donkeys and taken to the threshing floor. A gleaner who picked grain out of the bundles was often reprimanded and might even be asked to leave the field. Boaz wanted to be sure Ruth was not harassed in any way, so he told his workers to let her glean even from the bundles. Boaz goes even farther to assure Ruth will return to his fields. He tells his workers to pull some of the grain out of the bundles before they are tied and let it fall to the ground. Not just a small amount, but handfuls of grain. He wanted to be sure she and Naomi had plenty of grain to make bread for their meals.

INSPIRATIONAL LESSON:

Ruth had started out the day in a pretty grim situation. She was going to a stranger's field to beg, if necessary, but certainly to ask humbly if she could do hard work which might produce enough grain to allow her and Naomi to have bread for a day or two. She did not know what she would find … kindness or pain, but she went believing God would take care of her. By the end of the day she knew Yahweh had directed her to the field of Boaz, who had given her an enormous amount of grain to feed herself and Naomi. The world had changed from hopelessness to hope in just one day of work.

Have you ever been around a depressed person? They think their world is just terrible, so they sit around all day feeling sorry for themselves. Ruth could have been depressed. She certainly could have sat in the house all day worrying about where her next meal would come from. After all she was new in Bethlehem. No one would really expect her to work in the fields when she did not even know anyone yet. She did not do that. Instead she went to work. The time was right for work. The barley harvest had just begun and although she did not own a field or have a job, she went to the fields expecting to find food she could gather. She expected to work hard for it. She expected to sweat. She expected to ache at the end of the day. Yet she also expected that God would lead her to a field where the owner would allow her to work unmolested. What she found was an owner who not only let her work but provided lunch, water to drink, and extra grain for her to pick up. We should think and act like Ruth … work is the best cure for depression.

RUTH TAKES CARE OF NAOMI (Ruth 2:17-23)

*Ruth 2:17 "So she gleaned in the field until evening.
Then she beat out what she had gleaned, and it was
about an ephah of barley."*

Ruth worked all day long. It gets pretty hot in the
afternoons in Israel. Even though this was late Spring (early
Summer) time, the heat of the sun would have been plenty to
cause a worker to sweat while working. Ruth worked hard in
the field and then after everyone else quit, she kept working to
separate the grain from the stalks. Trying to carry the grain
attached to the stalks back home would have been too big a
burden for her to carry. Carrying just the grain was
manageable.

Ruth found a flat rock near the field and used a rounded
stone with sharp angles on one side or a strong stick to beat the
grain off the ends of the stalks. This in itself was a cumbersome
task to perform by hand, but Ruth willingly did it. Then she
would winnow the grain by lifting a small pile of grain up and
dropping it so the evening breeze would blow the chaff away.
She would do this over and over until she had finished all the
barley she had gleaned during the day.

After beating and winnowing the grain, she gathered it up
into her scarf or outer garment and bundled it tight so she could
carry it. An ephah of grain was quite a large amount for one
day's work. We do not know exactly how much an ephah was.
Some say it was about 20 to 25 pounds of grain. Others say it
was around 6 or 7 gallons. At any rate it was enough grain for
Ruth and Naomi to live on for five to seven days. That was a lot
more than most women glean in an average day, and we will
see later that Naomi was surprised at the huge amount of grain
Ruth brought home that first day. Of course, we know Ruth had

a little extra help from Boaz's instructions to his workers to purposefully pull out handfuls of stalks from the bundles and leave them behind for Ruth to glean. She could have stopped a few hours early if she had wanted to, but she did not. She worked all day and even worked a few hours longer than most.

> Ruth 2:18 "She took it up and went into the city, and her mother-in-law saw what she had gleaned. She drew it out and gave her what she had left, after she had been satisfied."

Ruth was probably so tired by the time she got home, all she wanted to do was go to bed. She had never gleaned before, so she did not know whether she had done well or whether Naomi would be disappointed in her.

Naomi would have had some meager meal prepared for them to eat when Ruth got home, but Ruth had a surprise for Naomi -- the parched grain that was left over from her lunch This delicacy was saved for Naomi, not for Ruth to eat later. Ruth was always thinking of Naomi's welfare first.

> Ruth 2:19 "Her mother-in-law said to her, 'Where did you glean today, and where did you work? May he who took notice of you be blessed.' So she told her mother-in-law with whom she had worked, and said, 'The name of the man with whom I worked today is Boaz.'"

> Ruth 2:20 "Then Naomi said to her daughter-in-law, 'May he be blessed of the LORD who has not withdrawn His kindness to the living and to the dead.' Naomi said to her, 'This man is a close relative of ours, one of our redeeming relatives.'"

Naomi had worried about how Ruth was doing all day. Did Ruth find a friendly field owner who allowed her to work, or had she moved from field to field for half the day before finding one where she felt safe. Remember Naomi is still laboring under the false concept that the field owners and/or workers are doing bad things as they did before she left Bethlehem 10 years ago. She probably spent the day worrying whether Ruth would be molested or harmed in some other way. Add to that the fact that Ruth stayed behind to beat out her grain after the other workers had left, and Naomi had time to imagine all sorts of bad things happening to her precious daughter-in-law. Just seeing Ruth come through the door was a great relief to Naomi, but then to see all the grain she was carrying. WOW! This girl knows how to work! On top of that she brought home parched grain!

Naomi could not control her excitement and curiosity, but Ruth sank into the nearest chair to rest her aching body. Ruth was not talking so Naomi was going to have to interrogate her. We can picture the scene. Ruth resting in that chair while Naomi walks around her not able to contain the curiosity. "Where did you work?" "Whose field was it?" "Tell me everything."

Ruth wearily tells Naomi, she worked in the field belonging to a man named Boaz who was very kind to her, although she did not know why. Naomi is about to burst with enthusiasm now, and blurts out … "Boaz is a relative of ours." For the first time since they came back to Bethlehem, Naomi is excited about their future. A near relative has taken notice of them and offered his help to them without treating them like some poor trashy burden of a relative. He has treated them with dignity. He could have said, "No relative of mine is going to glean in the fields. Go home and I'll send one of the workers over with a bushel of grain at the end of the day." He did not.

Instead he allowed her to work in an atmosphere of security and told the workers to be sure there was plenty for her to pick up. He respected her ambition and determination to work for what she and her mother-in-law ate.

Naomi also recognized this man as a "near" relative … perhaps the kinsman to redeem her and Ruth from poverty, by a levirate marriage with Ruth. Naomi did not bother Ruth with this information at the moment. She wanted to know more about Ruth's day.

Ruth 2:21 "Then Ruth the Moabitess said, 'He even told me, 'You should stay close to my servants until they have finished all my harvest.'"

Ruth 2:22 "Naomi said to Ruth her daughter-in-law, 'It is better, my daughter, that you go with his young women, for in someone else's field you might be harmed.'"

Ruth 2:23 "So she stayed close to the young women of Boaz to glean until the end of barley harvest and wheat harvest. And she lived with her mother-in-law."

Ruth was a Moabitess. She was born and raised in Moab. Many of her former lessons on how to act in society came from her childhood in Moab. She was rapidly adapting to life in Israel, but there were still nuances that she did not quite understand immediately. Boaz had told Ruth to stay near his young girls, but here we see Ruth telling Naomi that Boaz told her to keep near his servants. The King James Version says "young men". Did Ruth misunderstand Boaz? Or did she lie to Naomi? Probably neither. For Ruth in Moab, there may not have been any difference in opinion whether a young woman worked with the men or the women, so she used the masculine to explain what Boaz had said. As we see in the next verse,

Naomi (who grew up in Israel but had spent 10 years in Moab) corrected Ruth without chastising her. Naomi knew the difference, and she also recognized that Ruth would not automatically see a difference. Ruth speaks of the men in a sense of "all workers, both men and women", but Naomi repeats Ruth's statement agreeing with her but correcting the term to the feminine … Ruth should stay with his women workers. It was her way to let Ruth know without embarrassing her, that Boaz meant only the women workers. We know from the next verse that Ruth understood what her mother-in-law was trying to do, because she stayed with Boaz's young girls (maidens) to glean only in his fields.

The barley and wheat harvests lasted about seven weeks. If every day was as productive as the first, Ruth and Naomi had enough wheat and barley to make it through several months. Of course, there were also the grapes and olives to be harvested, so they could have had a good variety of food to last them if they had continued this way.

Ruth was a good-looking young woman and there were probably men in Bethlehem who noticed that, but Ruth was not looking around. She was still in mourning for her late husband, so no decent man would make an advance toward her. She went to work every day, except the Sabbath, and came home to live with her mother-in-law. There was no time for parties, no time to get to know the other young people in Bethlehem, except for some she worked with. She did not use her beauty to get special favors. In the fields she would not think she looked very good either. She was dirty, sweaty, and her hands were covered with calluses. Her hair fell into her face and was pushed back with a dirty hand. She was tired -- too tired to think of looking for a husband, if indeed she would be allowed to marry. She committed herself again to taking care of Naomi's needs, and she did it well.

INSPIRATIONAL LESSON:

When troubles surround you, what do you usually do? Do you sit around and think about all the bad things that have happened? Are you so paralyzed by the problems that you cannot think of anything else? Or are you like Ruth and get out and work. While reading the events of Ruth's life it is easy to forget that she just lost her beloved Mahlon a few weeks ago. She was still mourning his death, and at the same time she had moved to a strange land with her mother-in-law. On top of that they did not have much food. It was hopeless! She could have just sat around and cried all the time? I am sure she cried her share of tears for Mahlon, but she did not just sit around and feel sorry for herself.

We see in these verses many more qualities of Ruth's character. She was a woman of action. There was a job to be done (gleaning, winnowing, carrying home, etc.) and she did it. She was not a quitter. She could have told Naomi the work was too hard, or she was too sore from the previous day's work, or she could have said, "we have enough food now for a few days. I think I'll stay home until we need food again." Instead she got up every morning and went to the fields to work (except the Sabbath when no one worked).

Another quality was that she was not selfish. When she finished eating the parched grain Boaz had given her, she could have kept the leftover grain for herself. It would have been a nice snack during the afternoon or the next morning. Think of it like eating potato chips ... do we really want to share that bag of delightful potato chips with others? It is so tempting to keep it all to ourselves. Instead Ruth gave all the leftover parched grain to Naomi. She shared her delightful food with her mother-in-law.

Ruth trusted the Lord to help her and Naomi, but she did not just sit back and say, "OK Lord, give us food to eat." She said, "OK Lord, show me where you want me to work." She received a blessing for it. Not just the blessing from Boaz, but also the blessing of seeing her beloved mother-in-law happy again.

God tells us if we trust Him and keep his commandments that "The LORD will command the blessing on you in your barns and in all that you set your hand to do, and He will bless you in the land which the LORD your God is giving you" (Deuteronomy 28:8). He does not say to just sit still and I will just give you everything. There is work to be done and with the Lord's help we must do it. In Luke 10:1-2 we see Jesus sending out the seventy to do the work, "After this the Lord appointed seventy others, and sent them two by two ahead of Him into every city and place where He Himself was about to come. He said to them, 'The harvest truly is plentiful, but the laborers are few. Pray therefore the Lord of the harvest to send out laborers into His harvest.'" We are the laborers Christ sends out to do His work. Have you labored to tell others about Jesus? Are you too tired, too sore, or think it can wait a few days? What excuse are you using today? Are you like Ruth … you see a need to fill and go fill it?

RUTH LISTENS TO NAOMI (Ruth 3:1-6)

Ruth 3:1 "One day Naomi her mother-in-law said to her, 'My daughter, why should I not find a home that will be good for you?"

The grain harvests were over. Naomi had been planning for weeks what to do to get Boaz to live up to his obligations as a kinsman. Boaz was an honorable man, and would not pursue

Ruth while she was still mourning for her dead husband. He could see that she was still mourning by the clothing she wore. Also, Boaz was an old man compared to Ruth. How could he think that such a beautiful young woman would want to be married to him? After all, there were plenty of young men in Bethlehem that would make a good husband for her.

Naomi wanted Ruth to be happy, and she knew it was a husband and children for which Ruth longed. She also knew by now that Ruth was not going to make the first move on her own to attract a husband. Although Ruth's confidence in Jewish laws and customs was growing every day, Ruth still did not understand that she also had some rights under the law of the Lord, so Naomi would have to push her a little bit.

> *Ruth 3:2 "'Now is not Boaz our relative, with whose young women you have been working? Tonight he winnows barley on the threshing floor.'"*

This was not the first time Boaz had been winnowing harvested grain. He would have winnowed grain many times during both harvests. Many towns had one big threshing floor for the whole town to use, so naturally they had to take turns. A wealthy farmer could have built his own family threshing floor and Boaz was certainly wealthy enough to have done this.

We see that during this time when the famine was in Israel, in Judges 6:11 "Gideon threshed wheat by the winepress, to hide it from the Midianites." A winepress was often cut into the rock within the ground. It could be three feet deep. We found several in the area around Gezer when we were exploring the hills around the excavation. It would be a good place to hide the grain quickly if a raiding party came to steal the grain, but it was not in a good location for threshing the grain, which is why Gideon threshed there … to keep the

Midianites from finding and stealing what little grain his family grew. It was not the normal place to thresh grain, but shows the desperate times the people of Israel had gone through. That time was over and now threshing took place in the normal fashion.

A threshing floor was higher in the hills than the fields. It was above the farm land a bit, so the evening winds would come across it. Every evening a light wind would be present, so when the harvest was enough to fill the threshing floor, they would winnow the grain. Winnowing was done by first spreading the grain (still attached to the stalks) over the flat stone of the threshing floor. Then oxen or sometimes donkeys would pull a wooden sled with stones attached to the bottom over the grain. The stones would cut the grain away from the stalks, and cut the stalks into smaller bits. Large stone weights or sometimes children would ride on top of the sled to weigh it down against the grain.

After the grain and stalks were cut down into small pieces, the winnowing actually began. Large wooden pitchfork-like tools (sort of a cross between a shovel and a pitchfork) were used to scrape up the pieces of grain and stalks and throw them into the air. The breeze would blow the lighter chaff away and the heaver grain would fall to the ground. This had to be done over and over until all the chaff was gone. Then the grain would be scooped up and piled to the side of the threshing floor. The next morning the piled grain would be put into large jars for storage and carried down the hill to the home of the owner, or into town to be sold to others.

Winnowing was something of a festive time. The family would be there. The children enjoyed riding on the sled pulled by the oxen. The women would bring a meal … something like a picnic, but with work. Later the women and children would return home but the men would stay and guard the grain until morning when it would be taken back to the home, and/or barns to be stored and used later. If the owner had no wife and children, his servants would bring a feast to the threshing floor for the owner and his workers.

> Ruth 3:3 *"Now wash and anoint yourself, and put on your best clothes. Then go down to the threshing floor, but do not let the man know you are there until he has finished eating and drinking."*

Here is an often-misunderstood verse. It has been used to say Naomi was telling Ruth to seduce Boaz, but this was not the case. We can see from other scriptures what was really going on here. Ruth's husband had died in Moab shortly before she and Naomi came back to Bethlehem. Ruth was very much still in mourning for Mahlon. Her clothing reflected that. Even the fact that she did not put on sweet-smelling perfumes was an act of mourning. 2 Samuel 12:20 shows us another example of someone in mourning. King David mourned and prayed for his sick infant son for seven days. After the child died, David immediately washed, put on clean clothes, and anointed himself. When asked why he did this, his reply was that while the child was still alive there was a chance he would get well, but after he died there was no longer a chance he would get well. In other words, King David showed he had ended his period of sadness/grief over the child's condition and was moving on with his life. Just as a person who grieves for a dead loved one has to eventually stop grieving and move on with their life.

Another example of this comes from 2 Samuel 14:2, where King David's servant Joab tries to deceive the king by sending a woman to him to lie to him. Joab tells the woman to *"Act as if you are observing mourning rites. Put on mourning garments, and do not anoint yourself with oil, but act like a woman who has been mourning over the dead like this for many days.'"* Does this sound like what Ruth had been doing? She had been wearing mourning clothes and not anointing herself with oil (perfume). That is exactly what she was doing. (See also Daniel 10:2-3 for another example of people coming out of mourning).

Naomi was telling Ruth here that she had mourned enough for Mahlon, and now was the time to stop mourning and move forward with her life. No man would think of approaching Ruth or Naomi about marrying Ruth while she was still in mourning for her husband. How would they know when her time of mourning had ended? The way to tell the rest of Bethlehem including Boaz that Ruth was finished mourning, was for her to wash herself, anoint herself, and dress modestly. She did not care if all of Bethlehem knew her mourning time was over, only Boaz, and the way to do that was to go to the threshing floor and wait until he was alone.

Boaz was probably already at the threshing floor, so there would be no other time to tell him she was done with mourning. She was not going to the threshing floor to seduce Boaz, but to let him know her time of mourning was over. He could now take action to marry her if he so chose. Having sex before they were married was not part of it. Both Ruth and Boaz were honorable people who would never have considered such a thing.

> *Ruth 3:4 "'When he lies down, notice the place where he is lying. Go in and uncover his feet and lie down. He will tell you what you will do.'"*

Boaz would not be alone at the threshing floor. There would be plenty of his hired workers, and maybe even another farmer or two and their servants who were using the same threshing floor as Boaz to winnow their crops. Ruth did not want to let all of Bethlehem know she was finished with mourning until she knew what Boaz wanted to do. If he chose not to do his duty as the next of kin, then she could appear in public and take her chances as to whether or not any other man was interested in a Moabite wife.

Ruth was to stay in the shadows and "notice the place" … "remember" might be a better word for this. She was to remember where Boaz went to lie down. Then when all was quiet, and everyone else had gone to sleep, she was to go to him and uncover his feet. He was expected to be asleep when she finally went over to him. He had been working all day long and now was up late into the night winnowing. He would be so tired he would fall asleep almost instantly when he finally lay down.

Some would like to take this phrase "uncover his feet" to refer to uncovering him up to the waist. That is because a similar phrase is used in other scriptures to refer to a man going to the bathroom. However, that is not the same word used here, and actually the other scriptures which refer to feet in the sense of going to the bathroom actually say the person "covered" (להסך) his feet, not "uncovered" (וגלית) them (See I Samuel 24:3, and Judges 3:24).

If you have ever been in Israel in the summer or spring and spent the night in a tent, you will quickly see the logic of this statement. I spent two summers in Israel working at Tel Gezer where we lived in six-man army tents. The days were so hot we did not work from noon until late in the afternoon, but instead used the time to wash the pottery pieces we had dug up. You might think the nights were also hot, but that was not the case. When we arrived at Gezer we were assigned a tent and an army cot. We were given two wool army blankets, two sheets, a pillow and pillow case. Naturally those of us who were new thought the blankets were unnecessary. The first night I nearly froze and I had both blankets on top of me. A wise veteran of the excavation told me to put one blanket under me on the cot while using the other over me. It still was not enough, so someone else gave me another blanket. That helped, but I still wore a long sleeve shirt, jeans, and heavy socks to sleep in, and that was during the hot summer.

It was only spring when Ruth went to the threshing floor. She did as Naomi had said and waited for Boaz to fall asleep. Then she approached him. She quietly raised his cloak to reveal his bare feet and sandals. Then she lay down at his feet waiting for the cold night air on his feet to awaken him.

Ruth 3:5 "She said to her, 'All that you say to me I will do.'"

Ruth 3:6 "So she went down to the threshing floor and did all that her mother-in-law had instructed."

Ruth may not have fully understood what Naomi wanted her to do, but Naomi had never lied to her. She trusted Naomi with her very life, so she knew Naomi would not tell her to do something that would get her into trouble or hurt her. She quickly obeyed and did everything Naomi told her to do.

INSPIRATIONAL LESSON:

This whole day may have seemed hopeless to Ruth. The harvest time was over. That meant no more gleaning. It also meant no more food coming in daily. She had gleaned a lot of grain but would it be enough to get them through the rest of the year until harvest time next year? She did not know, so she sat around wondering. Naomi had other plans for her. There was another way to see that she was safely protected in Israel. If

Naomi could get a near kinsman to marry Ruth, she and Naomi would be cared for. First Naomi had to be sure Ruth would end her mourning for Mahlon. Naomi had seen over the past couple of months that the people of Bethlehem had changed a lot over the ten years she had been living in Moab. They had returned to worshipping God, and following His laws. The levirate marriage was one of God's laws and Naomi hoped and prayed Boaz would be willing to obey that law. There was once again hope in Naomi where there had been none before. God does provide for His people.

How many times do we give up without even consulting God's promises? When we are in a hopeless situation it helps to remind ourselves that God still loves us, and He is in control of our lives. Remember John 13:34, "*A new commandment I give to you, that you love one another, even as I have loved you, that you also love one another.*" Again, we have the promise of God's love from John 15:9, "*As the Father loved Me, I also loved you. Remain in My love.*" and many other passages of scripture. And don't forget the greatest love of all as told in John 3:16, "*For God so loved the world, that he gave his only begotten Son, that whosoever believes in him should not perish, but have everlasting life.*" God loved us from the first when He created Adam and Eve and He knew we would need that love always. How could anyone be depressed after reading of a love like that?

THE THRESHING FLOOR (Ruth 3:7-15)

> *Ruth 3:7 "When Boaz had eaten and drunk and his heart was merry, he went to lie down at the end of the heap of grain. Then Ruth came softly, uncovered his feet, and lay down."*

Ruth entered the threshing floor area very quietly so she would not be noticed. She stood off a little way to watch the activities. The men, including Boaz, had been working hard and stopped for a late supper before lying down to sleep. After such hard work all day and during the evening, they were pleased with what had been accomplished. It was a delight to finally sit and eat. We are not told what they drank. Some suppose it to be wine because the verse continues with "his heart was merry", thinking this meant he was drunk. This is probably not the case at all. Boaz's heart was merry because he had a good crop this year and the work was nearing completion. Remember only a few years before this, the Midianites had stolen all their crops and the people were going hungry because of the famine it caused. Boaz and his workers had reason to be happy or merry. They had finished the harvest of both barley and wheat. There would be enough food so none of them had to even think about starving. It was a good time, and a good place. They had worked hard and eaten a big meal. Perhaps there was even some music and dancing during the meal. The work and the merry making were finished and it was time to sleep for the night. They were happy about the results. Life was good.

Someone always slept at the threshing floor or more likely several men slept "around" the piles of grain. This was a habit they had gotten into to protect the grain from robbers. Boaz did not have to sleep at the threshing floor. After all he was the owner and had servants to do that sort of thing. We have seen before that Boaz was not just the "boss", he worked in the fields and at the threshing floor right beside his employees. He stayed through the whole night to see that the crops were safe.

Ruth watched from a discreet distance until Boaz said, "good night" to the workers and found a place near one pile of grain to sleep. He got comfortable and quickly fell asleep. Ruth was nervous. She had never done anything like this, but she trusted the counsel of her mother-in-law. As soon as Boaz and the other men were snoring, she quietly moved to Boaz's feet and uncovered them. He did not wake right away because the effect of the cold air would take a little while to make his feet cold enough to awaken him.

Ruth lay down at his feet. She did not lie beside him. She made a sort of upside down "T" at his feet. This way if she fell asleep, she would be awakened by his movement when he woke up. She was not right next to his feet, because if she had been, she might have blocked the cold wind from blowing across them. She was close enough to be touched by his feet if he woke up and stretched his legs and feet out. It is doubtful that she fell asleep. She was too nervous to sleep at a time like this.

Ruth 3:8 "At midnight, the man was startled and rolled over; and there, a woman was lying at his feet."

Awaken Boaz did! He woke up around midnight and was frightened. Why was he frightened? His feet were uncovered and cold. Had someone snuck into the threshing floor and brushed against his feet uncovering them as they passed by. Was there a thief among the grain? He turned himself to get a look at the pile of grain behind him, quietly so as not to scare the thief into doing something harmful to him or his men. There was enough light from the moon to allow him to see shadows of people moving around if there had been any. To Boaz's surprise it was not a thief, but a woman, and she was not stealing grain, she was lying at his feet. We see in the next verse it was not light enough to tell who someone was, but was it light enough to tell that a person lying on the ground was a woman? Probably not. What gave her away was the scent of the oils (perfumes) Naomi had told her to put on. The men working the threshing and the women doing the winnowing would not have anointed themselves with sweet smelling oils. The sweat of the work would have just covered up the nice smells. No, this was not some worker lying at Boaz's feet, and not some child. This was a woman. It could only be a woman, which may have frightened Boaz even more, because she was out of place.

> Ruth 3:9 *"He said, 'Who are you?' And she answered, 'I am Ruth, your maidservant. Spread your cloak over me, for you are a redeeming kinsman.'"*

Boaz was awake enough to realize it was a woman at his feet, but who was she? He did not yell out the question. His mind probably ran through several scenarios before he actually whispered the question. Could it have been the wife of one of his workers who in the dark mistook him for her husband? If so, he did not want to embarrass her by calling attention to her mistake and awakening the others, which would embarrass her and her husband more. Could it be the wife of a thief who was sent to distract him while her husband and his band of thieves stole grain? If so, he would not want to alert the band of thieves that he knew they were there. Was it one of his own female servants wanting to ask for a favor, but not wanting to awaken him? Again, he would not want to embarrass her or himself by awakening everyone at the threshing floor. So quietly he whispers, "Who are you?"

To his surprise it is Ruth who answers him. Many thoughts rush through his mind. Ruth is obviously finished with mourning for her late husband. Has she come to ask him to help her find a new husband? Does she want to marry within the family to preserve Mahlon's name? Has she already found a young man outside the family and wants to ask him to allow the marriage? Could she be interested in an old man like him?

Ruth quickly and nervously explains that she would like him to spread his cloak over her. The Hebrew word used here for cloak is (כָּנָף) kânâph which means a covering for protection such as a bird spreads her wings over her young for protection, or an army spreads it's troops over an area to protect its inhabitants. It is the same word used in chapter two, verse twelve where Boaz gives Ruth a blessing and asks the Lord to spread His wings over her. She is asking Boaz for protection, but it is more than just protection. She explains the protection she wants is only what a near "redeeming" kinsman can give and Boaz is that kinsman. The Hebrew word for kinsman here is go'el (גָּאַל) which means redeemer. Mr. Strong in his Concordance explains this as "to redeem that is, to be the next of kin (and as such to buy back a relative's property, marry his widow, etc.), avenger, deliver, purchase, ransom, redeem (-er), revenger." We will talk more about the redeemer later. But for now, understand that what Ruth asked of Boaz was something she thought only he could do. It was not just that he could do it, but that he had an obligation to do it, although he could refuse with certain penalties, as again we will see later in chapter four.

> Ruth 3:10 "He said, 'May you be blessed of the LORD, my daughter. You have shown your last act of kindness to be greater than the first, because you have not pursued young men, whether poor or rich.'"

> Ruth 3:11 "So now, my daughter, do not worry. All that you ask me, I will do for you. All of my fellow townsmen know that you are a woman of noble character.'"

Boaz praises Ruth again. He had probably seen her earlier in the day at the field gleaning any leftover grain. It was obvious to him at that time she was still in mourning for Mahlon because of the clothes she was wearing while working. Now she had changed. It was obvious she was ready for a new type of relationship. She could have gone to the village the next day and waited for a younger man to approach her while she was shopping or chatting with other women (or to approach Naomi and ask for permission to approach Ruth). She did not do that because she was interested in keeping the family name of her former husband, Mahlon, alive. This could only be done by marrying a close relative who was willing to raise children in the name of Mahlon.

Ruth thought Mahlon's nearest relative was Boaz, so she went to him even though he was a much older man. He may have been around 100 years old at this time, while Ruth was probably between 20 and 30 years old. Most young women would have hesitated to marry a man of Boaz's age even though he was still strong, smart, respected by everyone in the village, and wealthy. Ruth wanted to do what was right for her family, which meant what was right for Naomi, Mahlon, and Elimelek. She wanted to marry Boaz, and he obviously wanted to marry her.

Boaz respects Ruth and for good reason. She was virtuous and noble. She did not flaunt it, but her actions, the way she spoke, the way she worked, the way she cared for Naomi … everything she did showed the people she was a noble woman of virtue. Boaz was not the only one who noticed either. All the people in town knew it. There is no doubt the people of Bethlehem watched what Ruth did carefully, and probably talked (maybe even gossiped) about her. Why? Because she was the "new girl in town!" They could not help themselves. They had not had anything or anyone new to talk about for a long time now. It was only natural to want to know who she was, what she was doing, and if she was doing it correctly.

With all their watching and talking, all they could find to say was that she was a good girl. She was virtuous. Naomi had chosen wisely when she allowed her son to marry Ruth. She could not have done better, unless she could have chosen a Jewish girl, but they knew none were available in Moab.

Ruth 3:12 "'Now it is true that I am a redeeming kinsman. Yet there is another redeemer closer than I am.'"

This must have been a devastating blow to Ruth. Boaz promised to take the role of kinsman-redeemer, but he could not unless the nearer kinsman gave up that role. Either way, Ruth would be raising children to carry on Mahlon's name, and she and Naomi would be cared for by this other kinsman. There are two possibilities for a kinsman to be nearer to Mahlon or in this case to Elimelek. First, he would have to be older than Boaz but possibly only one year older. This would make him very old. Second, he may have been a full brother to Elimelek and only a half-brother to Boaz. We know Boaz was the son of Salmon and Rahab. If Salmon had outlived Rahab and remarried after her death, then Salmon's second wife gave birth to Elimelek and another son, this other son could be the unnamed relative (the nearer kinsman). Both Elimelek and his full brother would be younger (perhaps a lot younger) than their half-brother Boaz.

We do not know if Naomi knew about the nearer kinsman. It is not likely that she did, since she did not mention him to Ruth. If he was older than Boaz, Naomi might have assumed he had died already and therefore not given him a thought. If this kinsman was an older brother of Boaz (100 or maybe older), and Naomi had not seen his brother since she came back, it would have been a normal assumption that he was dead. Perhaps his sons had taken over running his farm and Naomi had seen them in Bethlehem buying, selling, and doing what family heads do to carry on their business. That too could have added to her assumption their father was dead.

If he was a younger half-brother of Boaz but full brother of Elimelek, Naomi might have assumed he had moved, or was too busy with a younger wife to want a Moabitess for a second wife. Whatever the reason, Naomi either had not seen him or hadn't thought he would be interested in a levirate marriage with Ruth.

Whether Naomi knew about the nearer kinsman or not, Boaz did. Boaz being an honorable man would not have tried to cheat his brother out of Naomi's property or the right to marry Ruth.

> *Ruth 3:13 "'Stay here tonight, and in the morning if he wants to redeem you, very well. Let him do so. Yet if he does not want to redeem you, then I will redeem you. I will, as the LORD lives! Sleep here until morning.'"*

> *Ruth 3:14 "So she lay at his feet until morning, but she arose before one could recognize another. Then he said, 'It must not be known that a woman came to the threshing floor.'"*

Boaz knew it was late. By now it was well after midnight. He was concerned about Ruth's safety if she tried to walk back to Naomi's place alone in the dark. There were wild animals in the countryside, or she could have taken a wrong turn and gotten lost. He wanted to keep her safe, so he told her to stay until morning. First though he assured her that he would settle the matter of who would marry her in the morning and that if the nearer kinsman would not do it, he certainly would.

Notice in verse 14, it specifically says she lay at his feet until morning. She did not move from the place she had been when he woke up, except to sit up to talk with him. He also did not move except to sit up to talk to her. They did not engage in any sort of "intimately friendly" activities (kissing, sex, etc.). All they did was talk, and when the talking was over, they simply laid back down the same way they had been before Boaz woke up.

The next morning before the sun was up ... at twilight or just before the sun is up, when you can see enough to not trip over something, but not well enough to recognize a person unless you were standing right beside or in front of them. Ruth and Boaz both got up. Boaz remarked they should not let anyone know she had been there. He was not trying to hide anything, but did not want to allow anyone to make any suggestive remarks about Ruth spending the night at the threshing floor with him or anyone else. It could have given them the wrong impression about her and he did not want her reputation soiled by innuendos or gossip. He also did not want others to start rumors about him having a woman come to the threshing floor. He wanted his reputation to be as pure as Ruth's so he would be someone she would be proud to marry and so this *perceived* improper behavior would not cast a blemish on her or his reputation. He was still trying to protect her.

In addition, it would not be fair to his brother, if his brother decided to marry Ruth, to allow others to say "Ruth and Boaz had been secretly together all night at the threshing room floor before Boaz offered her to his brother." Boaz was already very protective of Ruth's safety and her reputation.

> Ruth 3:15 *"He said, 'Bring me the shawl you have on you, and hold it.' So she held it, and he poured six*

measures of barley into it and placed it on her. Then
she went into the city."

The shawl or veil was Ruth's head covering. It was sort of a shawl she wore around her shoulders, but also used as a head covering. It was longer than an ordinary scarf, and made of heavier material. Ruth held it out and Boaz poured six measures of barley into it. We do not know how big a measure was, but it was a good amount. Some have said this was part of his dowry to Naomi for the bride. Maybe it was, or maybe Boaz was just trying to assure Naomi that he was serious about marrying Ruth and would take care of the matter of the other kinsman right away.

INSPIRATIONAL LESSON:

Ruth followed Naomi's instructions. She must have felt a little apprehensive about going to Boaz, someone she knew as land owner where she worked. Naomi wanted her to go to Boaz and ask a very important favor of him … to marry her and raise up a child to her deceased husband's name. This was a big step for her. What if he said "no"? Would she feel humiliated? Would he tell others she had asked and he refused? Boaz was someone she looked up to and admired. Would this request mean the end of their friendship or the beginning of a more wonderful relationship? What do you think Ruth was doing while she was laying at Boaz's feet waiting for him to awaken? I think she was praying … praying to the Lord, asking for His help … to say the right thing, to do the right thing, to help her not give Boaz the wrong impression. She was praying about Naomi, and about herself and about Boaz. She was praying about the past, the present, and the future.

Until this day she had never imagined herself lying at the feet of someone on a cold hard threshing room floor. She prayed, and God answered those prayers – perhaps not in the way she had hoped at first, but He did answer them. In Mark 11:24, Jesus tells us, *"Therefore I say to you, whatever things you ask when you pray, believe that you will receive them, and you will have them"*. Ruth believed the Lord God of Israel could protect her even though she was a Moabitess, and give her a future among His people in Bethlehem. She acted, she prayed, and left the rest to the Lord. What better way to deal with our problems or our doubts about the future than to pray? Always remember the words of James 5:16, *"The effectual fervent prayer of a righteous man* [or woman] *accomplishes much"*.

NAOMI'S REACTIONS (Ruth 3:16-18)

Ruth 3:16 "When Ruth came to her mother-in-law, Naomi said, 'How did it go, my daughter'"

Naomi had probably been sitting up all night, too nervous to sleep, wondering what Boaz's reaction to Ruth's proposal would be. By the time Ruth got home it was beginning to be daylight. Perhaps not light enough for Naomi to recognize Ruth from way off, but certainly light enough to tell who she was as she got closer to the house. Either way Naomi would not have been expecting anyone else to be coming to visit her that early in the morning. Her greeting was not to find out if the person approaching her home was Ruth or someone else. It was a question meant only for Ruth since it ended with "my daughter". Ruth was the only daughter Naomi still had since Orpah had left them to go back to her mother's house in Moab in chapter one. What Naomi wanted to know was "what did Boaz say"? Was Ruth now a woman who had a man to care for her, or was she still a widow? Had Boaz accepted her to be his wife or was she still single? Ruth could not actually answer that question, at least not totally. Instead she told Naomi everything that had happened.

> *Ruth 3:17 "She said, 'He gave me these six ephahs of barley, for he said to me, 'Do not return to your mother-in-law empty-handed.'"*

We are not told that Boaz said this in verse 15, but he did, or she would not have said it here. She had no reason to lie to Naomi about the grain. All the conversation was not told previously and this verse just expounds on what Boaz had told Ruth. Boaz wanted Naomi to know that Ruth had indeed found favor in his eyes and he was serious about taking care of the matter. He also wanted her to know that he intended to take care of her as well as Ruth.

> *Ruth 3:18 "Then Naomi said, 'Wait here, my daughter, until you learn what happens. For the man will not rest until the matter is settled today.'"*

Naomi had listened to everything Ruth told her. In her wisdom she told Ruth to be patient. We have all known people who could not stand to wait for someone to bring news. They pace the floor and stare out the window as if by sheer will-power they can make things happen faster. After a while they start to get on everyone else's nerves. Ruth was probably doing just that – pacing the floor, looking out the window, turning and asking Naomi, "How long do you think it will take for Boaz to settle this with the nearer kinsman?" Naomi tells Ruth to just sit down. It will be over when it is over, but you can bet that Boaz will not rest until it is decided and he will take care of it today.

INSPIRATIONAL LESSON:

We often act like Ruth when we take our cares to the Lord. We pray for the Lord to help us with a problem we are having. Then we pace the floor figuratively waiting for a sign or something that will let us know how to handle it. We pace in our minds, by going over and over the problem thinking God is going to reveal some magical solution to us. We pray about it again and again. When will it end? When will I know how it turns out? Lord why are you not doing something? Psalms 46:10 says, "*Be still and know that I am God*". Another way to say it is, "Sit down, because I am God and I can take care of it this day." No problem is too big for God. Sometimes we need to just let Him do the job. We need to completely rely on God to handle it and stop worrying about it. At times like these, we should just sit down and read the word of God.

There are many scriptures that deal with waiting on the Lord. One of my favorites is from Isaiah 40:31, "*but those who wait upon the LORD shall renew their strength; they shall mount up with wings as eagles, they shall run and not be weary, and they shall walk and not faint*" (see also Psalms 37:9, and Isaiah 30:18).

Some of you reading this are thinking, "Didn't she just tell us *not* to sit around and do nothing a few pages back?" You are right, I did say that, but this is a different situation. In the previous situation two things were different. (1) Ruth could do something with the Lord's help, so she did it. (2) There was no one else to do it, so it was either she does it or no one would. In the present situation Ruth could do nothing but wait and worry, and she had someone else who said he would take care of it. In Ecclesiastes chapter three we learn there is a time for everything. Now was the time for Ruth to sit down and wait.

KINSMAN REDEEMER (Ruth 4:1-12)

Ruth 4:1 "So Boaz went up to the gate and sat down there. And now the redeemer of whom he had spoken passed by, and Boaz said, 'Come over, friend, and sit here.' So he went over and sat down.

At this time in the Near East, most cities of any size had a wall around them. The wall was for protection. If it was a good enough wall, it would keep the enemy out. Many families had their primary home or a secondary home within the city walls, even if they had a farm outside the city. If an enemy came into the land, the inhabitants of an area would run to the city even if they did not live within the walls. As soon as all the people were within the walls the city gates would be closed. These were huge gates. The gateway in a city wall was the weakest part of the wall. To strengthen this weak portion one gateway could have as many as four actual gates, one after another, with open areas between each gate. These open areas had stone benches built against the walls where the people of the city would conduct business or just sit and chat with friends.

If you sat at the gate long enough you would see lots of your friends and relatives pass by. The elders of the town would sit at the gate daily imparting their wisdom to anyone who wanted to listen or ask questions of them. You could conduct court there, buy, sale, or trade there, or you could just sit and watch the people pass by on their way to or from work or just visiting others. It was the best place to wait for someone, to gain knowledge from the elders, or to conduct business where witnesses were needed.

Boaz obviously knew the habits of his brother, and knew he would be coming into the city that day, so he sat down and waited for him. When he saw him coming, he called out to him. We are not told what his name was. The Hebrew here is interesting. It is a play on words ... using two words that rhyme. The words are *Peloniy 'almoniy* (פלני אלמני) which actually mean about the same thing ... "a concealed one". We might call him "Mr. So-and-So". Boaz obviously knew his name and probably used it, too. The writer of the narrative chose not to tell us Mr. So-and-So's name to keep us from becoming involved with him. He is a minor part of these events, but an important one. Without him we would not see how much Boaz wants to marry Ruth, or how wise Boaz really is.

> Ruth 4:2 *"Then Boaz took ten men from among the elders of the town and said, 'Sit here.'"*

Ten men was a quorum. Ten were needed to witness the event so everything would be legal in every way. Boaz probably sat at the gate with Mr. So-and-So chatting about the weather, the family, how nice the crops were this year, etc. As an elder would come by, Boaz would just take a moment out of his conversation with Mr. So-and-So to ask the elder to come sit with them. More chit chat, and soon he had ten wise elders sitting with them.

> Ruth 4:3 *"He said to the redeemer, 'Naomi, who has come back from the land of Moab, must sell the plot of land belonging to our brother Elimelek.'"*

Without much change in his voice, Boaz turned the conversation of family to Naomi a relative of Mr. So-and-So and Boaz. Loud enough for all to hear he announces that Naomi, who had returned from Moab, wanted to sell the land that belonged to their brother Elimelek (Naomi's husband). It is very obvious by the way this statement is worded that Mr. So-and-

So, either did not know Naomi had returned, or had not bothered to visit or enquire about her welfare before this. He may have been busy with his own family, or harvesting, and not had time to check what was happening. Maybe he just did not care, but hearing Naomi wanted to sell the land, certainly caught his interest.

Some here have suggested Elimelek had sold the land before he left Bethlehem to move to Moab. Then they bring in the idea that a relative had to redeem the land to keep it in the family. This is simply not the case. Why would Elimelek sell his land if he was only going to Moab temporarily? If he had sold the land and in a couple of years moved back to Bethlehem, he and his family would have no place to live. On the contrary, Elimelek would have kept his land so he could easily move his family home when the famine was over.

Now Naomi was home and wanted to find a husband for her daughter-in-law. She could sell the land to anyone if she wanted, but if she sold it to a kinsman (redeemer) she could continue to live on it until she died. A kinsman redeemer would also marry Ruth and raise a child that would carry on the name of Mahlon (and Elimelek). Her husband's family line would not die out just because Elimelek and his sons had died. This son would then inherit the land and it would continue in his family name, but only if it was sold to a kinsman redeemer. Selling the land to anyone else would mean Naomi had no place to live, because the property would belong to the buyer until the year of Jubilee.

Boaz did not want to mention Ruth too soon in this transaction because he was not sure how So-and-So would react or how much So-and-So knew about Ruth. He only mentions the land at this point.

HOW DO WE KNOW BOAZ, ELIMELEK, AND THE UNNAMED KINSMAN WERE BROTHERS?

This is a question often asked. Many people take the word "brother" in Ruth 4:30 to simply mean that they were of the same tribe. I hear things like, "They were all brothers, since they were all Jewish." It is true the Hebrew word (לְאָחִינוּ - le'achinu) used in this sentence could mean "brother" in several senses of the word. According to Brown, Driver, and Briggs' Hebrew and English Lexicon, the root word is *ach*, and primarily means "brother" in the sense of two people born from the same father and mother, or "half-brother" as two people born from the same father and different mothers (or same mother and different fathers). As a secondary interpretation it could mean two people from the same tribe, or even two friends with no other connections.

Since we generally read a Bible that has already been translated into English by others, how do we know which is the correct translation of the Hebrew word? After all, didn't Boaz just call Ruth "my daughter" in chapter 2 verse 8, or again in 3:10 and 11? Did Boaz mean that Ruth was his biological daughter? The Hebrew word for my daughter (בִּתִּי – *bit ti*) can be used as a daughter, or a young woman of virtue, etc.

That brings us back to the question of "how do we know when a word that expresses a relationship is referring to a biological relative or just a close friend?" This is where we must be careful in studying our Bibles, and not just doing a quick reading of a verse.

There are three guidelines we must look at …

1. Prayer. We should always pray for God to lead us to an understanding of His scripture, before we read it.
2. Look at a verse in context. Don't read just one verse and then say, "I don't understand." Read the whole chapter, or even the whole book, so you can see what is going on that leads up to and follows that verse.
3. Let Scripture explain Scripture. If you don't find the answer in one place, look for other similar events throughout Scripture and compare to see how they are handled.

As for the two instances mentioned above, let's look at them in context. First, when Boaz first meets Ruth, he calls her "My daughter". That is in chapter 2 of Ruth. We read in chapter one that Ruth is a young Moabite woman. We read in chapter 2 that this is the first time Ruth and Boaz have met. Boaz is a wealthy Israelite land owner who has come to oversee his fields, and that he is a kinsman of Elimelek, so Boaz is at least old enough to be Ruth's father, perhaps even her grandfather. Obviously, he is NOT Ruth's father, so the phrase "My daughter" used here and in other verses in the book of Ruth, has to be a term of respect from an older man to a younger woman of honorable character.

Now looking at Ruth 4:30 where Boaz calls the nearer kinsman who is not named (Mr. So and So), and says to him that Elimelek was their brother, we see nothing in the verse or surrounding verses that would specifically make them biological brothers. However, in looking at the rules for a levirate marriage in Deuteronomy 25:5-10, we see that it was only a husband's brother who was bound by the levirate law to take his brother's widow as his wife to raise a son to inherit his brother's land. This makes even more sense today, because we know that the DNA of siblings is closer than any relative, and therefore a brother's DNA would mean the child would have the same or extremely close DNA as if he had been born of the husband who had died. The ancestry would be the same for the child. He would have the same grandfather and great grandfather, etc. as if he had been born of the original husband. There is no provision in Deuteronomy for any relative other than a brother to be bound by this type of marriage. If a man had no brothers, or all of his brothers were dead, there is no one else who can participate in a levirate marriage. Of course, Ruth could have married anyone she chose to marry, but their child would not be considered a son of her late husband, Mahlon, and could not inherit Mahlon's (and Elimelek's) property. He also would not have an obligation to take care of Naomi as he grew up.

With this in mind, Boaz has to be the brother of Elimelek and the unnamed kinsman. Normally he would have married Naomi who was the wife of his brother Elimelek, but as we are told earlier in the book of Ruth, Naomi was too old to bare children, so Ruth was the widow he needed to marry to raise up children to Elimelek's clan (in Mahlon's name). Note also that another name for levirate marriage was "the duty of a husband's brother", not "a husband's cousin" (see Deuteronomy 25:7-10).

Ruth 4:4 "'I thought I should inform you and say, 'Buy it in the presence of those sitting here and in the presence of the elders of my people. If you want to redeem it, redeem it. But if you will not redeem it, tell me so that I know, for there is no one prior to you to redeem it, and I am next after you.' So he said, 'I will redeem it.'"

Boaz changes words here. In the previous verse he said Naomi wanted to "sell" the land. Here he tells So-and-So to "redeem" the land. Perhaps he was hinting at the marriage of Ruth to see if his brother would catch the change. Boaz is very subtle in the way he is dealing with So-and-So. If Naomi just wanted to sell the land, she could sell it to anyone. It did not have to be a relative. But if she wanted to find a levirate marriage for Ruth, she had to sell the land to a near relative who was willing to take the land and Ruth so Ruth's child would inherit the land. This is why Boaz changes the word to "redeem" … to let So-and-So know there was more to the sale of the land than just buying land.

When So-and-So says he will redeem the land, Boaz's heart sank into his stomach. He had better think quick, and he did.

> *Ruth 4:5 "Then Boaz said, 'On the day you buy the field from the hand of Naomi, you also acquire Ruth the Moabitess, the wife of the deceased, to perpetuate the name of the deceased through his inheritance.'"*

Perhaps So-and-So did not understand that Ruth was attached to the land, so Boaz goes on to explain it more clearly. This was not just a matter of buying some piece of land to add to his farm. Buying the land meant redeeming Ruth as your wife so she could raise a child in her late husband's name and that child would inherit the land as soon as he was an adult.

Also, notice that Boaz purposefully says Ruth is a Moabitess. If So-and-So did not know Ruth which is very likely, he may have considered her a pagan as most Moabites were.

This could be enough to scare him off from wanting to marry her, even if it meant he could not get the land. Boaz was trying everything he could think of here.

> Ruth 4:6 *"The redeemer replied, 'I am not able to redeem it for myself lest I ruin my own inheritance. Take my redemption rights for yourself, for I cannot do it.'"*

It is not clear exactly how redeeming the land and Ruth would ruin So-and-So's inheritance. There are many possible scenarios here. If he was already married, he may have had several sons who were currently arguing over who gets what when dear old Dad dies. Obtaining another piece of land and then telling them they cannot have it because a child born to his new wife would get it, might have made that worse.

Another possibility was that his wife might have been a jealous woman who would never allow him to have another wife. Still another scenario could be that he was afraid if he married a Moabitess it would mean he would become an outcast among the Jews. Whatever the reason, Boaz's comments worked. So-and-So gave up his right to redeem Ruth and the land. Boaz had won.

> Ruth 4:7 *"(Now this was the custom in ancient times in Israel for redeeming and exchanging: to confirm a transaction, a man would remove his sandal and give it to his neighbor. This was a binding act in Israel.)"*

> Ruth 4:8 *"Therefore the redeemer said to Boaz, 'Buy it yourself,' and he removed his sandal."*

The only place we see this practice of taking off the shoe as a sign of a change of property is in Deuteronomy 25:7-10 where it talks of a widow's right to a levirate marriage.

Deuteronomy 25:7-10: "If the man does not want to take his brother's wife, then let his brother's wife go up to the gate to the elders and say, 'My husband's brother refuses to raise up his brother's name in Israel. He will not perform the duty of my husband's brother.' Then the elders of his city shall call him, and speak to him, and if he persists and says, 'I do not want to take her,' then his brother's wife must come to him in the presence of the elders and remove his sandal from his foot, and spit in his face, and answer and say, 'So shall it be done to that man who will not build up his brother's house.' His name will be called in Israel, 'The house of him who has his sandal removed'."

Although this passage does not refer to buying or selling land, it does show how seriously the people were to follow the levirate law. If a man refused to accept his role as husband to his dead brother's wife to raise up a child to carry on the name of the deceased, he was humiliated in public by the widow. Of course, Ruth had no intention of doing this since she wanted to marry Boaz, not Mr. So-and-So. Also, Ruth did not bring So-and-So before the elders of the city, Boaz did, and he did it in a friendly manner so So-and-So would not feel threatened. Ruth was not even at the city gate. She was home waiting with Naomi to hear how all this turned out.

The actual custom of one taking off his shoe and giving it to another to finalize the buying or selling of land may have grown out of the above-mentioned practice. No one spit into So-and-So's face. This was not a situation of humiliation, but just a situation of one brother giving up his rights to another.

Ruth 4:9 "Then Boaz said to the elders and all the people, 'You are witnesses today that I have bought everything that belonged to Elimelek, Kilion, and Mahlon from Naomi.'"

Ruth 4:10 "'Moreover I have also acquired Ruth the Moabitess, the wife of Mahlon, to be my wife, in order to preserve the name of the deceased man for his inheritance, so that his name will not be cut off from among his brothers or from his town. You are witnesses this day.'"

Boaz had staged this public gathering for one main purpose ... to have witnesses that what he was doing was right. Of course, it was right, but he could have gone to So-and-So and settled it privately. For Boaz, though, this was not a private matter. Boaz was an honorable man and he did not want to be in any situation where one could say he had acted in a way that was not honorable. He also knew that Ruth was an honorable, virtuous woman and he did not want anyone to be able to say she had acted in any way less than virtuous.

To handle this situation privately would have left them both open to questions, gossip, and perhaps attacks on their integrity. So-and-So could have said, he did not know Naomi was selling the land or that Ruth was part of the deal. He could have accused Boaz of tricking him into letting Boaz have the land and Ruth. Without witnesses, there would be no way to tell who was giving a truthful account of the transaction.

Boaz knew his brother, and knew what sort of man he was. Since he refused to do his duty as a kinsman redeemer, he was perhaps less than honorable. Boaz therefore sought to make the whole transaction public and in front of ten elders of the city. This was equivalent to taking So-and-So to court to settle the matter. The court took place at the city gate where it was expected to be. Although they started with only ten elders, it was obvious to people passing by that something important was going on. Here was Boaz and his brother discussing something. More and more people would have gathered around to hear and see what was going on. These were two men from a well-respected family in the village; they all wanted to know what it was about. When it was finished, Boaz asked all present to serve as witnesses. There was no way So-and-So could come back later and say, "wait a minute. You tricked me out of what was rightfully mine." If he did, all Boaz had to say was, "Let's talk to some of the witnesses." Boaz was not only an honorable man, a man of wealth, and a man of strength, he was an intelligent man!

> Ruth 4:11 *"Then all the people who were at the gate, along with the elders, said, 'We are witnesses. May the LORD make the woman who is coming to your house like Rachel and Leah, who together built up the house of Israel. May you do well in Ephrathah and be famous in Bethlehem!'"*

> Ruth 4:12 *"'May your house be like the house of Perez, whom Tamar bore to Judah, through the offspring that the LORD will give you by this young woman.'"*

All the people that were at the gate said "We are witnesses." That must have been a thunderous shout from the people. We can just imagine them shouting "We are witnesses" and shaking their heads in agreement as they did it. Then one by one they started blessing Boaz. This was a marriage that not only was approved by the people of the village but they blessed it. The fact that Ruth was a Moabitess made no difference to them. She had lived and worked among them long enough for them to know she was an honorable virtuous woman and even more than that, they knew she worshipped Yahweh. She was not a pagan foreigner. She was a worshipper of the true living God of Israel. Their praise for her to be like the mothers of all Israel was a wonderful reminder of this. Rachel and Leah were the wives of Jacob (Israel) and with their maid servants produced the 12 children who made up the tribes of Israel (see Genesis 29ff). They compared Ruth to the women who with Jacob produced the nation of Israel. They went on to compare her to Tamar who helped to produce the house of Judah and to Pharez who was a direct ancestor of Boaz. Pharez was not only one of the fathers of Judah's tribe but was the father of this clan of the tribe of Judah who had settled in Bethlehem. WOW! Could the villagers have had more love and respect for these two people? Ruth and Boaz were blessed by these people to be like the very heads of the tribe and the clan. And Boaz was not even looking to raise children to himself, but to another man's name. Of course, only the first born would bear Mahlon's name. Any other children would bear Boaz's name.

INSPIRATIONAL LESSON:

Boaz was a man who knew what he wanted, but he was also a man of integrity. He could have secretly married Ruth the next day and then announced it to the world that they were married, without mentioning Naomi's land. Ruth did not have to marry the nearest kinsman and Naomi could sell the land to anyone. Boaz was not a man who hid things or did things in secret. Doing something in secret and then announcing it later gives the impression there was something wrong with what was done. Even if there was nothing wrong with the act, it still gives the impression of evil happenings.

We are told in the New Testament to deal honestly with our brother in the Lord. 1 Thessalonians 4:6 tells us, *"and that no man take advantage of and defraud his brother in any matter, because the Lord is the avenger in all these things, as we also have forewarned you and testified."* We should always be honest with others. That means carrying on business and private matters in a manner that anyone can see and know we are participating in an honest dealing.

We are told in Romans how to deal with our brethren. *"So then each of us shall give an account of himself to God. Therefore let us no longer pass judgment on one another, but rather determine not to put a stumbling block or an obstacle in a brother's way. I know and am persuaded by the Lord Jesus that nothing is unclean in itself, but to him who considers anything to be unclean, to him it is unclean"* (Romans 14:12-14). If it appears to be wrong to others and would cause them to doubt God and His salvation, then it is wrong for us to do it. If Boaz had married Ruth without first telling his brother about the land and giving him a chance to buy it, it would have been wrong. Even though Boaz could legally have married Ruth without telling Mr. So-and-so, it would have been wrong.

Jesus told us to do only one thing in secret. We are to pray to the Lord in secret. We are not to make huge public prayers just for show, so others will think we are so much better than they are. *"But you, when you pray, enter your closet, and when you have shut your door, pray to your Father who is in secret. And your Father who sees in secret will reward you openly"* (Matthew 6:6). There is nothing wrong with public prayers, as long as they are meant to uplift the people hearing them. They are only wrong when they are meant to uplift us in other people's eyes, instead of uplifting others in God's eyes. If we want to truly discuss our daily lives with God we are to go into a private place like a closet and pray. God will hear us and grant our needs if we do this. This is the only time we are told to do something in secret.

RUTH'S SECOND MARRIAGE (Ruth 4:13-18)

> *Ruth 4:13 "So Boaz took Ruth, and she became his wife. When they came together, the LORD enabled her to conceive, and she bore a son."*

Some say here that Ruth was barren and the Lord needed to intercede for her to become pregnant. That may be, or it might just be that the Lord enabled her to conceive on the first night of marriage, so the rest of Bethlehem could see how the marriage of Boaz and Ruth was blessed by the Lord. Either way the Lord obviously blessed the union of these two who on the outside seemed so different. Ruth was a foreigner, Boaz an Israelite; Ruth was young, Boaz was old; Ruth was poor, Boaz rich; Ruth had nothing, Boaz had everything. Even with all those differences there was one overwhelming thing they had in common … they both loved the Lord and wanted to follow Him.

> *Ruth 4:14 "Then the women said to Naomi, 'Blessed be the LORD, who has not left you without a redeemer. May he become famous in Israel!'"*

> *Ruth 4:15 "'He will be a comfort for your soul and support you in your old age. For your daughter-in-law, who loves you and who is better to you than seven sons, has given birth to him.'"*

Here the women are referring to the child as Naomi's kinsman redeemer, not Boaz. The child is now the nearest relative to Naomi. The child was legally Naomi's grandson, and he would be the one to take care of her in her old age. Of course, this does not mean Ruth and Boaz did not help take care of Naomi. Naomi probably moved in with them, at least while the child was an infant. This child gave Naomi a new outlook on life. There is nothing like having a child around to make you feel young.

Notice here the women compare Ruth to seven sons. Seven was considered the perfect number (God created the whole universe and rested on the seventh day), and sons were looked on as the perpetuation of life. A father's name was carried on by his sons. Although in ancient Israel people did not go by last names, sons were spoken of by their given name followed by "son of" and the father's name. We still see this used today in countries where the use of "von", "van" or "ben" before the last name means "son or child of". We have seen these many times in scripture. For Ruth to be compared to "seven sons", was like saying she was the best of the best of the best as far as children go. Naomi could not have given birth to a better child than Ruth had become by love.

Ruth 4:16 "Then Naomi took the child, laid him on her lap, and became his nurse."

Ruth 4:17 "The neighbor women gave him a name, saying 'A son has been born to Naomi!' And they named him Obed. He was the father of Jesse, the father of David."

Naomi had an important part in raising the child. She became a nurse to the child. This does not mean she nursed the child. Obviously, she was too old for that, but she took care of him and helped teach him. He spent a lot of time with her. This did not diminish his time with his parents either. They were happy to see the attention Naomi gave her grandson, and I am sure Ruth was happy for the help raising him.

As we can see here, Obed did become famous as the grandfather of King David, and ultimately as an ancestor of the Lord Jesus Christ.

INSPIRATIONAL LESSON:

What is fame? When we think of famous people, we often think of movie stars, athletes, scientists, politicians, and great speakers ... the people with adoring fans hanging around all the time. While it is true this is a sort of fame, but this fame lasts for only a short time. It often leads to the "famous" person thinking he/she can do no wrong. The next thing you know they are treating others badly, taking drugs, and they lose the respect of their fans.

How many times do we think of parents or grandparents as being famous? Maybe they do not have a lot of adoring fans hanging around, although when a grandmother bakes cookies, it can often seem like that because she has a group of small adoring fans sitting around waiting for those cookies to come out of the oven. That is not the type of fame we are talking about either. What we are talking about is fame that comes from raising children to know the Lord. In Proverbs it says, *"Train up a child in the way he should go, and when he is old, he will not depart from it."* (Proverbs 22:6). What better legacy could a parent or grandparent leave to their children and grandchildren than to train them how to live a godly life in service of the Lord? *"Her children rise up, and call her blessed"* comes from Proverbs 31:28 and is talking about the virtuous woman (mother). Are you famous today? Do you teach your children about the Lord Jesus Christ, or do you expect them to learn about the Lord from Sunday school or friends? We know how disastrous that can be. We should all dare to be a famous person by raising godly children and grandchildren like Boaz, Ruth, and Naomi did.

GENEAOLOGY (Ruth 4:18-22)

Ruth 4:18 "Now these are the descendants of Perez: Perez was the father of Hezron,"

Pharez was one of twin sons born to Tamar and Judah. But Tamar was not Judah's first wife. Tamar was actually married to Er, Judah's oldest son. Er died without children and Onan, Er's brother took Tamar for his wife. He also died and Judah told Tamar to stay a widow until his last son Shelah was old enough to marry. Judah did not intend to give Tamar to Shelah though for fear that Shelah would also die. When Tamar realized this, she tricked Judah into thinking she was a prostitute beside the road. He slept with her and she became pregnant by him, and gave birth to Pharez and Zarah. You can read about Tamar and Judah in Genesis 38.

The only thing we know of Hezron was that he was the son of Pharez and the father of Ram (See Genesis 46:12). Also that he was the father of the family of the Hezronites (see Numbers 26:21).

Ruth 4:19 "Hezron the father of Ram, Ram the father of Amminadab,"

We know very little about Ram except his place in the genealogy. He had two brothers, Jerahmeel, and Chelubai. (see I Chronicles 2:9).

Amminadab was the son of Ram. We do not know his wife's name, but they had at least one son named Nahshon and at least one daughter named Elisheba. We will read more about Nahshon after the next verse. Elisheba was married to Aaron. Aaron was Moses' brother and the first High Priest of the Israelites. From this marriage came four sons: Nahab, Abihu, Eleazar, and Ithamar who were also grandsons of Amminadab (see Exodus 6:23). Aaron's four sons were also priests (see Exodus 28:1 and Numbers 3:2-3), but Nadab and Abihu were evil (see Leviticus 10:1 and Numbers 3 and 26:61). Nadab and Abihu died without any children. Eleazar and Ithamar were good priests who ministered with Aaron before the Lord (see Numbers 3:4).

> Ruth 4:20 "Amminadab the father of Nahshon, Nahshon the father of Salmon,"

Nahshon was alive during the Exodus from Egypt. He is listed as the "leader of the sons of Judah", (KJV says "prince" instead of "leader") so he had some standing as a leader of the tribe of Judah during the time of the Exodus from Egypt and wandering in the wilderness (see I Chronicles 2:10). He was chosen by Moses to help with the numbering of the Hebrews, and to be a leader of his tribe (see Numbers 1). He was also called the "captain of the children of Judah" (see Numbers 2:3). Nahshon's offering at the dedication of the alter that stood in front of the tabernacle was listed as …

> Num 7:12-17 "He that offered his offering the first day was Nahshon the son of Amminadab, of the tribe of Judah. And his offering was one silver charger, the weight of which was one hundred and thirty shekels, one silver bowl of seventy shekels, after the shekel of the sanctuary, both of them full of fine flour mixed with oil as a grain offering; one spoon of ten shekels of gold, full of

incense; one young bull, one ram, and one male lamb in its first year as a burnt offering; one goat kid as a sin offering; and as a sacrifice of peace offerings, two oxen, five rams, five male goats, and five male lambs in their first year. This was the offering of Nahshon the son of Amminadab."

He was obviously a leader among the Jews and a wealthy man. His offering was the first of the leaders' offerings from among the tribes of Israel.

Salmon was the son of Nashon. Salmon was born during the wandering in the wilderness. His name was also spelled Salma in I Chronicles 2:11. (There is also another Salma listed in I Chronicles 2:51 and 54 as the father of Bethlehem. We should not confuse Salma the son of Nashon with Salma the father of Bethlehem. They are not the same person.) We know from Matthew 1:5 that Salmon was married to Rahab. Rahab was the prostitute in Jericho who hid the Jewish spies Joshua sent to check out the city and surrounding area. Because of her help, she and her relatives were spared when God led the Israelites to destroy the city (see Joshua 2 – 6; Hebrews 11:31). Salmon may have been one of the two spies Joshua sent out to Jericho. We have no way to verify this, since the Bible does not name the spies.

Ruth 4:21 "Salmon the father of Boaz, Boaz the father of Obed,"

Boaz we know about from this study of Ruth to be a wealthy and highly respected leader among the people of Bethlehem. He is not mentioned again in the scriptures except in genealogies in both the Old Testament and New Testament (See I Chronicles 2:11-12; Matthew 1:5 and Luke 3:32).

Obed is also only mentioned in the genealogies in Ruth 4, I Chronicles 2:12; Matthew 1:5; and Luke 3:32. Although we know Obed was the son of Boaz and Ruth, we do not know much else about him. We do know he was a comfort and helper to Naomi in her old age and that she helped raise him.

Ruth 4:22 "Obed the father of Jesse, and Jesse the father of David."

Jesse lived in Bethlehem and was visited by the prophet and judge Samuel many times. The first time was when the Lord sent Samuel to Jesse to anoint David king of Israel. David was still a lad tending his father's sheep when Samuel arrived. He was so young that Jesse did not think he was old enough to be called to the house while Samuel was there. The Lord had other plans though and after rejecting all of Jesse's other sons, David was called away from the sheep to the place the rest of the family was waiting with Samuel so Samuel could anoint him. Jesse had eight sons. Jesse was a shepherd as were his sons (see I Samuel 16 and following). In I Samuel 17:12, Jesse is also described as an "Ephrathite of Bethlehem Judah" just as Elemelech was in Ruth 1:2. If we accept the idea that an Ephrathite was an aristocrat of the city, then Jesse was probably a wealthy and definitely a respected leader of the people in Bethlehem.

David was a man after God's own heart (I Samuel 13:14). He was the boy who slew the Philistine giant Goliath (see I Samuel 17), and armor bearer to King Saul (see I Samuel 16:21). He also played his harp to calm King Saul when the evil spirit troubled him (see I Samuel 16:23). David was the husband of King Saul's younger daughter Michal (see I Samuel 18:27). He was the captain of an army of outcasts (see I Samuel 19-27). Finally, he was King of Judah and all the nation of Israel (see 2 Samuel 2:4 and 5:3). He was the best-known king who followed God's laws and led the people to do the same. He was also a sinner, but he confessed his sins and continued to worship the Lord.

INSPIRATIONAL LESSON:

Even though King David is described as a man after God's own heart, he was not perfect. David sinned with Bathsheba. The important thing here is not that David sinned. We all sin. Romans 3:23 says "For all have sinned, and come short of the glory of God;" The important thing is, "What did you do after you sinned?" David's first reaction was to cover it up. David had Bathsheba's husband (Uriah) sent home from the battlefront, with the hope that he would spend the night with his wife and then would think the baby she carried was his. That did not work, because Uriah said he would not spend the night with his wife while his men were still at the battlefront. In a few months there would be no way to hide the fact that Bathsheba had committed adultery. David's servants knew she had been with him, so there would be no way he could hide the fact that he had committed adultery either. He compounded the first sin with another. He sent word back to the battlefield to have Uriah put in the front of the battle and then have the troops withdraw leaving Uriah there to be killed. This meant Bathsheba was a widow and could marry David which she did. The first son born to that marriage was sickly, and died a few days later. Only then did David repent, go to the tabernacle to pray, and ask God for forgiveness … which he received. After that he continued to serve the Lord (See 2 Samuel 11-12 for the whole story).

We all sin. From the time of Adam mankind has sinned. The real test of the Christian is how do we deal with our sin? Do we, like David, try to hide it? If no one saw me, maybe it was not a sin? God saw us, so we were seen. Do we try to reconcile it, saying, "I had to do it. There was no other way to handle the situation." Or do we go to God in prayer, confess our sin to Him, and ask for forgiveness? God promises to forgive us if we do this. 1 John 1:9 tells us, *"If we confess our sins, he is faithful and just to forgive us our sins, and to cleanse us from all unrighteousness."* The Bible cannot make it any clearer than that. Confess, and we will be forgiven and cleansed. It is a promise from the Lord and the Lord keeps His promises.

FAMILY GENEALOGY FROM ABRAHAM TO KING DAVID

ABRAHAM and SARAH
ISAAC and REBECCA
JACOB and LEAH
JUDAH and TAMAR
PHAREZ
HEZRON
RAM
AMMINADAB
NASHON
SALMON and RAHAB
BOAZ and RUTH
OBED
JESSE
DAVID

Matthew 1:17 *"So all the generations from Abraham to David are fourteen generations,"*

Chapter Five: OUR KINSMAN REDEEMER

The entire Bible points us to Jesus Christ and the book of Ruth is no exception to this. Throughout the Old Testament we can see examples of God's plan for salvation. These examples are called "types". In Ruth we see the only real example (or "type") of the redeemer spoken of in the law. Job 19:25 says, *"For I know that my Redeemer lives, and He will stand at last on the earth"*. In Psalms 19:14 King David says, *"Let the words of my mouth, and the meditation of my heart, be acceptable in your sight, O LORD, my strength, and my Redeemer"*. They are not talking about an earthly redeemer, but the earthly redeemer we see in Boaz is a type of redeemer which leads us to Jesus Christ as our redeemer.

WHAT CAN BE REDEEMED?
This is a very good question. What can be redeemed? Is there anything that cannot be redeemed? The twenty-fifth and twenty-seventh chapters of Leviticus give us God's list of what can and cannot be redeemed. God says He owns the land, but gives it to the Israelites for a possession as long as they obey His laws. God gives specific areas of land to specific

tribes, clans, and families. If a person finds himself poor and cannot pay his bills, he can sell the land to another Israelite. Later if his fortune changes or if he can find a relative who is not poor, the land can be redeemed from the buyer and put back into the original family's hands. If the seller's family never has the money to redeem the land, during the year of Jubilee the land automatically reverts back to the original owner. If he is no longer alive, it goes to his family (See Leviticus 25:23-28). The Year of Jubilee was every fiftieth year when the land would be left unplanted and the Israelites would celebrate their freedom (See Leviticus 25:9-13).

A house that is located in a walled city can also be sold if the owner is poor, but this house has a different value because of its location. If it is sold, it can only be redeemed within a year. If it is not redeemed within a year from the time it is sold, it becomes the permanent property of the buyer and never goes back to the original owner (See Leviticus 25:29-30). The only exception to this rule is any house within the cities of the Levities. The Levities were not given huge areas of land as the other tribes were. Instead they were given twelve cities with the surrounding area to inhabit, because they were to serve as the priests of the Lord (See Joshua 14:4, and Joshua 21). If a Levite sold his house within the Levitical city, he or someone in his family could redeem it. If it was not redeemed it would automatically revert back to the original owner during the year of Jubilee.

Houses located in an open field are treated different from houses within a walled city. If sold, the house in an open field could be redeemed at any time by the original owner or someone within his family. If not redeemed these houses reverted back to the original owner during the year of Jubilee (See Leviticus 25:31).

People could also be sold. Israelites were not allowed to purchase other Israelites as slaves. If an Israelite bought another Israelite, he was to be treated as a hired servant and paid for his work. However, a foreigner living within Canaan could buy a poor Israelite and keep him as a slave until the Year of Jubilee when he would be freed. If at any time before the Year of Jubilee the Israelite or his next of kin could afford it, they could redeem him from his slavery by paying the buyer back.

Above we saw a list of people or things that could be redeemed if sold to someone else. There is another category of people and things that can also be redeemed ... those vowed to the Lord. Leviticus 27 deals with this category. A person (man, woman, child, or senior citizen) could be vowed to the Lord. Even a baby could be vowed to the Lord by his or her parents before or shortly after they were born. Samuel is a prime example of a child vowed to the Lord by his mother before he was born (See I Samuel 1:11). If this person or a family member wanted to get him or her out of their vow, they could be redeemed (see Leviticus 27:1-8). Animals vowed to the Lord could be redeemed by paying the value of the animal plus a fifth more (See Leviticus 27:9-13). Even a house vowed to the Lord could be redeemed but it was always held as holy afterwards (see Leviticus 27:14-15).

While things and people vowed to the Lord's service could be redeemed, there is a difference between being vowed to the Lord and being devoted to the Lord. Animals and people devoted to the Lord could never be redeemed. They were the Lord's forever.

We have one more category of objects that must be redeemed. These were never sold nor vowed to anyone or the Lord. Numbers 18:15 says that every firstborn of man must be redeemed. Also, the firstborn of any unclean animals must be redeemed. The firstborn of clean animals is not to be redeemed. Instead, they are to be sacrificed to the Lord.

All of the above refers to individual people, animals, or things, but there is one more reference to redeeming that should also be noted. Exodus 6:6 says the Lord will redeem all of the Israelites out of Egypt. This was God's way of telling the Israelites He was going to rescue them. 2 Samuel 7:23 and I Chronicles 17:21 confirm that God did indeed redeem the Israelites from Egypt for the purpose of being a holy nation to Himself.

WHO CAN REDEEM AND HOW IS IT DONE?

Looking again at the scriptures in Leviticus chapters 25 and 27 we see that God did provide for a method of redemption for the Israelites. If a man sold his property or himself, a brother or other near relative such as an uncle or cousin could redeem the property or person. Or the man, who sold his land or sold himself, could redeem himself. There is no provision in the law for anyone else to do the redeeming.

In the case of a person vowed to the Lord's service, the person who made the vow may redeem himself or herself from the vow. In the case of an animal that is vowed to the Lord, the person who vowed the animal to the Lord may redeem it.

In all these cases of redemption the way to redeem, whether it is property or persons, is to pay the price. In the case of property or a person sold, the price would be determined by figuring the worth of the property or slave labor until the next year of Jubilee. The year of Jubilee was decreed by God in the first part of Leviticus 25. It was every fiftieth year after the children of Israel entered the promised land of Canaan. During that year, there would be no planting, no harvesting, and all properties would be returned to their original owner or his family if he was no longer alive, and all Hebrew persons sold into slavery would be freed.

When the property was redeemed by paying the price, it was immediately returned to the original owner. If a relative of the original owner paid the cost of redemption for the property, it was still returned to the original owner. There was no provision made for the original owner to pay back his relative, but one would expect that he was grateful and would at least try to repay the kindness, if not with money then with good deeds for the relative.

To redeem a person (man or woman) sold into slavery to a foreigner living in Canaan, either the slave or a near relative would have to pay the cost of what a slave's duties were from that time until the year of Jubilee. If a near relative (brother, uncle, or cousin) paid the bill, then the former slave could go live with the redeemer and work for him receiving wages as any hired worker. If the former slave still owned land, he could go home to his land. Again, there is no provision for the former slave to pay back what the redeemer has paid for freeing him. Perhaps this is because there was no way for the former slave to pay back the redemption price since he owned nothing of value.

For a person vowed to the Lord, either by a parent or him/herself, he could also be redeemed from the vow by paying a predetermined price. Leviticus 27 sets down the cost of the vow by looking at the age and sex of the person. There was one price for an able-bodied adult male, another for a male child, another for a male senior citizen, and yet another for a woman in each of these categories. God wanted His people to take the use of vows seriously, so to get out of one (even one made in haste) there had to be a redemption paid. The same was true for an animal vowed to the Lord. If the owner of the animal vowed to give an animal to the Lord and then changed his mind, he had to pay to the priests the cost of the animal plus one fifth more. We should always be careful before we promise God something, we do not really want to give Him, whether it is our life or our possessions.

THE OLD TESTAMENT EXAMPLE OF A REDEEMER:

The only example of redeeming we see in the Old Testament comes from the book of Ruth. As the only living heirs of Elimelech, Naomi and Ruth had land with a house on it, but they were poor and could not support themselves on it. The only recourse was to sell it. They could have sold it to anyone, but that would not help their situation. If they had sold it outside the family, the money they earned from selling the property would have run out after a while, leaving them with no place to live and no money to buy food. The next step would be to sell themselves as servants or slaves.

If they sold the land to a near kinsman … a redeemer … he would also take on the job of caring for the widows and they could either continue to live on their land, or live with the redeemer. Since Mahlon and Ruth had no children before Mahlon died, the redeemer could also take on the levirate marriage with Ruth and provide an heir to Mahlon's (and Elimelech's) estate.

For this to happen there were several things that also had to happen. First, they had to find a near relative to Mahlon. A brother was out of the question, since Mahlon's only brother was also dead, but a brother of Elimelech would do. Boaz fit the bill for this one, but so did the unnamed nearer kinsman. Next they needed a relative who was wealthy, so he would be able to pay the price for the property, and the support of the widows. Again, Boaz fit the bill perfectly. We are not told if the unnamed kinsman was wealthy, but certainly he was wealthy enough to buy the land, so we will assume he was also wealthy enough to support the widows. Only one more thing was needed … this near relative that was also wealthy, had to be willing to do it. That is why Naomi sent Ruth to Boaz at the threshing room floor … to find out if he was willing. He was very willing to do everything that was needed, but the unnamed kinsman was a nearer kinsman, so he had first choice whether or not to fulfill the position. The only thing left was to find out if the nearer relative was willing. He was not, so that left everything up to Boaz.

As we know the Old Testament shows us types … people whose actions and lives give us an example of the means of salvation as seen in the New Testament. Boaz was a redeemer for Naomi and Ruth and a type of the redeemer to come for the rest of the world.

DO WE NEED TO BE REDEEMED?

What would we need to be redeemed from today? Are we in poverty? That depends on what type of poverty we are talking about. In Ruth, the poverty was a lack of means for Ruth and Naomi to support themselves. For us today the poverty is living an unrighteous life. We are slaves to sin. We have sold ourselves to sin. Jesus said in John 8:34 *"Truly, truly I say to you, whoever commits sin is a slave of sin."* The law could only redeem us if we kept it perfectly, and only one person has ever done that throughout history … Jesus Christ. If we have ever sinned, we have lost our salvation. As the apostle Paul says, *"For all have sinned, and come short of the glory of God;"* (Romans 3:23). We are under a death penalty for our sins. *"Therefore as sin came into the world through one man [Adam] and death through sin, so death has spread to all men, because all have sinned*" (Romans 5:12). We need someone to redeem us from our slavery to sin. Without a redeemer we will remain slaves to sin, and continue in that slavery. Many times, people say, "I don't want to sin. I just can't help myself." This is part of the slavery we are living in. We are living in poverty caused by sin. What will happen to us as a result of our sin? *"For the wages of sin is death"* (Romans 6:23). Without a redeemer we will have to pay the penalty of our sin. We need to be redeemed, but who can redeem us?

WHO CAN REDEEM US?

As seen from our look at Leviticus 25, there are two ways we can be redeemed. We can redeem ourselves. That means we can pay the price of redemption ourselves. How do we do that? We keep the law perfectly. We do not start sinning … ever! We can work hard and keep ALL of the law as explained in the Old Testament and be saved. Watch out! That means we cannot commit even one sin. Keeping 99.99% of the law is not enough. It has to be all of it or there can be no redemption. We know this is impossible, so likewise it is impossible for us to redeem ourselves. We just do not have the price to pay for our own redemption.

The second way to be redeemed is to find a redeemer. Where can we look? Who can redeem us? Again, we go to the book of Ruth and look at the example of a redeemer and at the laws given in Leviticus to see what can be done to redeem us from this slavery to sin. We find that only someone who is a near relative can redeem us. What near relative can do this? Matthew 5:16 says *"Let your light so shine before men, that they may see your good works, and glorify **your Father** who is in heaven."* Many times in the New Testament Jesus spoke of God as our Father (see Matthew 5:45, 48; 6:1, 4, 6, etc.). Other times Jesus spoke of God as His Father … *"he who does the will of **my Father** who is in heaven"* (Matthew 7:21; see also John 15:24; 16:10, etc.). If Jesus has the same father we have, that makes Him our brother. According to scientists today, siblings are closer in DNA than any other people. If a person needs an organ or bone marrow transplant doctors will look for a sibling first, because they know siblings have the closest DNA. You cannot find a nearer relative than that of a sibling. We have a near relative in our brother, Jesus Christ.

Next we need to find someone who can afford to pay the price. In our case, it has to be someone who has not sinned; someone who has kept the law perfectly. Again, we look to Jesus. Does he have the price to pay for redeeming us? John 3:17 says he does … *"For God did not send His Son into the world to condemn the world, but that the world through Him might be saved."* God sent Jesus to the world with the price of our redemption, so He can save us.

There is only one other requirement of the redeemer. Is he willing to redeem us? We look to our brother Jesus Christ and find him praying to our/His Father on the eve of being arrested. We see in Matthew 26:42 that Jesus prayed to God, *"O my Father, if this cup cannot pass away from Me unless I drink it, Your will be done."* The cup referred to here was the price of redemption. Not an actual cup but an event that would buy us out of our slavery.

We can see here that Jesus does meet all the requirements to be our redeemer. He is a near relative … our brother. He can afford to pay the price, and He is willing to pay it. What was the price He had to pay?

HOW CAN WE BE REDEEMED?

What price did Jesus pay for our redemption? Boaz had only to pay the price of the field Naomi was selling and marry Ruth, in order to redeem Ruth and Naomi. Is it money Jesus must pay for our redemption? If a person could buy their salvation with money, only the rich would be saved, but that is not the case. In fact, Jesus said, *"It is easier for a camel to go through the eye of a needle, than for a rich man to enter into the kingdom of God"* (Matthew 19:24). I have done a lot of sewing and I can tell you I have never seen a needle large enough for a camel to get through. We know it is not money that will pay the price of our redemption.

We know Jesus lived a perfect life and you will remember that I said before that a person could redeem themselves by keeping the law perfectly. Jesus did that, but is that the price of our redemption? That would only pay the price for the person who kept the law perfectly, but not for others. We know that was not the price of our redemption, but that was a requirement to be able to pay the price.

What is that price? What was required of the Hebrews for forgiveness of sins?

Lev 1:1 *"And the LORD called Moses, and spoke to him from the tent of meeting, saying:"*

Lev 1:2 *"Speak to the children of Israel and say to them: 'When an individual among you brings an offering to the LORD, you shall bring your offering from the livestock, either from the herd or from the flock.'"*

Lev 1:3 *" 'If his offering is a burnt sacrifice, and it is from the herd, he shall offer a male without blemish. At the door of the tent of meeting, he shall offer it of his own free will before the LORD.'"*

Lev 1:4   *" 'Then he shall lay his hand on the head of the burnt offering, and it shall be accepted for him to make atonement for him.'"*

Lev 1:5   *" 'And he shall slaughter the bull before the LORD, and the sons of Aaron, the priests, shall bring the blood and sprinkle the blood on all the sides of the altar that is at the door of the tent of meeting.'"*

The Hebrews had to present a sacrifice to the Lord. A pure, without blemish, male animal from their cattle was all that would do. The blood of the animal was shed and sprinkled around the altar. Nothing less would do for an atonement of sin. Atonement means to cover something. This sacrifice was to cover the sins of the person, until the ultimate sacrifice was brought before the Lord. This sacrifice as listed In the Old Testament was only temporary. The price of our redemption had to be a sacrifice, but an animal would not do. It had to be a man. Not just any man would do, because it had to be a pure unblemished, sinless man. We know of humans that "all have sinned", so where could we find a sinless man to give his life to redeem us from our slavery to sin? We are as unable to provide redemption for ourselves as Naomi and Ruth were. Like Naomi and Ruth, we have to look to someone else to provide that redemption. We look to the only source available – God. God provided His Son (our brother), Jesus Christ who was sinless, as the sacrifice.

The only thing that would pay the price of our redemption was the perfect sacrifice. Jesus gave His life for us as that perfect sacrifice. Even Pilate could find no fault in Him (Luke 23:4; John 18:38 and 19:4). Lies were told about Him (Matthew

215

26:59; Mark 15:56; Luke 23:2). He was beaten, tortured, and nailed to a cross to die (Matthew 27; Mark 15; Luke 23; and John18-19). At that moment He took on all of our sins, so we could be presented to God pure and sinless. What can we do to repay Jesus for this sacrifice? NOTHING! Absolutely nothing! It was given freely and the work of redemption is finished.

That does not mean everyone is going to heaven. We are still creatures of freewill. We can choose to accept or reject the salvation given us by Jesus' act of redemption. How do we accept it? We start by believing in Jesus Christ (see Acts 8:37). We repent of our sins (see Acts 2:38; 3:19; etc.). We confess our belief in Jesus before others (see Romans 10:10). We get baptized (see Acts 2:38). When we accept salvation, we then show our gratitude by living a righteous/Christian life as presented in the Bible (see Galatians 6:10; Hebrews 13:21; I Peter 3:11).

PLAN OF SALVATION

HEAR	Romans 10:17 *"So then faith comes by hearing, and hearing by the word of God."* (see also: John 3:16-18)
BELIEVE (FAITH)	Acts 10:43 *"To Him [Jesus Christ] all the prophets bear witness that whoever believes in Him will receive remission of sins through His name."* (see also: Mark 16:16; John 8:24; Acts 8:37; Romans 10:9)
REPENT	Luke 13:3 *"... but unless you repent, you will all likewise perish."* (see also: Matthew 3:2; 4:17; Mark 1:15; 6:12; Acts 3:19; 17:30)
CONFESS	Romans 10:9 *"that if you confess with your mouth Jesus is Lord, and believe in your heart that God has raised Him from the dead, you will be saved."* (see also: Matthew 10:32; Luke 12:8; Romans 10:10; Philippians 2:11)
BAPTISM	Acts 2:38 *"... Repent and be baptized, every one of you, in the name of Jesus Christ for the forgiveness of sins, and you shall receive the gift of the Holy Spirit."* (see also: Acts 22:16; Galatians 3:27; Colossians 2:12; Romans 6:4; and 1 Peter 3:21)
STUDY GOD'S WORD (BIBLE) AND LIVE A CHRISTIAN LIFE	Galatians 6:10 *"... let us do good to all people, especially to those who are of the household of faith."* (see also Hebrews 13:21; 1 Peter 3:11; 2 Peter 3:18; 2 Timothy 2:15)

ADDENDUM A: RUTH IN LITERATURE AND MEDIA - INTRODUCTION

One does not have to go far to find Ruth's story portrayed in poetry, literature, films, and songs. From the early 1700's one can find poetry that speaks of Ruth in terms of happiness and sadness. Modern writers still find Ruth's life worthy of poems and short stories. In written prose we find full length novels that tell the account of Ruth's life, but fictionalize the events not mentioned in the Bible. If the author has done his or her homework into the background and history of Moab and Israel, these novels can be very interesting as well as helpful to people who are curious about what might have been going on in the background during the days of Ruth's life. As with any books about Ruth, these should not be read without first reading the Biblical book of Ruth, and definitely should not be taken as scriptural.

The newest form of reworking the book of Ruth to provide entertainment for the public is movies and films. Hollywood got right into reproducing Biblical events almost from the beginning. Most of us are too young to remember the 1927 release of Cecil B. DeMille's silent film about Jesus called _The King of Kings_, but we can remember watching the _Ten Commandments_ starring Charlton Heston. I still enjoy watching it on TV almost every Easter and at any other time, since it is also available on DVD. Hollywood writers used many events from the Bible to create films of lesser quality than Cecil B. DeMille's blockbusters, and

Ruth was no exception. People everywhere enjoy a good love story, even though Ruth is much more that "just" a love story. It has so much more to offer.

Now fast forward to today and the advent of the computerized movie. You can find many groups creating films that are designed for the general public to watch at home with or without their children. Just like the poetry, short stories, and novels, one should never accept a film version of a Bible event without first reading the Biblical account to make comparisons. The Bible is the only inspired version of any of these historical events and should be treated as the only true version when there are discrepancies between the two.

You can use these movies and films as a sort of game when you watch them with your children, or even in a classroom situation. First, read the Bible book of Ruth to the children. Then show them the movie or film, but ask them to see who can find the most discrepancies in the movie or film. You can even offer a small prize to the child who gets the most. It can be the basis for a good discussion after the movie.

ADDENDUM B: RUTH IN POETRY

The account of Ruth's life as a happy and/or sad love story has captured men and women's hearts through the ages. As such, it was often mentioned in poetry and we have several examples starting from the 1700's onward. Perhaps the earliest poem that still exists about Ruth is one written by John Bunyan. Bunyan turned the entire book of Ruth into poetry in his book of Scriptural Poems printed in London in 1701. "The Book of Ruth" is one of six portions of the Bible completely re-written as poetry by Bunyan. He divided his poem on Ruth into four chapters each coinciding with a chapter in the Bible.

Bunyan follows the Biblical account of Ruth very well. The only discrepancy I could find is in line 17 of the first chapter where he refers to Ruth and Orpah as Naomi's "step-daughters". Elsewhere he refers to Ruth as Naomi's daughter or daughter-in-law which fits perfectly with the Bible. It would be normal for Naomi to refer to Ruth affectionately as daughter rather than using the formal "in-law" part, so I see no problem with that. She actually refers to Ruth as "daughter" in several verses within the Biblical book as well.

From the late 1700s to the early 1900s, we have poems by John Keats and Francis Ledwidge. Neither of these poems has Ruth as the subject, but only uses her as an illustration within the poem. Keats lived from 1795 to 1821, and used Ruth incorrectly in his poem "*Ode to a Nightingale*" where he compares the nightingale's song to Ruth's tears and sad heart. Ruth is supposedly standing and crying in the alien corn field of Bethlehem, although Keats does not actually say Bethlehem. Those who have read the Biblical book of Ruth know where the cornfield was, and that Ruth shed no such tears over her homeland of Moab. Although it makes good poetry, it does not follow the real Ruth's life.

Francis Ledwidge, who lived from 1891 to 1917, also used Ruth as an illustration in his poem "*Behind the Closed Eye*." The woodbine plant bending to intertwine with the thorn is illustrated by Ruth's activities in the corn field. Gleaning grain would require a lot of bending and stooping to pick up the ears of grain. Ledwidge uses that as part of his view of a scene from his past. It is a valid reference and one I am sure most people of his day would easily recognize.

Perhaps a better example of poetry from this time written about Ruth would be Thomas Hood's "*Ruth*". Hood lived from 1799 to 1845. His poem is a mixture of light heartedness with a bit of seriousness. Containing five stanzas of four lines each, it describes Ruth standing in the corn field. It appears from the last stanza that we are seeing Ruth through Boaz's eyes since he asks her to "share my harvest and my home" in the last line. It has nothing of God's work in Ruth's life, but does describe her as praising God with her "sweet looks". Obviously, the poet assumed his readers would understand who this Ruth was, as do we today.

From the other side, we see Boaz through Ruth's eyes in a poem titled "*Boaz Asleep*", by Victor Marie Hugo. Hugo also fits into the 19th century poetry scene having lived from 1802 until 1885. "*Boaz Asleep*" is a description of Boaz who is a wealthy, honorable man. Boaz is described as an older man who has lived well, worked hard, and easily gives to the poor. The scene in the poem takes place on the threshing room floor where it ends with Ruth's decision to choose Boaz even though she is a woman easily desired by younger men.

A more modern poem written by Linda Gayton and published on the world wide web on March 29, 2005, is titled "*A*

Song to Boaz." This poem takes place on the threshing room floor and has Ruth bringing grain to Boaz. Ruth starts out by explaining who she is. She ends by asking Boaz to be merciful while taking her and her grain in. The poem is short -- only 13 lines ---, but does not follow the real Ruth's personality. Ruth in this poem talks about gleaning "for" Boaz, making him sweet cakes, and bringing him grain at the threshing floor. We know from the Bible that Ruth gleaned for Naomi and herself, and that it was actually Boaz who gave Ruth grain at the threshing floor. While this poem is interesting, it does not follow the Bible account of Ruth's actions.

Another twentieth century poem found on the internet was written on January 3, 2006. This poem called "*Leftovers*" was written by a young lady known only as Riihele. Again, this is a short poem of only four stanzas, but covers a lot. It speaks of Ruth and Naomi coming to Bethlehem with only leftovers. Then goes on to speak of how they lived on leftovers, but finally says that God used those leftovers to create a banquet and a legacy to a beautiful woman known as Ruth. It looks at Ruth from a different point of view and creates a very beautiful sentiment about how God used Ruth even though all she had was leftovers. It also shows how God uses us even though we do not have anything of worth to bring to Him.

Several poems about Ruth have been published in a book titled Reading Ruth: Contemporary Women Reclaim a Sacred Story. This book is not strictly a book of poetry, but contains articles, commentaries, short stories, and poetry, all written by different women and all written about Ruth. The first of the poems is by Marge Piercy and titled "*The Book of Ruth and Naomi*". This poem is about the book of Ruth, more than about Ruth herself. The first two stanzas are strictly about the book, while the last four are about the friendship of Ruth and Naomi.

"*Ruth's Journey*" by Ruth Whitman is a light-hearted poem that has Ruth speaking. She tells her own story, but this story ends the night she goes to Boaz at the threshing room floor. While this poem is fun to read, it is mostly fiction. For instance, it begins by fictionally filling in Ruth's early life in Moab before and after she marries Mahlon. Naomi takes care of Ruth as her daughter-in-law, and teaches her how to cook, sew, and do all the other things she needs to know to be a good wife and woman. After ten years Elimelech and his sons die. Ruth and Naomi travel the southern path around the Dead Sea passing through Hebron on the way to Bethlehem. Starving in Bethlehem Naomi tells Ruth to go to her cousin's field to gather leftovers. We know from the Bible; it was really Ruth who suggested that she go to glean. She did not know whose field she would glean in until she was there. Boaz is nice to her and the next night Naomi tells Ruth to go to the threshing room floor. The poem ends its fifth part with Boaz recognizing Ruth at the threshing floor.

Merle Feld writes a part poem, part prose story of Ruth called "*At the Crossroads*". Feld goes through important times in her own life where her life parallels that of Ruth and Naomi. She looks at how other women affected her life ... women like her mother, her neighbor, her Israeli friend, her mother-in-law ... comparing these to times in Ruth and Naomi's lives. These include happy times, bad times, even grieving times. All are expressed in prose and poetry which makes very interesting reading. She shares a bit of herself as she writes about each event.

Kathryn Hellerstein, the most prolific poem writer in this Reading Ruth book, writes four poems about Ruth and Naomi. She writes short poems that take you through the book of Ruth from chapter 1 through chapter 3. "*Naomi: Loss*" is an interesting look into the mind of Naomi as she looks back on her life after the deaths of her sons. It is well written and covers the years from the time Elimelech decided to take his family to Moab until Naomi has to face the fact that she will have no grandchildren to share her future.

"*Ruth and Orpah*" shows a brief discussion between the two sisters-in-law about whether they should go with Naomi to Bethlehem and what they will leave behind in Moab if they do. Both end up packing in silence, determined to do what is right to care for their mother-in-law.

The third poem again looks at Naomi's thoughts, but this time she is thinking of Bethlehem and how she left it ten years ago with her family at her side. Now she returns bitter and alone except for her foreign daughter-in-law, Ruth. This poem is titled "*Naomi: Call Me Bitter*", and covers the entrance of Naomi into Bethlehem when she tells the women not to call her Naomi but instead to call her Mara.

Ruth's thoughts speaking to Naomi are covered in the fourth poem, "*Ruth to Naomi: After the Threshing*." Ruth thinks of what Naomi has told her to do as she waits for Boaz and the other men to go to sleep. Then she follows Naomi's advice and lies down at Boaz's feet. The poem ends with Ruth going home and Naomi's greeting of "who are you?".

All four of Hellerstein's poems stay true to the scriptures, and show a very good understanding of what Naomi, Ruth, and Orpah may have thought during the times of sadness, uncertainty, and hopefulness.

Following that line of thinking is a poem called "*Awakening Ruth*" by Barbara Helfgott Hyett. In this poem, Ms. Hyett gives voice to Ruth's thoughts as she lies at the feet of Boaz. It does not cover anything mentioned specifically in the Bible but simply speculates on what Ruth was doing and thinking as she lies there waiting for Boaz to awaken.

BIBLIOGRAPHY

POETRY:

Bunyan, John. "The Book of Ruth", Scriptural Poems Being Several Portions of Scripture Digested into English Verse. London: London Bridge (for J. Blare, at the Looking Glass), 1701.

Feld, Merle. "At the Crossroads", Reading Ruth: Contemporary Women Reclaim a Sacred Story. New York, NY: Ballantine Books, 1994. pp. 166-181.

Gayton, Linda. A Song to Boaz. 2005. (http://www.authorsden.com/visit/viewpoetry.asp?AuthorID=25 327&id=133461)

Hellenstein, Kathryn. "Naomi: Loss". Reading Ruth: Contemporary Women Reclaim a Sacred Story. New York, NY: Ballantine Books, 1994. pp. 236-237.

_____. "Ruth and Orpah". Reading Ruth: Contemporary Women Reclaim a Sacred Story. New York, NY: Ballantine Books, 1994. pp. 237-238.

_____. "Naomi: 'Call Me Bitter' ". Reading Ruth: Contemporary Women Reclaim a Sacred Story. New York, NY: Ballantine Books, 1994. p. 238.

_____. "Ruth to Naomi: After the Threshing". Reading Ruth: Contemporary Women Reclaim a Sacred Story. New York, NY: Ballantine Books, 1994. pp. 239-240.

Hood, Thomas. Ruth. (1799-1845)
(http://www.lang.nagoya-u.ac.jp/~matsouka/Hook.html)

Hugo, Victor Marie. Boaz Asleep. (1802-1885)
(http://www.poemhunter.com/poem/boaz-asleep/)

Hyett, Barbara Helfgott. "Awakening Ruth". Reading Ruth:
Contemporary Women Reclaim a Sacred Story. New
York, NY: Ballantine Books, 1994. p. 241.

Keats, John. Ode to a Nightingale. (1795-1821)
(http://rpo.library.utoronto.ca/poem/1131.html)

Ledwidge, Francis. Behind the Closed Eye. (1891-1917)
(http://rpo.library.utoronto.ca/poem/2544.html)

Piercy, Marge. "The Book of Ruth and Naomi". Reading Ruth:
Contemporary Women Reclaim a Sacred Story. New
York, NY: Ballantine Books, 1994. pp. 159-160.

Riihele. Leftovers.
(http://blog.360.yahoo.com/riihele05?tag=bible), 2006.

Whitman, Ruth. "Ruth's Journey". Reading Ruth: Contemporary
Women Reclaim a Sacred Story. New York, NY:
Ballantine Books, 1994. pp. 161-165.

ADDENDUM C: RUTH IN MUSIC

We come next to musical versions of or about Ruth. Since most of this section will deal with songs and the lyrics of songs are usually poems, I thought it prudent to put this section next. I found only three actual recordings using Ruth in some way. The first was part of a children's read-a-long book and cassette by Jean Horton Berg titled The Story of Ruth. The book will be reviewed in more detail in the section on children's books later in this book. What we want to look at now is the cassette tape that accompanies the little book. The audio cassette tape is performed by three people who represent each of the main characters: Ruth, Naomi, and Boaz, as well as taking turns being the narrator. There is a musical background score that adds to the enjoyment without being overpowering. The best part of all is three songs beautifully performed at the end of the story: "Your People and Your God", "Who is She?", and "Home". The songs were composed by Erik Johansson and performed by Erik Johansson and Marylee Hursh. The songs are very professionally written, sung, and recorded. It would be great to be able to get a tape of just these three songs, since they are the best thing about the tape and book. "Your People and Your God" shows how we, like Ruth, should be willing to trust God and go where He wants us to go. The chorus is Ruth singing to Naomi asking her not to make Ruth leave her. Ruth says they will go together making Naomi's people and Naomi's God Ruth's as well. The stanzas tell the rest of the story of Ruth. "Who Is She?" tells the story of Ruth working in the fields. Boaz responds to her and blesses her. It is mostly the story of that first day in the field when Boaz meets

229

her. The last song "Home" is a song about being at home with God. "Following God, we'll never feel alone. Where we go with God is home" is the chorus of this short song. The stanzas tell us we should have faith in God and we will never be alone.

On a more classical tone, in the 1930's Kurt Weill wrote an opera in German titled The Eternal Road (or perhaps a better translation of the German is "The Road of Promise"). The Eternal Road is an opera but with music that covers many genres from cabaret and Broadway musical to pageant tones. It was originally performed in New York in 1937 where it was a hit from the beginning. However, the extensive six-hour length, along with the massive number of performers, and changes in elaborate background scenes took a lot out of the performers as well as the audience. That combined with the enormous cost led to bankruptcy and doom, causing it to be closed after only 153 performances. It has been revived in audio by the Berlin Radio Symphony Orchestra who performs highlights from the opera on a CD that came out in 2003. The Opera was written more as a political statement against the Nazi's, than as Jewish history and was hoped to be a medium to convey to the world what Hitler was doing to the Jews in Germany. Its short run prevented it from doing this on the grand scale it was hoped it would.

Looking at it more closely, it does cover a good amount of the Old Testament. The opera takes place in a synagogue in Germany where the occupants are hiding from a Nazi pogrom. During their time hiding together the occupants of the synagogue begin talking about their fears along with how fear and bravery has affected their history. They start acting out many stories of the brave, noble Jews from times past, including stories of Abraham, Isaac, Jacob, Moses, Ruth, Isaiah, and Jeremiah, as well as others. It is very clear the author considers Ruth, Naomi, and Boaz as brave heroic people from Jewish history. While many of Israel's greatest leaders are left out of the opera, Ruth is there with her profession of devotion to God and Naomi.

We are, of course, only concerned in this study with two of the musical numbers from the opera. Both are found in Act 3: Scene 24 – "Naomi and Ruth", and "Ruth and Boaz". Ruth's speech to Naomi is taken from Ruth 1:16-17 and while rewritten, it does cover what Ruth is saying very well. Ruth professes her love of God saying, to lose that would be torture. She goes on to say she will never leave Naomi, telling Naomi not to ask such a thing. Naomi accepts and the scene changes.

Next the opera is in the grain field of Boaz and Boaz asks the head reaper who the woman is. The reaper says she is the woman who came from Moab, and Boaz instantly knows who she is and that she is a worthy woman. He then tells his master reaper to be sure she gets food, drink, and vinegar when she needs it.

At this point the Rabbi comes in to basically change the scene to the threshing room floor. He makes a few comments on how brave Ruth is, taking us into the next song which is Boaz being startled by a woman at his feet. There is not enough time to tell the whole story. It does convey that Boaz thought Ruth honorable because she did not go after young men, and he agrees to claim her as his bride the next day. He urges her to stay until morning assuring her that her purity will be whole. Then the scene changes to the people of the village blessing them and God. For being only ten minutes long, this part of the opera does get the main story of Ruth across without adding false information.

One thing that did confuse me about this opera is that the Act where Ruth is portrayed is titled "The Kings", not "The Judges". In fact, there are no actual kings mentioned in the highlight's CD at all. The next section goes on to "The

Prophets". With no Judges listed, and no kings actually included, it seems the groupings of the songs are wrong for the Act. Although they move along somewhat chronologically through the Old Testament, there is a lot left out of the Bible ... but then, they only had six hours for the whole performance, and they were only telling stories of the bravest of the Jews.

Looking at a more modern music find; singer Lyle Lovett recorded a very successful CD in 1992. He titled the CD Joshua, Judges, and Ruth after the three books of the Bible. Do not be deceived by the title! I have listened to this CD several times and find nothing in any of the songs that points to Ruth, Joshua, or Judges. The CD contains a song titled "Church" that is about a preacher who preaches too long and the congregation gets hungry, longing for cornbread among other things. Apparently, this cornbread is more nourishing than what the preacher is saying. There are songs about places such as "North Dakota," "Memphis," and "Baltimore", none of which remind us of Moab or Israel. There are also songs about girls leaving him, girls making him feel good, family ties, and death, but nothing I could link to the Bible or specifically to Ruth. Lovett sings in a sort of country/jazz style. Most of the songs are interesting and sometimes fun to listen to, but why he chose the title of Joshua, Judges and Ruth is beyond my comprehension. The album does not even have a theme that brings all the songs together. It deals with some aspects of religion, but mostly speaks of heartbreak, loss of love, and life.

Looking for more music about Ruth, I did a search on the internet and found two songs as sheet music, although all had a sound byte or downloadable digital music version on the website. Both deal with the passage in Ruth 1:16-17 where Ruth makes her now famous speech asking Naomi not to tell her to leave her because "whither thou goest, I will go..."

One of these websites containing sheet music with a sound byte is called "A Song of Ruth". Written by Steven Warner with arrangement by Karen Schneider Kirner, this song deals with the same subject, Ruth's expression of love for Naomi. It is listed as being used for marriage, commitment, wedding, love, unity, and love of God for us. It was written for soprano/baritone duet to be played on a violin or C Instrument, guitar and/or keyboard. While the words to the song are a total re-write of the passage in Ruth, the meaning is the same and it does express the need to be united in the love of one God.

The second and last song I found is also called "Song of Ruth" (apparently song titles do not have to be very different to be accepted, since it is enough to just leave "A" off the title) and was written by someone who calls himself "mrxmas". It is a simple verse of only four lines, which gives a brief overview of only the verses Ruth spoke to Naomi.

BIBLIOGRAPHY

Music

Berg, Jean Horton (author), and Palm, Felix (illustrator). Audio
tape with musical underscore narrated by Felice C.
Meyer, June Hamblin Mitchelll, and Larry Weber. Songs
composed by Erik Johansson and performed by Erik
Johansson and Marylee Hursh. The Story of Ruth. Boston,
MA: The Christian Science Publishing Society, 1981.

Lovett, Lyle (performer). Joshua Judges Ruth. Produced by
George Massenburg, Billy Williams, and Lyle Lovett.
Universal City, CA: Curb Music Company/MCA Records, Inc.,
1992.

Mrxmas (writer). Song of Ruth.
(http://www.songramp.com/mod/mps/viewtrack.php?trackid=2
3656), 2004.

Warner, Steven (writer), and Karen Schneider Kirner
(arrangement). A Song of Ruth. Schiller Park, IL:
World Library Publications, 1999.

Weill, Kurt (composer) and Franz Werfel (lyrics). Eternal Road
(Highlights). Milken Archive of American Jewish Music.
[Berlin Radio Symphony Orchestra. Performers:
Barbara Rearick, Constance Hauman, Hanna
Wollschlager, Ian Denolfo, James Maddalena, et al.),
Audio CD - September 30, 2003.

ADDENDUM D: RUTH IN FICTIONALIZED NOVELS

While I could find only three novels written about Ruth, I found three different ideas of what could have been happening in the areas of Naomi and Ruth's lives, which are not mentioned in the Bible. It is also interesting that all three novels are written by women. Not that I would make anything positive or negative about that, it is just interesting. I would like to have seen the story fictionalized from a man's point of view as well. Let us take a look at the three novels.

The first was written in 1965 and is meant more for juveniles, but still interesting reading for adults as well. Beverly Larsen's book Damsel from Afar: The Story of Ruth is told in a narrative style. It starts as the caravan Naomi, Ruth, and Orpah are traveling with stops for the night. This is where Naomi expects Ruth and Orpah to leave her the next morning. Ruth is up early and, while contemplating how bad her life was in Moab before she married Mahlon, the Lord speaks to her. The Lord tells Ruth to go on with Naomi instead of back to Moab. She does go on with Naomi all the way to Bethlehem. The book sticks closely to the Biblical account of Ruth and Naomi's lives. While it is an interesting book, the fictionalized parts show a lack of background research on the part of the author. On the plus side, the book has some nice illustrations throughout the story which help the reader visualize the content of the story.

In 1981, Lois Henderson wrote Ruth: A Novel which was published by Guideposts. Ms. Henderson has used her vivid imagination to fill in the gaps of the Biblical story of Ruth. From Ruth's sister's baby being sacrificed to the pagan Moabite god Chemosh, including her first meeting with Naomi as a child of 14 years, to her realization of a God who cares about women, the story is filled with interesting and well researched events. Although for the most part fictional, the story flows right through the marriage with Boaz and birth of Ruth's first child, all the time showing the author did much research on the historical times she writes about. Where she writes about events that are told in the Bible, she remains true to the Biblical account.

Our last novel about Ruth was written by Francine Rivers in 2006. The book is titled <u>Unshaken</u> and is the third in a group of books Ms. Rivers has or is writing about the women who are mentioned in Christ's genealogy in Matthew. This fictionalized novella tells the story of Ruth and Naomi while staying close to the Biblical account. Ms. Rivers has one glaring error in the book that cannot be ignored. She keeps saying Naomi's family was in Moab for 15 years, and later even says they were gone for 20 years. While this may be a little thing it is clearly stated in the Biblical book of Ruth that they were gone for 10 years. Other than this the author stays true to the Biblical account of Naomi and Ruth, and uses her imagination only to fill in the gaps. She portrays Elimelech as a man who abandoned his belief in God to worship idols, and likewise abandoned the Promised Land for a land where he thought it would be easier to get rich. She describes the journey of Naomi and Ruth very well, showing it to be exhausting and possibly dangerous. When Naomi and Ruth return to Bethlehem, they have to live in a cave outside of the city because Elimelech had mortgaged his land before leaving Bethlehem years before, and because the people of Bethlehem do not want to offer shelter to a woman of Moab. There are excellent sections in the book where Ms. Rivers has the women of Bethlehem gossiping about what is going on, and then, (not to show favor to one sex over the other -- we all know gossip is not something only women do), shows what the men were gossiping about as well. The story presented in this book is overall a beautiful love story showing Ruth and Boaz finally discovering they have more feelings for each other (love) than just doing their duty to raise up an heir for Elimelech and Mahlon.

This book goes beyond just fictionalizing the story of Ruth. It ends with a section written by Peggy Lynch called "Seek and Find". In the "Seek and Find" section are six short studies to be used in a group (or alone) to better study the book of Ruth. This is a great touch to make studying the Bible more enticing. First, you read the fictionalized account of an already interesting story. Then you are encouraged to go directly to the Bible to see the true story and study it to see what God wants us to learn from it. When reading fictionalized accounts of Biblical events, we should always study the Bible as well to be sure we do not confuse what is imagination and what is real in what we are reading. I would reverse the order and suggest reading the Biblical account first.

BIBLIOGRAPHY

FICTIONALIZED NOVELS

Henderson, Lois T. Ruth: A Novel. Carmel, NY: Guideposts, 1981.

Larsen, Beverly. Damsel from Afar: The Story of Ruth. Minneapolis, MN: Augsburg Publishing House, 1965.

Rivers, Francine. Unshaken. (Lineage of Grace #3). Detroit, MI: Thomson Gale, 2006.

ADDENDUM E: RUTH IN CHILDREN'S BOOKS

      Rewriting Biblical events for children to understand is also another way of fictionalizing the parts of Biblical events that are not told in the Bible. This author looked at ten children's books written about Ruth and found a wide variety of stories told under the guise of being about Ruth. What is most amazing is what is left out of the children's stories, as well as how some things have been explained for young children to understand. We are talking about children from pre-school age to about 8 or 9 years old. These are the ages where pictures are important, and where parents and grandparents as well as babysitters either read to children, or the child who is just learning to read will read it to him/herself.

      I have divided children's books into four categories: (1) those that use modern children in their stories; (2) those that tell the complete or nearly complete story; (3) those that leave critical parts out, and (4) those that add unnecessary information that can confuse a child.

      Children are often attracted to books about other children who fall into their age group, so the books in category one can be a plus to get your child interested in books about the Bible. The down side of this type of book is that a third or more of the story is taken up by a separate narrative about a modern child who has nothing to do with the Biblical adventure. This means the author has to tell the story of Ruth in much less space (less words, and less graphics), then a book dedicated totally to telling the story of Ruth. We will look at three books that fit into this category.

The first is written by Alice Joyce Davidson and designed by Victoria Marshall. The book is titled <u>The Story of Ruth and Naomi</u> and is part of an *Alice in Bibleland Storybook* series. In this book, a little girl named Alice is visited by the airmail bird. This bird turns the book she is reading into a screen she can walk through. Since she is reading the book of Ruth, Alice watches Ruth, Naomi, Boaz and others as they are living their lives first in Moab and later in Bethlehem. She does not interact with the characters but simply watches them.

Next is a book by Damon J. Taylor who wrote and illustrated the book titled <u>To Cheese or Not to Cheese: The Story of Ruth</u>. This book is about a small child named Coleman who does not want to go to his great-grandmother's 92nd birthday party, because he would rather be with his friends. His sock puppet friend tells him the story of Ruth and Naomi to illustrate how unselfish Ruth was. The story of Ruth is told in a way for a pre-school child to understand, meaning many things are left out that a child that age might not understand, such as the meeting on the threshing room floor and Boaz's meeting with the nearer kinsman at the city gate. Overall, it is a good book for the age group.

Third and the worst of the three is a book written by Charlotte Lundy and illustrated by Miriam Sagasti called <u>Thank You, Ruth and Naomi</u>. Keana is a third-grade student who has had a best friend since the first grade. When another girl moves into the neighborhood, Keana becomes worried that her best friend is replacing her with the new girl. Keana's Mom tells her the story of Ruth and Naomi to show her that people can remain friends even though another person comes into their lives. The story of Ruth and Naomi is told very succinctly, totally leaving God out. In fact, the only time God is mentioned in this storybook is at the very end where Keana thanks God for sending Ruth and Naomi to help her understand what true friendship is.

As mentioned above, it is difficult to get the whole story of Ruth into a book in this category, because of space limitations. I did not find one book in this category that told the whole unbiased story of Ruth as represented in the Bible. While this type of book may be good for catching a young child's attention, be sure you talk to your child about the story. Each of these books has a different statement to make. One talks of unselfishness, one illustrates friendship, and one looks at jealousy. Only one actually allows the telling of the story for the child to see as it is in the Bible. Make sure your child knows there are many lessons to learn from Ruth's story, so they will not be confused when one book looks at Ruth from one viewpoint and another book looks at it from another viewpoint. All are valid viewpoints and can be easily explained to your child.

Our next category is that of books that do tell the whole story. These books cover a wide period of time, the oldest having been written in 1958 and the newest in 2005. Let us hope there will be more of these type of books in the future as well.

A book called <u>Ruth and Naomi</u> written and illustrated by Jean Marzollo, is a good example of this type of book. The story starts with Ruth and Naomi going from Moab to Bethlehem. Orpah is not mentioned in this book. The author says it is simplified for children ages 4 to 8 years old. The story is very well written with explanations of things like "widow", and how the harvest was accomplished. Boaz is called Farmer Boaz. There are even song lyrics about the story to be sung to the tune of "The Farmer in the Dell". At the bottom of every page is a row of tiny rabbits that make comments about the story to help children remember it. The drawings are somewhat abstract but very colorful. This is a very good introduction to the account of Ruth for very young children.

Next, we have a book titled Ruth Woman of Courage written by Paula Jordan Parris and illustrated by Robert H. Cassell. This storybook is written for young children to read themselves. It is true to the Biblical book of Ruth, but starts with Naomi telling her daughters-in-law that she is going back to Bethlehem. Of course, it explains that Elimelech, Mahlon, and Chilion have died and that is why Naomi is leaving. The story adds an important message, telling children that Jesus is a descendant of Ruth and Boaz. Each small chapter ends with questions to help the child remember what has been read, and the book ends with two pages of reflections on the entire story. Both of these are nice touches to help children remember an important story.

Authors and illustrators Maud and Miska Petersham have created a beautifully illustrated book simply titled Ruth, with every other page being a full-page illustration, some in color, and some in black and white. The story is told following the Biblical account but the narration uses more modern English words, which changes when a person speaks. When a speech is quoted, it is quoted using the King James Biblical text exactly, even using the "thee", "thy", "thine" and 'est at the end of words such as goest, lodgest, etc. Even though this book was first written in 1958, it is still an excellent book to read to small children or for school age children to read for themselves.

Last in this category is Ruth's Story as told by author Catherine Storr and illustrated by Geoff Taylor. This book is a nicely told story for young children. Nothing is left out of the story. It starts with Elimelech taking his family out of Judea to Moab because of the famine, ends with the birth of Obed, and gives the genealogy in one sentence at the very end. The illustrations are colorful and good, and there is even a colorful map of Bible lands at the end of the book. The map is drawn and colored to attract the attention of a child. It includes the location of Bethlehem as well as several other cities and countries, but does NOT include the location of Moab, which is a rather odd omission since part of the story takes place in Moab.

Books to avoid, in my opinion, are those that leave parts out. I am sure most of these authors are well meaning people who think a child would never understand these points and maybe they are not that important to the story. I would disagree with this sentiment totally. It was important enough to put these parts in the Bible and it is important that a child learn them as well. This is another reason why an adult should read to or with their children ... so they can explain that this storybook they are reading is just a retelling of the real story as presented in the Bible which may contain even more information.

Two books that leave important things out are <u>Ruth - A Woman Whose Loyalty Was Stronger Than Her Grief</u>, written by Alex Marlee, and <u>Ruth's New Family</u>, written by Penny Frank. Both of these are beautifully illustrated but leave important things out of the narrative. Ms. Marlee leaves the entire part of the nearer kinsman out. Ms. Frank leaves God's help out of her book. She only mentions God as an afterthought in a few "thank yous". It does not show how God works in people's lives and this is important to the Biblical account of the book of Ruth.

One last book I will mention here is actually in many ways a good book. It has already been mentioned in the "Addendum C: Music" section of this book. The book is called <u>The Story of Ruth</u>, written by Jean Horton Berg. It comes with an audio tape that is fantastic. It is a read-a-long book, so the child who is learning to read can listen to the tape and watch the words as the story is told. It leaves a few things out, but the part that bothers me most about this book is what is added that does not need to be there. Things like foreigners living in Moab could not do much because of their status; widows automatically returned to their mothers' homes; no one in Bethlehem had to let Ruth work in their fields because she was a foreigner; and Ruth was resting when Boaz came to the field. None of these is valid and can be misleading to a child. While these may seem like little things, children tend to remember stories the way they first hear them their whole lives, so why not make sure we give our children and grandchildren the truth from the beginning?

I know some of you are now saying, why should we purchase a children's book about Ruth for our child? Why not just read the story from the Bible? That is a good point and you can certainly do that and be blessed for so doing. In fact, I encourage you to do that. Keep in mind that the Bible is written in somewhat grown up language, and the book of Ruth is written about a time long ago. While we may see it very clearly, a child may need lots of things explained. I cannot think of a better way to spend time with your child than to spend it going through the Bible talking about the events told there. However, a child also learns by seeing and since you cannot take a child back to the time of the Judges in Israel, you can show them pictures drawn in books for just that purpose ... to illustrate the times of Ruth's life. I encourage you to examine a children's book before you purchase it. Look at the pictures. Read the story, and most importantly of all, read the Bible book of Ruth to compare it to the child's book. Know where the child's book leaves something out, so you can add it while reading to your child. Know what the child's book adds that might not be right, correct it explaining what the Bible says. Explain that we should always take what the Bible says as truth, because it is the word of God and does not lie.

BIBLIOGRAPHY

CHILDREN'S BOOKS

Alex, Marlee (author), and Ruano, Alfonso (Illustrator). <u>Ruth - A
Woman Whose Loyalty Was Stronger Than Her Grief</u>.
Outstanding Women of the Bible Series. Grand Rapids,
MI: William B. Eerdmans Publishing Company, 1987.

Berg, Jean Horton (author), and Palm, Felix (illustrator). Audio
tape with musical underscore narrated by Felice C.
Meyer, June Hamblin Mitchell, and Larry Weber. Songs
composed by Erik Johansson and performed by Erik
Johansson and Marylee Hursh. <u>The Story of Ruth</u>.
Boston, MA: Christian Science Publishing Society,
1981.

Davidson, Alice Joyce (author), and Marshall, Victoria (designer).
<u>The Story of Ruth and Naomi</u>. An Alice In Bibleland Storybook.
Danbury, CT: Grolier Enterprises, Inc., 1991.

Frank, Penny (author), and Morris, Tony (illustrator). <u>Ruth's
New Family</u>. Belleville, MI: Lion Publishing Corporation,
1984.

Lundy, Charlotte (author), and Sagasti, Miriam (illustrator).
<u>Thank You, Ruth and Naomi</u>. Mooresville, NC: Bay
Light Publishing, Inc., 2004.

Marzollo, Jean (Author and illustrator). <u>Ruth and Naomi</u>. New
York, NY: Little, Brown and Company, 2005.

Parris, Paula Jordan (author), and Cassell, Robert H. (illustrator). Ruth Woman of Courage. Biblearn Series. Nashville, TN: Broadman Press, 1977.

Petersham, Maud and Miska (authors and illustrators). Ruth. New York: The Macmillan Company, 1958.

Storr, Catherine (author), and Geoff Taylor (Illustrator). Ruth's Story. Milwaukee, WI: Raintree Childrens Books, 1986.

Taylor, Damon J. (author and illustrator). To Cheese or Not to Cheese: The Story of Ruth. Child Sockology Series. Grand Rapids, MI: Kregel Kidzone, 2003.

ADDENDUM F: RUTH IN MOVIES AND FILMS

Hollywood quickly grabbed on to the Bible as a good source of material to make into movies. From Cecil B. DeMille's silent movie _The King of Kings_, to his blockbuster _Ten Commandments_, to movies by other directors such as _The Story of Jacob and Joseph_, _Samson and Delilah_, _The Bible_ (which was actually a movie about the first 22 chapters of Genesis), _David and Bathsheba_, and many more, Hollywood has been fascinated by events from the Bible. You can find Biblical movies from the silent era of movies to the recent _Passion of Christ_ on DVD. Some are better than others. Some had huge budgets, some small budgets, but all were designed to catch the viewer's attention and hold them as if riveted to their seats. Naturally, some succeeded better than others. That is true of all the movies and films I have discovered about Ruth. Some are made with a huge Hollywood type budget while others are made with the lowest budget imaginable. In some cases, maybe even no budget at all.

I have found ten movies or films on DVD that either use the story of Ruth as the focus, modernize the story, or simply mention Ruth in an important way. Of these ten movies, we will look at movies designed specifically for children, movies designed for family viewing, and movies designed for adult audiences only. Like books for children, you should always watch movies with your children and talk about them afterwards. Most of the movies I watched are good, but again like the books, some leave parts out or do not explain some things about which your child may be curious. Always watch the movie with your children the first time they watch it. Of course, it is also a good idea to watch the movie before you allow your children to watch it, so you can be prepared for some questions and/or discussion afterwards.

First, let us look at the children's films. A lot of these DVD's contain more stories from the Bible than just Ruth, but we will only deal with Ruth in this study. One of the best children's films I found is part of the Testament series. It is titled Testament: the Bible in Animation - Ruth and is a full feature film done in Claymation. The film tells the story of Ruth in 30 minutes using characters completely made of clay. These clay models of the characters are done so well they are almost life-like. One can hardly tell they are watching an animated movie. This short film was originally produced for BBC television as part of a series of individual Bible stories. It is very well done with only a few fictional items added between the Biblical events to help the story flow more smoothly. The movie was designed to appeal to children of all ages ... even grown up ones.

Another film series for children is called Jacob's Ladder. Volume 2, episodes 3 and 4 are about Ruth, and are titled Naomi and Ruth, and Ruth and Boaz. This series involves a group of teenagers known as the "teenpack" who are sent into the past by a lighthouse keeper. One or two of the teens are changed into characters that are part of the past (a neighbor or relative of a main Bible character). In episode three, the past is in Moab, where one of the girls is transformed into a cousin of Ruth. The other teens are simply sent into the past as they are and can observe and participate in what is happening, but mostly try to observe and protect. The lighthouse keeper warns them not to interfere, but they are teens, after all, and do not always listen. In episode four, one of the girls becomes a servant of Boaz and one of the boys becomes Boaz's nephew. They all try to talk Ruth and Boaz into seeing they are in love with each other. The stories are designed to put "action" into the narrative to make them more appealing to children and teens. Little attention is paid to historical or Biblical accuracy. The village in both Moab and Bethlehem could have come out of the medieval period in Europe rather than the period of Judges in Israel. Episode three is closer to the Biblical account than episode four, which leaves a lot of the Biblical text out. Of course, the language was updated to modern speech, which works just fine. In episode four, the teens were more into protecting Ruth and Naomi. They keep interfering with the action instead of letting Ruth and Boaz find their way as time passes. The lighthouse keeper finally has to go there and warn them not to interfere anymore. This movie will definitely catch older children's attention, and can be fun for the whole family to watch as well.

Morning Light Media produced a good series of Biblical stories for younger children. The one on Ruth is called <u>Happily Ever After, the Story of Ruth</u>. This children's film shows the Biblical account of Ruth through drawings which are slightly animated (eyes move, fade out, fade in with new picture, etc.). The story is narrated by David Mead, who also breaks in at various points to explain the drama, or ask questions to make children think about the action of the story. The narrative is not read directly from the Bible, but the language is modernized to attract young children. Although it does say that Ruth was the wife of Chilion and Orpah was the wife of Mahlon, the film is written very well for small children. The film tells the viewers repeatedly to open their Bibles for more great stories. The DVD also contains the stories of Joseph and His Brothers (<u>Discovering Dreams Come True</u>), and The Passover (<u>Discovering the Way Out</u>), as well as Ruth. Each story is approximately 25 minutes long, and ends with a short question and answer session to help the children watching review the story.

The Children's Bible series gives you the whole Old Testament in 25 stories on one DVD. The Story of Ruth and Naomi is less than five minutes in length. This is a good example of a low budget film, although that by itself does not make the film bad. The narration is done by a woman, which is a nice touch, although her pronunciation is lacking in places. The drawings, which form the background for the narration, are childlike drawings ... like something you would find in a child's coloring book. What little animation there is consists of taking a cutout of one of the characters from a drawing and moving it stiffly across the scene. The story only loosely follows the Biblical account of Ruth and Naomi, leaving out important things, like the scene at the threshing floor, the scene at the city gate, the naming of Obed, etc. They say Ruth went to the "woman" who was in charge of the women workers and asked permission to glean. Boaz *orders* Ruth to come to him when he sees her the first time and he tells her she has won his affection because she is a good worker. Boaz then takes Ruth into his house for a meal. This film is definitely lacking in every way, story, animation, drawings, etc.

Family films are those designed for the whole family to watch together. These are movies that generally have adult actors rather than children or animation. Even though I love a good animated movie, I also realize those movies are primarily directed at small children. Now let us look at the family movies and films.

Hollywood's big movie about Ruth was called The Story of Ruth and was directed by Henry Koster with Norman Corwin as the screenwriter. It was created and sold by Twentieth Century Fox Film Corporation in 1960. I saw this movie on DVD and bought it thinking it was going to be a great presentation of the Bible, but was sadly disappointed. This movie is 131 minutes of Hollywood's idea of how to improve on the Biblical account of Ruth. The writer was not content to fictionalize just the gaps between the events in the Biblical book of Ruth. He fictionalizes the entire story. Other than the names of the characters, the only thing that resembles the Biblical account of Ruth is that it starts out in Moab, Ruth and Naomi travel to Bethlehem, and Ruth eventually marries Boaz. The rest of the story including the people of Bethlehem hating Ruth and the nearer kinsman "demanding" that Ruth marry him is totally fictional. Not just embellished but twisted, totally ignoring what the Bible says about these events.

A more recent movie about Ruth released in 2016 by Universal Pictures Home Entertainment, is the movie titled <u>The Book of Ruth: Journey of Faith</u>. While this 91-minute movie is closer to the actual events told in the Biblical book, it is very loose with details. It is advertised as being true to the book of Ruth, but like the above movie, it leaves out the first few verses that explain why Elimelek's family is now living in Moab. Instead it starts the story in Moab, and shows Naomi's family living in desperate times because their land in Moab does not produce much in the way of food. The family is starving. It does fill in areas left out of the Bible, such as a possible way that Chilion and Mahlon die; how Naomi hears that the famine is over in Israel; etc.; most of which is plausible.

It leaves out some important things. For instance, Boaz does not greet his workers, but instead starts questioning them about the woman gleaning in the field. He treats his workers in a mean way. It is another man who is gleaning that tells him who Ruth is and that she has been working hard all morning. The field is not Boaz's, but he is the overseer of the field for Neb (the closer kinsman), and he and Neb do not get along.

Another instance that varies from the Bible is when Ruth goes to the threshing floor (in the movie it is called a harvest festival, which is sort of correct since it would have been a party or feast), and lays down next to Boaz (not at his feet), she does not uncover his feet, but instead raises his cloak off his feet just enough so she can put her feet next to his and cover both sets of feet with his cloak.

The worst part of all about this movie, is the scene where Boaz is going to take care of the problem with the nearer kinsman. In the movie, it is the nearer kinsman (Neb) who calls the elders to the steps/gate to settle the matter because he has been told that Boaz is giving away half of the grain that has been harvested … to Naomi. At this point Boaz explains he wants to buy Naomi's land, which the kinsman (Neb) says he wants and proclaims he is the nearer kinsman so he will exercise his right to buy it and marry Elimelek's widow. Then Boaz proclaims it is not Elimelek's widow, but Mahlon's widow, Ruth, that he must marry. At that point Neb gives up his right to the land, because he hates Moabites.

One nice thing about this movie is that it is told by Obed to his grandson, David, who in the beginning of the movie is practicing with his slingshot. David questions how he can serve God, since he is the youngest and least experienced of his brothers, and Obed tells him that he must have faith that God will show him the way when the time comes. To illustrate this point, he then tells David the story of two people (Naomi and Ruth) who had nothing left but still relied on their faith in God. The result of that faith was that wonderful things happened. We see Obed and David briefly at the beginning of the film, and then again at the end. It is only at the end that we find out who they are.

Before I continue with other films about Ruth, I would like to add another Hollywood movie that is not specifically about Ruth. I am sure you have heard of it, and probably seen it once or twice. Fiddler on the Roof is an excellent movie about Jewish life around 1905 in Russia. Tevye is a milkman living with his wife and five daughters. As his three oldest daughters reach marriageable age, he has to contend with changing times, which tests his faith in God. While this film is not specifically about Ruth, there is a sentence in the Sabbath prayer song which says, "May you be like Ruth and Esther" signifying the importance of these two women even in twentieth century Russian Jewish life. It is followed by a line calling for them to be deserving of praise, showing that Ruth is regarded as being praise worthy. Consider watching this movie with your family and when it gets to this line in the Sabbath prayer, ask your children why they think Tevye and his wife would want their daughters to be like Ruth or Esther. It is a good way to get your children interested in finding out more about Ruth and Esther.

For shorter films, look at Concordia Films' The Living Bible Collection. The Old Testament from Abraham to Samuel is included on Disk 1 of this series. Ruth: A Faithful Woman is one of ten stories. The actors do a very good job of acting out the story of Ruth while a narrator tells us what is going on. Occasionally in very short scenes, the actors will talk. In approximately 15 minutes, the entire account of Ruth is acted and narrated, but it is done beautifully and stays very close to the Biblical account. Nothing has been added. The only scene that is lacking is the threshing floor scene where it shows both Ruth and Boaz standing as they briefly discuss Boaz taking care of Ruth and Naomi. Then he quickly gives Ruth grain for Naomi and sends her on her way in the middle of the night. By contrast to that scene, the scene showing Ruth and Naomi entering Bethlehem is done very well. The women are at the well when Naomi and Ruth arrive and one of them walks up to Naomi and says, "Is this Naomi, the Pleasant One?" Then Naomi makes her statement saying, do not call me pleasant, call me bitter, etc. This short movie is definitely worth the time it takes to watch it.

Another series worth watching, although not as entertaining, is the Wonder Book of Bible Stories. Disk 1 contains the Old Testament and Ruth is among these stories. Paintings from classical artists are used on screen along with the text of the story. One half of the screen shows a painting, as well as actors and actresses who portray the characters of Ruth, Naomi, Boaz and others, while the other half presents the printed story being read by a narrator. Ruth is only 6 minutes and 55 seconds in length. The story being told is not quoted from the Bible, but a retelling of the Biblical book. The first half of the story is good; filling in background information such as Bethlehem is 6 miles south of Jerusalem, and giving a more detailed account of Ruth and Naomi's journey from Moab to Bethlehem. However, when Boaz enters the scene, he is told by his master reaper that Ruth has been working in the fields since yesterday, which is not what the Bible says. Then they cover the encounter at the threshing floor as if it took only seconds with no mention of Ruth spending the night or even asking Boaz to become her kinsman redeemer. She simply asks him to be kind to her. There is no mention of the nearer kinsman or the encounter at the city gate. It is almost as if they were doing a great job writing the story until they got to the middle. Then they were told it had to be finished in one minute, so they just said, "Ruth and Boaz married, had a child, who had a child, etc. and Ruth became the mother of kings. The end." If they had carried the whole story through as they did the first half, it would have been a beautiful retelling of the Bible book of Ruth. I did not care much for the voices used for the characters. Ruth and Oprah sound like robots when they speak together, and Boaz has a monotone voice, which lacks all sense of emotion. However, the narrator was reasonably good.

Going to privately produced films, I found a very well-done one-woman play (actually several plays), called Women of the Bible written, directed and acted by Anita Gutschick. This particular DVD contains episodes about Queen Esther, The Woman at the Well, Ruth, and Rebekah, as well as her own testimony. Ms. Gutschick performs her one-woman play in costume. Her performance of Ruth shows all the emotion of Ruth and Naomi's decision to stay together, the long tiring trip to Bethlehem, joy of finding Boaz, etc. She uses props to help with the performance. Most of all she sticks right with the Biblical account of the story of Ruth. Nothing is left out. Afterwards her own testimony is delightful to hear as she tells how God called her to this ministry -- a ministry she did not really take seriously at first. God kept after her through various encounters with other people, until she did take it seriously. She is also developing a workbook to be used with the DVD's.

Now for possibly the worst movie made that claims to be about Ruth. Golem, L'esprit de L'exil (Golem, Spirit of the Exile) was written and directed by Amos Gitai who claims it is a modern adaptation of the story of Ruth from the Bible. It has Elimclech's family living in Paris, France in the 1990's. It is not rated and is not recommended for all ages due to some nudity. The story begins with a rabbi creating a mythical creature called a Golem, which is then ordered to watch over travelers and exiled people. This is the third in a series of movies made by Gitai about the Golem, and the only one that deals with the Biblical book of Ruth. The story is done in several languages (French, Hebrew, English, etc.) all being spoken during different scenes. Even with English subtitles, it is difficult to follow the story, because the Golem keeps commenting on the events. It is not always clear whether the Golem is talking or one of the other characters. Gitai has little regard for the Bible. Elimelech is portrayed as a drunken construction worker, who falls to his death. Mahlon and Chilion are murdered. Orpah leaves Naomi, returns to her parent's home, and immediately finds another

255

man to sleep with (no mention of marriage). Ruth returns to Bethlehem with Naomi after they are evicted from their apartment in Paris. While there are frequent quotations from the Bible, they are not necessarily from the Biblical book of Ruth, but could come from anywhere at any time. There is frequent reference to David and Goliath, as well as quotations from the Song of Solomon. Do not be fooled into thinking this film has anything to do with the Bible. Other than the names of the main characters, it is not about the Biblical book of Ruth.

As you can see from our discussion of literature, music, and films, the story of Ruth is one that fascinates people. For some it is the love story, for some the devotion to God and family, or for some it is a way to get publicity for a movie that really is not about the Bible. The important thing, when choosing something to read, listen to, or watch, is to be sure to read or re-read the Biblical account of Ruth ahead of time so you will know when the story takes a turn not in the real account of Ruth's life. If it is a book, song, or movie for your children, be there with them so you can explain things mentioned (or not mentioned). Always explain to others that the only real account of the events in Ruth's life is recorded in the Bible for everyone to read and mediate on. While it's fun to try to fill in the parts of Ruth's life not mentioned in the Bible, we really cannot know for sure exactly what her life outside of the Biblical account was like. Did Ruth have a happy childhood in a home where her parents loved and cared for her? Was she sold into the priesthood of Chemosh? Did she worship the idols of Moab? We do not know, but what we do know is she came to love the one true God and worshipped Him in every way. This we can encourage our children to do also.

BIBLIOGRAPHY

FILMS AND MOVIES:

Beda, Galina, dir. Testament: The Bible in Animation - Ruth.
(screen writers Martin Lamb and Penelope Middelboe).
Voices of Adjoa Andoh, Doreen Mantle, and Clive Russell.
Christmas Films and Eliza Babakhina, 1996.

Dew, Edward, dir. Ruth: A Faithful Woman. The Living Bible
Collection: Old Testament, Disc 1. (writer, Betty Luerssen).
Concordia Films, 1952.

Gitai, Amos (director and writer). Golem, L'esprit de L'exil (Golem,
Spirit of the Exile). Performances by Hannah Shygulla and
Marisa Paredes. Facets Video, 1992.

Gutschick, Anita (director, writer, actress, speaker). Women of the
Bible. (Women of the Bible, Severna Park, MD), 2003.

Jacob's Ladder (Volume 2 -- episodes 3 and 4). Naomi and Ruth;
Ruth and Boaz. Storyworks, Ltd. (distributed by Vision Video,
Worcester, PA), 2005.

Jewison, Norman, dir. Fiddler on the Roof. (screen writer Joseph
Stein, based on Sholem Aleichem's stories). Performances by
Topol, Norma Crane, and violinist Isaac Stern. Mirisch
Corporation and United Artists Films, 1971.

Koster, Henry, dir. <u>The Story of Ruth</u>. (screen writer Norman
    Corwin). Performances by Stuart Whitman, Tom Tryon,
    Peggy Wood, Viveca Lindfors, Jeff Morrow, and Elana
    Eden. Twentieth Century Fox Film Corporation and
    Samuel G. Engle Productions, 1960.

Morning Light Media. <u>Happily Ever After, The Story of Ruth</u>.
    Performance by David Mead. The Great Bible Discovery
    Series #8 (Volume 2 on DVD). Creative Communications for
    the Parish, 1997.

<u>Ruth</u>. Bible Stories: The Wonder Book of Bible Stories (Disk 1
    Old Testament). (compiled by Logan Marshall). Voices
    of Ed Perkins, Paul Schneider, Nancy Kay, Hans Nelson,
    Shawn Murphy, and others. Michael Stevens Productions
    Inc., 2006.

<u>The Story of Ruth and Naomi</u>. The Children's Bible: 25 Tales from
    the Old Testament. Delta Entertainment Corporation, 2006.

Walker, Stephen Patrick, dir. <u>The Story of Ruth: Journey of Faith</u>.
    (Screen Writers: Stephen Patrick Walker, Richard Raucci, and
    Salvatore DiSalvatore). Performances by Sherry Morris,
    Carman, Eleese Lester. Universal Pictures Home
    Entertainment, 2016.

ADDENDUM G: RUTH IN COMIC BOOKS

I have to admit, I hadn't thought about looking for Comic Books when looking for other books about Ruth. Then a book popped up in one of my searches, which naturally piqued my interest. I realize today Comic Books are called Graphic Novels, which may be a more specific phrase as it does describe the nature of the book … being more pictures than words usually. However, the one I found does call itself a "comic", so I will continue to use that phrase to refer to it.

This book is part of a series of comic books called the "Word for Word Bible Comic" illustrated by Simon Amadeus Pillario. Each comic book in the series deals with a different book of the Bible. There have been four others published at this time (Mark, Joshua, Judges, Ruth) and the website for the books says there is another coming out soon (Esther). We will look at only the one on Ruth in this study.

The book is designed much like any other comic, with pictures drawn in frames located side by side with some larger and some smaller at times. Ruth is told using only the World English Bible translation. The whole book is designed and drawn for adults, but is also very good for children. It is definitely a good reproduction of the Biblical book of Ruth.

The drawings are well done. There is even a section at the end that shows why the illustrator, Mr. Pillario, chose the particular likenesses for the main people in his comic. I'm not a big fan of the colors chosen for the graphics though. They are dark colors, mostly browns and muted blues … no bright colors, which gives the impression of sadness and darkness when viewing them. If you read the back of the book you will find this is the way Mr. Pillario views the time of Ruth … "The promised land has become war-torn and desolate. Famine and death jolt this story into motion …" That does describe the beginning of the book of Ruth, but if the colors were chosen to represent that time, they should have changed as the lives of Ruth and Naomi changed for the better. They did not change.

All in all, I found this little comic of 48 pages to be very good. It is family oriented so can be read as a family or as an individual. Only about half is the actual comic book about Ruth. That is followed by a page of "Relevant passages from other books of the Bible" which includes references about Levirate Marriage, Gleaning, and other genealogies. Also included is a map of Israel during the time of the Judges. All are very good for helping the reader whether adult or child understand the events in the Ruth and Naomi's lives. While I enjoyed the comic book very much, it would have been easier to read if it had used more natural colors in the graphics, or maybe it's just my eyes. This certainly is a personal preference and has nothing to do with the events themselves.

BIBLIOGRAPHY

COMIC BOOKS:

The Holy Spirit (Illustrator: Simon Amadeus Pillario). "The Book of Ruth." Word for Word Bible Comic. United Kingdom: Word for Word Bible Comics, October 2018 (Version 2).

ANNOTATED BIBLIOGRAPHY: RUTH

This bibliography is not meant to show every book ever written about Ruth, but rather shows all the ones I could find in various libraries, the web, and used bookstores as well as several friends' personal libraries. As King Solomon said in Ecclesiastes 12:12, "of making many books there is no end". We could add ... of making many books about Ruth there seems to be no end.

COMMENTARIES:

Asimov, Isaac. <u>The Story of Ruth</u>. Garden City, NY: Doubleday & Company, 1972.
Well known writer of science fiction, Isaac Asimov has written a small book for children explaining the Biblical book of Ruth. The first part of the book is a history of the Israelites, used to explain when Ruth was written and by whom. Mr. Asimov thinks someone he calls only the "Writer" (an unknown author) who lived during post-exilic times (somewhere between 450 and 380 BC), took an oral Jewish tradition and added information from his own imagination to come up with the book of Ruth. The purpose of this writing was to counter the laws of Ezra who wanted the Jews to divorce their foreign wives. Mr. Asimov's position on both the history of the Jews and the book of Ruth is very far from the facts of both. His real reason for attempting this book is shown in the last chapter where he makes a plea for people to accept all people and not be prejudiced against anyone just because they are different or

from a foreign country. While this reason for writing a book is noble, his views on the history of the Jews and on the book of Ruth are extremely liberal and unfounded.

Auld, A Graeme. Joshua, Judges, and Ruth. The Daily Study Bible Series. Philadelphia, PA: The Westminster Press, 1984. pp. 258-280.
While Mr. Auld thinks Ruth is a good book to study, he puts it's writing into a category of a "midrashic" writing period. This would put the writing of Ruth into a post Biblical time period. In his opinion Ruth may simply be the re-telling of Tamar's story. Also, he does not see Judah as an area good for farming, so sees famines as normal in the area. The book of Ruth is also only seen as a way of explaining a social custom that helped widows and foreigners in Israel. Once again this is liberal thinking, trying to make the book of Ruth something that doesn't belong in the Bible.

Barber, Cyril J. Ruth, A Story of God's Grace (An Expositional Commentary). Chicago: Moody Press, 1983.
A very readable style of writing makes this commentary a book for everyone to read. You do not have to be a scholar to understand Barber's reasoning. He has some very good comments about why Samuel should be considered the author of the book as well as why it is in the Old Testament canon.

Baxendale, Rev. Walter. The Preacher's Commentary on the Book of Ruth With Critical and Exegetical Notes. New York: Funk & Wagnalls, 1892.
A good look at what many authors before 1892 wrote on the book of Ruth. Rev. Baxendale has compiled what writers before him have published, putting it all in very easy to follow

categories. There isn't much original writing in this book, but it is still very helpful for seeing what a lot of others thought about things like authorship, dating, and the text itself. This was published in a volume that includes Ruth through Samuel.

Campbell, Edward F. Jr. <u>Ruth: A New Translation with Introduction and Commentary</u>. (The Anchor Bible, Volume 7). Garden City, NY: Doubleday & Company, 1975.

It is amazing that the Anchor Bible gave Ruth a whole book by itself. This 189-page book deals exclusively with the Biblical book of Ruth. Mr. Campbell takes the stance that Ruth is a work of Hebrew prose in the form of a novella and interprets a novella as a fictional story. He assumes the book was more of an oral tradition and written down much later than its story would lead us to believe. He spends much time translating from the LXX versions of the book with only minor discussion of the actual Hebrew text There is a good explanation of the Ruth fragments found in the Dead Sea Scrolls at Qumran which covers about a page, and a good explanation of the location of the country of Moab which covers about a page and a half. There are a lot of notes on each verse which cover text criticisms, geography, history, etc. This book is written for the scholarly reader who has studied the languages of the early Bible versions (Hebrew, Greek, and Latin).

Coffman, James Burton and Thelma B. <u>Judges & Ruth</u>. James Burton Coffman Commentaries. Abilene, TX: Abilene Christian University Press, 1992, pp. 326-379.

This is a commentary on the book of Ruth and as such goes into more detail on background information than many other books. According to the Coffmans, the most likely candidate for writing the book of Ruth is Samuel and it was written during the life of David during a time before he became king of Israel. While it is unknown exactly where the events of the book of Ruth fit into Israel's history, they suggest the most likely place is between the judgeships of Abdon and Samson, but do not rule out the possibly of Boaz being the judge Ibzan. Much of the comments within this commentary are very succinct. Many times, I would have liked to read more about a particular subject. Much research has gone into the writing of this book as can be seen by the extensive quotations from others' works. However, the footnotes are difficult to follow since he only lists the initials of the author (which then have to be matched up with the correct book in the bibliography section) and page number of the quotation.

Cook F. C. (ed.). Joshua - I Kings. The Bible Commentary, Vol. 2. New York, NY: Charles Scribner's Sons, 1915. pp. 224-241.

Even though originally published over 100 years ago, this book is an excellent book for examining words used within Ruth and looking at all the other places that particular word or words are used throughout the Old and New Testaments. It is not a definitive study of the words, but has references listed of places where a particular word is used along with a brief explanation of the word or phrase. It is very interesting reading for anyone wanting to study Ruth. There is a brief two-page introduction to the book, including date of writing, etc., as well as some interesting comments on the genealogy at the end of the book.

_____ (ed.). Exodus -- Ruth. The Bible Commentary. Grand Rapids, MI: Baker Book House, 1977. pp.471-479.

This is actually a reprint of the original commentary (mentioned above), having been edited and *abridged* by J. M.

Fuller. Mr. Fuller apparently thought it important to take out whole sentences of material he considered unimportant reducing the material covered to less than half of the original. Only eight pages of this commentary are left for the entire discussion of the background and comments on the book of Ruth. According to this book, the importance of the book of Ruth is to show God's grace and begin the ingathering of the Gentiles into God's kingdom. Also important is the genealogy which shows the genealogy of King David and ultimately Jesus Christ through the entire period of the Judges.

Dray, Stephen. <u>Judges and Ruth</u>. Great Britain: Christian Focus Publications, 1997. pp. 127-158.
Although only 31 pages, this is an excellent introduction to the book of Ruth and its wonderful spiritual lessons. Each chapter is ended with questions to ponder individually, or discuss in a Bible Study group. It is conservative in nature and sticks to the story of Ruth as told in the Biblical book of Ruth.

Feinstein, Rabbi David. <u>Kol Dodi on Megillas Ruth</u>. Brooklyn, NY: Mesorah Publications, Ltd., 2006.
This is an excellent introduction to Jewish tradition about the book of Ruth. It explains the thinking of generations of Jewish thought. Rabbi Feinstein goes through the Biblical book of Ruth offering comments on words and/or phrases. It includes many comments on the Hebrew of Ruth, as well as comments on Jewish numerology as it pertains to Ruth.

Gray, John. <u>Joshua, Judges, and Ruth</u>. New Century Bible. Greenwood, SC: The Attic Press, Inc. 1967. pp. 293-314.
Using the Revised Standard Version of the Bible throughout, this commentary takes a more liberal position on the

whole book. Mr. Gray is confusing on the date, giving many different views and leaning himself to an exilic or post-exilic date for the writing. He says the purpose for writing the book has much to do with the date of the writing, using reasons such as giving encouragement to the exiles or the marriages of Jews and pagans during the post-exilic period as valid purposes for writing the book. He also thinks the book of Ruth is a work of fiction, especially the names used in Ruth. Other possibilities Mr. Gray suggests in passing are that Ruth and Naomi were sacred prostitutes around whom the story was built; the name Boaz can be taken as meaning "Baal is strong"; the grain Boaz gives to Ruth for spending the night with him was the equivalent of what a prostitute would receive for visiting the threshing floor; and the genealogy at the end of Ruth was added at a later time by a different writer.

Hubbard, Robert L., Jr. The Book of Ruth. (The New International Commentary on the Old Testament). Grand Rapids, MI: Wm. B. Eerdmans Publishing Co., 1988.

Mr. Hubbard's commentary on Ruth is extensively researched and written to cover all aspects of the book of Ruth. Although he does go into the original Biblical languages and makes comparisons, he writes in a style anyone can understand. His commentary is good, as is his background on the book. He also explains the fragments of Ruth found at Qumran and how they compare to other Hebrew versions of the Old Testament. Mr. Hubbard thinks the book may have been written by a woman. He rejects Samuel as its author, and puts it's writing in a pre-exilic time, perhaps during the life of Solomon.

Kates, Judith A. and Reimer, Gail Twersky (editors).
<u>Reading Ruth: Contemporary Women Reclaim A
Sacred Story</u>. **New York, NY: Ballantine Books, 1994.**
A compilation of the writings of many Jewish women
(from all walks of life, professional women and non-professional
women) on various aspects of the book of Ruth is what this
book contains. It is more than a commentary. It contains
commentaries from several women on the background of Ruth,
but also contains poetry, short stories, and just thoughts of
individuals as they look at the story of Ruth using traditional and
contemporary standards. There are many new thoughts in this
book, including one who incorrectly thinks Ruth and Naomi
shared a lesbian love. That is only one writer's view. Many
writers praise Ruth as a model woman we should look up to,
while others say she was too submissive to Naomi's and later
Boaz's wishes. Still others say Naomi was the best role model
for Ruth, while some say she was too conniving and
manipulative. Overall the consensus was that the story of Ruth
had little effect on them as young girls, but they had a totally
different attitude to the story when re-reading it as adult women.

Keil, C. F. and Delitzsch, F. <u>**Commentary on the Old
Testament -- Joshua, Judges, Ruth, I & II Samuel**</u>.
**Volume 2. (Translated by James Martin) Grand
Rapids, MI: William B. Eerdmans Publishing
Company, 1980. pp.465-494.**
German was the original language of this commentary
although it is now published extensively in English. It is an
excellent commentary for those wanting to take an in-depth look
at the Hebrew as used in the early manuscripts, as well as the
Greek used in the LXX, and Latin in the Vulgate versions of the
Old Testament. The background of the book, location in the
canon, and date is explored by looking at early manuscripts.

While the authors see no reason to date the book of Ruth to a late date, they admit they do not have a date for it. They place Boaz as a contemporary of Gideon, and say the famine that caused Elimelech to leave Bethlehem was caused by the raids from the Midianites as recorded in Judges at the time of Gideon. They also state that the genealogy at the end of the book of Ruth has left some generations out, in order to make it an even 10 generations from Moses to David. The notes at the bottom of the pages in this commentary are just as filled with information as the text itself.

Kennedy, J. Hardee. <u>Ruth</u>. The Broadman Bible Commentary, (Volume 2, Leviticus-Ruth). Nashville, TN: Broadman Press, 1970. pp. 464-480.
Dr. Kennedy is professor of Old Testament and Hebrew at New Orleans Baptist Seminary. He presents a fairly conservative point of view on the book of Ruth with several extraordinary sections on Ruth's devotion to Naomi, and the idea of the kinsman-redeemer's usage through the Bible. He falls short of the mark though by saying the law forbidding Moabites and children of Moabites into the congregation of Israel from Deuteronomy 23:3 must have been written at a later date than the book of Ruth since it is ignored in this instance.

Kent, Dan G. <u>Joshua, Judges, Ruth</u>. Layman's Bible Book Commentary, Volume 4. Nashville, TN: Broadman Press, 1980. pp. 141-154.
As the title of the commentary series says, this book is written with the layman in mind. It does not go into detail on the original language of Ruth, nor into controversies associated with the book. It is however a very good look at the story of Ruth itself. Dividing the book by geographical sections (Moab, Bethlehem, the threshing floor, etc.), Mr. Kent looks at each

scene and explains its significance to the overall story of Ruth. It is written in easy to read language and gets the point across that God works in our everyday lives.

Lewis, Arthur. Judges/Ruth. Everyman's Bible Commentary. Chicago, IL: Moody Press, 1979. pp. 106-126.

This is an easy to read commentary. Mr. Lewis puts Ruth in the time of the judgeship of Gideon. While conservative in nature, Mr. Lewis does think there is something missing in the genealogy of Boaz. This is also the first commentary that gives a meaning to the word Ephrathah, which he says means "fruitful place". Though short, this is a good introduction to Ruth.

Luter, A Boyd, and Davis, Barry C. God Behind the Seen. Expositor's Guide to the Historical Books. Grand Rapids, MI: Baker Books, 1995. pp. 11-95.

Dr. Luter writes the section of this book that deals with Ruth. He spends much time looking at the mirrored structure of the writing of the book of Ruth. The book of Ruth starts and ends on the same or similar notes and every part within the story does the same sort of thing. The book has brief charts to demonstrate this. The text of the book is interesting reading and informative. He writes from a conservative point of view. He gives a chapter to the genealogy at the end of the book and says it is an important part of the book and has been since it was originally written.

McGee, J. Vernon. Ruth. Thru the Bible Commentary Series, Volume 11. Nashville: Thomas Nelson Publishers, 1991.

McGee sees the plan of salvation throughout the book of Ruth, from the sinner (Naomi and her family leaving the

Promised Land), to repentance (Naomi and Ruth coming home to the Lord as evidenced by their returning to the Promised Land), to the Kinsman-Redeemer (Boaz, as an example of Christ, redeeming the lost women by marrying Ruth). Even the Old Law is represented by the nearer Kinsman-Redeemer who could not save Ruth and Naomi even though he wanted to at first. Everything is very well presented in a very readable and logical style. McGee also puts a lot of emphasis on the meaning of the names in the book of Ruth.

Morris, Leon. Ruth. Tyndale Old Testament Commentaries. Downers Grove, IL: Intervarsity Press, 1973.
This book is actually called Judges, Ruth with the Judges part written by Arthur E. Cundall, but since our study here is with Ruth, I am only dealing with the 101 pages of the commentary on Ruth written by Dr. Leon Morris. Dr. Morris' extremely well written conservative view point is brought out by looking at all view points and then explaining why one is wrong and another is right, or even saying "we just don't know" when appropriate. Dr. Morris is very well versed in the original language of Ruth, and frequently goes to the meaning of the Hebrew word to find the best English translation. He compares various texts of the Bible in English, Hebrew, Latin, and Greek in his search for the original meaning of a word, verse, or section of the book, but does not bog the reader down in complex language studies. Besides the introduction to the book of Ruth, and a verse by verse commentary, Dr. Morris also includes additional notes on the Hebrew word *sadday* (Almighty) as it pertains to God, and on the meaning of the Hebrew word *go'el* (redeemer).

Sasson, Jack M. <u>Ruth: A New Translation with a</u> <u>Phiolological Commentary and a Formalist-Folklorist</u> <u>Interpretation</u>. **(Second Edition). Sheffield, England: Sheffield Academic Press, 1995.**

Reading this commentary is not for the casual reader to tackle. It is a comprehensive look at the Hebrew text of Ruth. In doing that Mr. Sasson provides his own translation of the Hebrew, then explains it using his own thoughts and that of other authors. He also takes a brief look at the literary genre of the book giving it a new category all its own. Also provided is a brief look at the canonicity of the book of Ruth, author and date.

Slotki, Judah J. <u>Ruth: An Introduction and Commentary</u>. **Soncino Books of the Bible. London: The Soncino Press Ltd., 1965. (pp. 34-65 of** <u>The Five Meggiloth</u> **volume).**

This commentary written and published for the Jewish community is very conservative and well written. It gives a translation of the book of Ruth along with comments and notes about individual verses and words. It also contains some interesting background on the book, date of Boaz, who Boaz possibly was, aim of the book, etc. Without being dogmatic about many of the background comments the author leaves it to the reader to decide if he/she wants to accept certain Jewish legends that surround the Midrash and other commentaries on the scriptures. Definitely interesting reading for anyone whether Jewish or Christian.

Spence, H. D. M. and Exell, Joseph S. (ed.). Ruth, I and II Samuel. The Pulpit Commentary. Volume 4. Grand Rapids, MI: Wm. B. Eerdmans Publishing Company, 1976, pp. i - 73.

This book begins with an 18-page introduction of Ruth that discusses date, author, canon, etc. The author thinks Ruth may have been written by King David himself and gives many reasons for this including the lack of use of the word "King" before David's name in the genealogy, and because King David was a prolific writer as seen in Psalms. It may also have been written by David to show the King of Moab that he had relatives in Moab when David took his father and mother to Moab for their safety. This commentary series contains an exposition of the book plus several homiletic and homilies written by various authors. The book of Ruth is divided into sections based on subject matter. Each section is then given an exposition which looks at not only the subject matter, but also the translation of the actual Hebrew words used and how they were translated into various versions such as the LXX (Greek), Vulgate (Latin), and King James (English) versions. The exposition section is followed by several homilies based on the same subject matter.

Thatcher, G. W. The Century Bible - Judges and Ruth. Edinburgh: T. C. & E. C. Jack, n.d. (probably 1910), pp. 173-195.

This small commentary written over a century ago, presents the Revised Version of the books of Judges and Ruth with notes at the bottom of the pages. In the introduction to the book of Ruth, Mr. Thatcher takes the liberal point of view on the date, saying the book was probably written during the exilic or post-exilic times. He admits the style of writing is the same as that of the books of Samuel, but would rather attribute this to the writer's ability to copy that style rather than say that Samuel might have been the author. Thatcher gives little discussion to the date of the events of the book of Ruth other than to say they happened during the time of the Judges, or some time before the monarchy in Israel. His notes on the text itself are brief. The book does have a nice color map of Israel during the time of the Judges in the front.

Winter, Willard W. <u>Studies in Joshua Judges and Ruth</u>. Joplin, MO: College Press, 1973, pp. 578-628.
Dr. Winter drew on his many years of experience as Professor of Old Testament at Cincinnati Bible Seminary to write this commentary. Although only 50 pages out of 625 are given to the study of Ruth, this is a conservative well written commentary on the book. A good discussion of the background, date, and circumstances of the book, as well as questions to ask yourself while reading the book of Ruth.

Yerushalmi, Rabbi Shmuel. <u>The Book of Ruth</u>. MeAm Lo'ez. (translated into English by E. Van Handel). New York: Maznaim Publishing Corporation, 1985.
This book contains Jewish traditions, historical information, and folklore about the Biblical book of Ruth as well as all the people within the book. It goes into detail on backgrounds of Boaz who is identified with the Judge Ibetzan (Ibzan), and Elimelech, as well as Ruth and everyone else, named and unnamed in the book. It gives the name of Tove to the unknown nearer kinsman. It also leans heavily on Jewish *gematriya* (numerology). Many famous Rabbis as well as the Talmud and Jewish traditions are used to explain many unimportant things missing in the Biblical text. Nearly a third of the book is given to explaining how Elimelech sinned by going to Moab and why he died first. The chronology of this commentary does not fit well since Ruth and Orpah are

supposed to be sisters and daughters of King Eglon of Moab. Goliath is supposed to be a descendant of Orpah, thus showing a descendant of Ruth (David), killing a descendant of Orpah (Goliath). He also explains that Ruth lived to see Solomon on the throne of Israel which would have made her extremely old.

INSPIRATIONAL AND GROUP STUDY BOOKS:

Baltz, Evan D. The Road to Hope: Studies in Ruth. AZ: Exangello Ministries, 2004.

This small book is an excellent overview of lessons from Ruth. There are four chapters which each coincide with chapters in Ruth. Evan Baltz asks the question of whether your hope is grounded in the Lord. He sees the theme of HOPE in every chapter of Ruth: Hope Forsaken, Hope Renewed, Hope Pursued, and Hope Fulfilled. Although only 60 pages it is an excellent look at the book of Ruth and how God cares for His people.

Bingham, Derick. Joseph & Ruth: God's Providence in Difficult Circumstances. Belfast, Northern Ireland: Ambassador Publications, 1999, pp. 101-156.

Mr. Bingham looks at how God works in Ruth and Naomi's lives and compares that to how God works in our lives today. This is not an in-depth look at the book of Ruth itself. Instead Bingham looks at God working in Ruth's life and how she reacts to God in the various circumstances of her life, and explains how we as Christians should have a similar reaction to the same circumstances in our lives today -- whether we are facing the death of a loved one, moving to a new land/city, loneliness, love, working with in-laws, etc. God is always there to help us through ... just like he was always there for Ruth and Naomi, even when sometimes they did not see it right away.

Bos, Johanna. <u>**Ruth and Esther: Women in Alien Lands**</u>. **NY: General Board of Global Ministries, The United Methodist Church, 1987, pp. 1-39.**

Ms. Bos uses her own translation of the Hebrew text of Ruth throughout this small book. The book is a commentary on the events of the story of Ruth. She only briefly mentioned Ruth's connection to Christ at the end of the book as she mentions the genealogy also located there.

Chittister, Joan D. (Art by John August Swanson). <u>**The Story of Ruth: Twelve Moments in Every Woman's Life**</u>. **Grand Rapids, MI: William B. Eerdmans Publishing Co., 2000.**

Ms. Chittister uses the examples of Ruth and Naomi to illustrate how the Christian woman has choices when it comes to dealing with twelve events that happen to women as they live their lives. These twelve important "moments" are listed as loss (of any type), change (in position), transformation (when a woman can no longer be the person she used to be), aging (wisdom comes with age, but how do you use it), independence (making independent decisions helps us be an asset to others), respect (for who we are, not who we are connected to), recognition (for achieving something on our own efforts), insight (of her own worthiness), empowerment (her role will help shape the next generation of women), self-definition (a woman must define herself to be a moral agent of God's), invisibility (knowing what it means to be treated like less than a woman by the outside world), and fulfillment (of life within themselves).

DeHaan, M. R. The Romance of Redemption -- The Love Story of Ruth and Boaz. Grand Rapids, MI: Zondervan Publishing House, 1958.

Sermons delivered over the airways are what this book contains. The sermons all deal with the book of Ruth, and there is much repetition in the themes of the sermons. DeHaan finds a parallel between Naomi's life and the history of Israel which he brings out in his sermons. He also compares Boaz to Christ as redeemer.

Fortner, Donald S. Discovering Christ in Ruth -- The Kinsman Redeemer. Auburn, MA: Evangelical Press, 1999.

Mr. Fortner presents several interesting and very readable pictures of the events of Ruth's life. He also presents three likely possibilities of representatives of the nearer kinsman who could not redeem Ruth. These include the Law, Angels of God, and the old/sinful nature of man. He also says that God will find his elect wherever they are and use whatever events are needed to bring them into fellowship with Him.

Gardiner, George E. The Romance of Ruth. Grand Rapids, MI: Kregel Publications, 1979.

Mr. Gardiner's book is not meant to be an all-inclusive look at ever verse of the book of Ruth. His book looks at Ruth and Boaz as types. Ruth is the "type" of the sinner (us) who needs saving (redemption), and her actions show us all how a sinner should approach Christ ... humbly, with a servant attitude, asking for redemption, etc. Boaz is a "type" of Jesus Christ, and likewise, his actions are those of Christ to us. He notices us in our sin, he provides for us, and when we come to him humbly asking for redemption, he gives it freely.

Glimmers of Hope in Dark Times: Judges and Ruth.
   Schaumburg, IL: Regular Baptist Press, 2005. pp.
   97-103.
   Meant to be a group Bible study, this book focuses on
Judges, and has only one small chapter that covers the entire
book of Ruth. It contains small explanations of what is going on
in Ruth followed by questions to be answered in individual Bible
study or in a group Bible study. There is also a leader's guide
available for use in a group study setting. The questions are
insightful but limited.

Haggee, Diane. Ruth: The Romance of Redemption: A
   Love Story. Nashville, TN: Nelson Books, 2005.
   A conservative rendering of the story of Ruth as
presented in the Bible. Mrs. Haggee presents her view of the
Biblical book having done much research into it from both
Christian and Jewish viewpoints. She seems to use Jewish
numerology a little too much for my taste, but her points are well
presented even if the numerology were not used. This is a very
well written book ... easily readable by everyone.

Hammond, Michelle McKinney. Ending the Search for Mr.
   Right. Eugene, OR: Harvest House Publishers, 2005.
   While this book does quote verses from Ruth at the
beginning of every chapter, it is not really a book about Ruth. It
is about love relationships and how a Christian woman can be
fulfilled without a man in her life. If she is following God's plan
for her life, she will be fulfilled with or without a husband. Ms.
Hammond is president of Heart Wing Ministries and has
devoted her life to helping others with their love lives. This is a
very good book on how to be a Christian woman. It tells women
not to look for Mr. Right, but to make their lives what God wants
them to be, and God will bring Mr. Right to them. There is some

279

very good advice in here, but very little said about Ruth even though it is listed in the Library of Congress cataloging as being under the subject of "Bible. O. T. Ruth -- Criticism, Interpretation, etc."

Hammond, Michelle McKinney. Finding the Right Woman for You. Eugene, OR: Harvest House Publishers, 2005.
Like the book by Ms. Hammond above, this book barely discusses Ruth. It is a good book to help Christian men in their look for Ms. Right, but it is not a book about Ruth. This is the companion book to the one mentioned above. It has the same chapter headings (except to change "woman" to "man" in chapter 9), and quotes the same verses at the beginning of the chapters. Again, there is lots of good advice here, but very little to connect it with Ruth except the Library of Congress cataloging which is the same as above.

Heijkoop, H. L. The Book of Ruth. Sunbury, PA: Believers Bookshelf, Inc., 1969.
While this is an interesting book to read, Mr. Heijkoop does tend to ramble a bit perhaps to give the book more pages, or perhaps in an effort to be sure he gets his points across. He agrees with many others that the period of Judges was a time of "ruin and decline" because of the statement in Judges 21:25 that says "everyone did what was right in their own eyes". The theme of GOEL (redeemer) is seen as the most important part of the book of Ruth.

Hess, Margaret. Love Knows No Barriers. Wheaton, IL: Victor Books, 1979.
Ruth is used as the basis for solving many of life's problems. From painful separations such as death, or moving,

to love's fulfillment and reward, the book takes examples of Ruth's behavior to show how we should live today. God wants to bless us in our relationships as He did Ruth, if we will just listen to Him.

Jones, Debby and Kendall, Jackie. <u>Lady in Waiting,</u>
<u>Developing Your Love Relationships</u>. Shippensburg,
PA: Treasure House, 2001.
An excellent book for single women who are trying to live Christian lives while waiting for their knight to come along. It uses examples from Ruth to show how a single woman should prepare herself for a godly life first and not worry about searching for a husband. God brought Boaz to Ruth at the right time, and God can do the same thing for women today if they will just trust Him. An excellent point is made that women should concentrate on doing the Lord's work while single as well as becoming the best Christian they can, because after marriage there are other demands on their time from husband and children. Much space is used in the book to show women what to look for in a godly husband, as well as how to be content being single.

Lee-Thorp, Karen (ed). <u>A Life-Changing Encounter with</u>
<u>God's Word from the Books of Ruth & Esther</u>. Life
Change Series. Colorado Springs, CO: NavPress,
1987. pp. 9-60.
Questions are the main part of this book. Questions to make you think about what Ruth says, how to react to it, and how to study it. The book is designed to be a group study guide, so the questions will also help with discussion during the group time. Between the pages of questions is a page or two of explanations of words or phrases within the text to help the reader understand the text as they read it. Even more than

that, this book shows how and why to study the scriptures by offering suggestions and questions to help the reader's study habits.

Lucado, Max. Life Lessons From the Inspired Word of God -- Books of Ruth & Esther. Dallas, TX: Word Publishing, 1996, pp. 9-42.
This book is meant to be a study guide for group study. As such the only original writings in the book are the questions used to make the reader think about what he/she is reading in the book of Ruth. While the questions are very insightful, they give no answers. Each person's answers are meant to be discussed in a group situation. The book quotes sections from Ruth in both the New Century Version and the New King James Version of the Bible. Each chapter has an inspirational quotation from another book, a prayer, a place for journal entries and additional thoughts. It also gives additional Bible verses to read that deal with the same subject being considered in that chapter.

MacArthur, John. Ruth & Esther: Women of Faith, Bravery and Hope. MacArthur Bible Studies. Nashville, TN: Word Publishing, 2000, pp. 1-44.
This book is actually more of a devotional Bible study. The book contains the scripture text as well as text of cross references, and other scriptures to study in conjunction with the book of Ruth. There are also lists of key words with brief explanations included with each chapter of Ruth. To help the reader think more deeply about the meaning of the scriptures, questions are listed with spaces to fill in the answers. MacArthur puts Ruth in the time of Jair's judgeship. He also says the genealogy at the end of Ruth is not complete saying there are more generations between Salman and Boaz, even

though this is not supported by any other genealogy in the Old or New Testament.

McGee, J. Vernon. <u>Ruth and Esther: Women of Faith</u>. Nashville, TN: Thomas Nelson Publishers, 1988.
This is the first book I have found that deals with both Ruth and Esther and yet gives more pages to Ruth (200 pages) than to Esther (133 pages). This shows how important the redeemer quality found in the book of Ruth is in relation to our salvation. Boaz is a redeemer to Ruth and Naomi, as Jesus Christ is our redeemer. McGee finds love to be a vital part of redemption ... love that is personal, love that does not count the cost ... this type of love the Lord Jesus has for us -- His creation.

_____. <u>Ruth, the Romance of Redemption</u>. Nashville, TN: Thomas Nelson, Inc., 1981.
McGee explains the position of Boaz as the kinsman-redeemer (*goel*) of Ruth, Naomi and all of Elimelech's land. Further he shows how this position of Boaz is the only place in the Old Testament where there is an example of the kinsman-redeemer. This makes Boaz a type of Christ in the sense that Christ was the ultimate kinsman-redeemer. This idea of the kinsman-redeemer is vital to the doctrine of scripture and is explained in depth in the last seven chapters where the qualifications of the kinsman-redeemer are discussed ... near relative, willing, able, free, and wealthy. The last chapter discusses the need for a kinsman-redeemer to the world, and its relationship to sin in the world. [NOTE: This is actually a previous publication of the Ruth-part of the book listed above.]

Newell, Ray. Joshua, Judges, and Ruth. **Nashville, TN:**
Abingdon Press, 1997. pp. 99-106.
Keyed to the New International Version of the Bible, this
study guide is made up primarily of questions to be answered in
a group Bible study program. A teacher book is available for
Genesis-Esther which would include this book. The questions
are basic. Following the questions are three pages of "What
does the Bible mean?" In this section it is said that Ruth went to
the threshing floor looking for a consummation of the marriage
with her. Part three of the book is titled "What does the Bible
mean to me?" and is much more insightful in it is thoughts and
questions to ponder then the other two sections.

Nywening, Willy. Sister Stories: Daily Inspiration from the
Lives of Ruth and Esther. **Grand Rapids, MI: CRC**
Publications, 1997. pp. 12-35.
Twelve chapters each showing a different aspect of
Ruth's life are what make up the part of this book that deals with
Ruth. Faith, love, pain, etc. are the themes of these chapters.
Each chapter is two pages long ... enough for a daily devotion ...
and is followed by a short prayer. The thing that makes this
book unique is that after the short prayer, is a "Follow-Up" which
gives the reader something to actually do to work on this aspect
of their present life. For instance, at the end of the chapter on
"the power of love" the follow-up is to visit a shut-in expecting no
recognition or thanks.

Obbard, Elizabeth Ruth. Ruth & Naomi: A Story of
Friendship, Growth, and Change. **Cincinnati, OH:**
St. Anthony Messenger Press, 2003.
Elizabeth Obbard is a Carmelite nun, and as such leans
heavily on the Catholic church teachings as she interprets the
book of Ruth. She looks at Ruth through her own needs as a

child feeling like an outsider in her own family which consisted of herself, one full brother, one half-sister, her father and step-mother (who loved her own daughter more than Elizabeth). Although the book is written in a very readable fashion with each chapter ending with a prayer, there are some rather glaring errors in the first chapter, such as saying Bethlehem is 20 miles south of Jerusalem when there is in fact only about 5 or 6 miles between the two cities. Even with these errors, she has some interesting points to consider. She compares the journey of Ruth and Naomi to Abraham's call out of Ur by God. She says Ruth went with Naomi out of need rather than love. Later she compares Boaz giving Ruth wine/vinegar and bread to communion bread and wine. While she gives no date to the book of Ruth, she does place the activities of the book during the judgeship of Ehud. While the book has some inspirational value, it is written from a liberal point of view as evidenced from her statement in the last chapter that the genealogy was not part of the original text of the book, but added later.

Wakefield, Dr. Norm, and Brolsma, Jody. <u>Men Are From Israel, Women Are From Moab</u>. Downers Grove, IL: InterVarsity Press, 2000.
An interesting book about relationships between men and women. While it does use illustrations about Boaz and Ruth from the book of Ruth to show how men and women should act towards each other, these illustrations are a minor part of the book. It is a good book for learning how Christians should relate to each other, particularly to the opposite sex, but not a book for studying Ruth in depth.

Wiersbe, Warren W. Be Committed. (An Old Testament Study -- Ruth and Esther). Wheaton, IL: Victor Books, 1993. (pp. 13-63).

Dr. Wiersbe sees Ruth as a person who is an example of a committed and faithful servant of the Lord. Ruth decides to follow God's will no matter what it costs her. According to Dr. Wiersbe the theme verse of the book of Ruth is Ruth 2:12 *"May Yahweh repay your work, and a full reward be given you from Yahweh, the God of Israel, under whose wings you have come to take refuge."* He sees the book as largely historical in nature but says we should not overlook the message of total commitment to the Lord found within the book.

Zeisler, Steve. A Conspicuous Love -- The Enduring Story of Ruth, Romance & Redemption. Grand Rapids, MI: Discovery House Publishers, 1999.

While Mr. Zeisler has a lot of good things to say about love (friendship and marriage), he sees Naomi as a bitter, crabby old woman who has decided God has deserted her. On the other hand, Ruth is the complete opposite ... a young woman who has complete trust in the God of Israel to take care of her and Naomi. Zeisler also thinks Naomi was not willing to wait for the Lord to bring Boaz and Ruth to marriage, so Naomi thinks she can do the job better than God. Naomi suggests Ruth go to the threshing floor at night to seduce Boaz, so he will have to marry Ruth. Only because both Ruth and Boaz are virtuous people did they avoid getting into a sexual situation. Mr. Zeisler does have a great section on Ruth's declaration to Naomi to go with her to Bethlehem.

BIBLE DICTIONARIES, ENCYCLOPEDIAS, AND CONCORDANCES:

Orr, James (General Editor). <u>The International Standard Bible Encyclopaedia</u>. (5 volumes). Chicago, IL: The Howard-Severance Company, 1915.

While this is a rather old set of encyclopedias, it is still an excellent set to consult on Biblical matters. Most articles are conservative in theology. This encyclopedia does lean heavily on Hebrew and Greek, so some parts may seem a little over the average reader's head, but even if you have to skip a paragraph or two here and there, you will still find the articles helpful. Articles consulted in these books included "Ruth", "Ruth, Book of", "Naomi", "Orpah", "Moab", "Moabite Stone", Septuagint, "Moabitess", "Agriculture", and "Elimelech". [Note: There is a more modern updated version of this encyclopedia published between 1979--1995 in four volumes by Eerdmans Publishing Company. The newer edition includes more archaeology, but this older version includes more of what the Holy Land was like before modernization ... things that had not changed for hundreds of years, so both editions can be helpful to the Bible scholar.]

Pfeiffer, Charles F. (editor). <u>The Biblical World</u>. Nashville, TN: Broadman Press, 1976.

This dictionary of Biblical archaeology gives a fairly conservative viewpoint. Although the use of the Revised Standard Version of the Bible is not the best choice, it does a good job of giving a history of archaeological findings and places that relate to the Bible and Bible times. Articles consulted in this book include "Moab, Moabites", "Moabite Stone", "Judah", "Bethlehem", and "Agriculture". Many articles have a brief bibliography at the end along with the author's name.

Strong, James, et al. The Strongest Strong's Exhaustive Concordance of the Bible. Grand Rapids, MI: Zondervan Publishing House, 2001.

This is one of the best reference tools for someone studying the Bible.   This edition was revised and corrected by John R. Kohlenberger and James A. Swanson. It lists words with references to every usage of the word. It contains a numbering system originally set up by Mr. Strong, which refers to the Greek and Hebrew word used in the Hebrew and Greek dictionaries also included in the book. There are loads of other Bible helps within this book, including Nave's Topical Bible Reference System, Social concerns of the Mosaic Covenant, Old Testament sacrifices, Hebrew Calendar, Hebrew Feasts and Holy Days, Weights, Lengths and Measures of the Bible, Prophecies of the Messiah, Parables of Jesus, etc. This concordance is geared to the King James Version of the Bible.

Tenny, Merrill C. (General Editor). The Zondervan Pictorial Bible Dictionary. Grand Rapids, MI: Zondervan Publishing House, 1967.

Like the pictorial encyclopedia mentioned below this is an excellent dictionary of the Bible. It contains articles on a vast number of subjects that are mentioned in the Bible, but in a small more condensed format than the encyclopedia, so is great for a quick overview of the subject. Articles consulted include "Bethlehem", "Moab", "Moabite Stone", "Naomi", "Orpah", "Ruth", "Ruth, Book of", and "Farming".

_____ (General Editor). **The Zondervan Pictorial Encyclopedia of the Bible**. (5 volumes). Grand Rapids, MI: Zondervan Publishing House, 1980.

This set of encyclopedias is written for every student of the Bible, whether it be a formal classroom type of study or an at home interest in daily Bible reading and study for personal benefit. The articles are written by numerous people most of whom have a conservative point of view. Through photos and text, the reader is given an overview of Biblical material from archaeology to canonicity to general opinions. Every article has a brief bibliography at the end along with the name of the author of that particular article. For Ruth study, the articles on "Ruth", "Ruth, book of", "Naomi", "Orpah", "Moab, Moabites", "Moabite Stone", "Winnowing", "Weights and Measures", "Harvest", "Elimelech", and "Gleaning, Glean" can all be useful in understanding the times in which Ruth lived.

GENERAL BOOKS ON BIBLE WOMEN:

Deen, Edith. **All of the Women of the Bible**. New York: Harper & Row, Publishers, 1955.

Looking at all the women of the Bible is a huge task, yet Ms. Deen does it well. Her commentaries are fairly conservative. There is a chapter listing and explaining all the names of the women in the Bible as well as those not named. There are also chapters giving more detailed biographies of the more well-known women of the Bible. Most of what is written about Ruth is good, except she does indirectly say that Ruth worked in other fields before coming to Boaz's field, and that Ruth worked for several days in the field of Boaz before meeting Boaz which is not what the Bible says.

Lockyer, Dr. Herbert. The Women of the Bible. Grand Rapids, MI: Zondervan Publishing House, 1975.

A conservative look at the women mentioned by name and those not mentioned by name. The book also contains chapters on symbolic women, the ideal woman, aids for women's groups, and messages for Mother's Day. The section on Ruth deals with the qualities shown in her life: wife, widow, convert, humble, mother, etc. It is a very good overview of Ruth's life.

Meyers, Carol (ed.). Women in Scripture. Boston: Houghton Mifflin Company, 2000.

This dictionary of women contains information about women in the Old and New Testaments as well as those mentioned in the Apocryphal/ Deuterocanonical books. Both named and unnamed women located in the scriptures are included. It is written from a liberal feminist point of view, speaking of Naomi as being "subordinate" to Elimelech since she is listed as "his" wife, "his" widow, etc. The book of Ruth is referred to as historical fiction.

CHRONOLOGIES and CHARTS:

Brown, Mike. The World History Chart. (Available for free download online at: http://www.creation-science-prophecy.com/timeline.htm), 2008.

Although this is not a World History Chart, because it contains mostly Biblical History, it is a conservative chart. It prints out easily to two sheets of paper in black and white. The first page contains Bible history from Creation at 4000 BC to the beginning of the Kings of Israel about 1000 BC. It contains names of people in Genesis including the age when a son was born, and the total age of the person. It would be better if more room was given to the time of the Judges and afterwards, but for the amount of information covered by this chart, it is excellent. It is not specific as to the individual times of the Judges, but gives a total time period listing their names within it. The second page of the chart is somewhat more confusing. It covers the time from 1000 BC to 2000 AD. Again, the chart is too small for all the information Mr. Brown tries to put into it. After Christ ascends into heaven, Mr. Brown tries to cover the Catholic Church and reformation along with prophecies about each. This page was of no help for our study in Ruth.

Jones, Floyd Nolen. <u>The Chronology of the Old Testament</u>. Green Forest, AR: Master Books, 2007.

Lengthy explanations of his chronologies provide the student with more than just a chart of the history of the Old Testament. Although he may not be 100 per cent on each date, he comes close to establishing a date for everything in the Old Testament. This large format book of 337 pages also includes a CD with all of his charts on it in PDF (Acrobat Reader) format. The disappointing thing is that you can look at the charts on your computer, but if you print them out, they have a line or lines drawn across them. If you really want his charts you can order them for $39.95 more.

McFate, Richard W. <u>Bible and World History Timeline</u>. Vancouver, WA: Visquar, 2006.

This giant wall chart is very impressive looking. It is a good tool to get an overview of how Biblical events fit into the context of events taking place in other parts of the world. He lists events as falling between certain dates, such as the

Exodus being between 1400 and 1500 BC, but does not get any more specific than that. Mr. McFate puts Ruth into Ehud's judgeship which is pretty unlikely since the Moabites would not have been willing to allow Israelites to move there after Ehud killed their king and drove them out of Israel. While McFate's times are acceptable since they are not specific, he has one fatal flaw with the chart. He does not start it with Adam, but starts with the Geological Table which shows a definite evolutionary leaning. Without that, the chart is otherwise very helpful. He also color codes the lines of Shem, Ham, and Japheth which is even more helpful.

SERMONS ON TAPE OR CD:

Hammack, Trevor. Sermon Series on Ruth. Ovalo, TX: Victory Baptist Church, 2004. (http://www.sermonaudio.com/main.asp)
This sermon series consists of eight sermons delivered on the Victory Baptist Church's radio show in 2003 and 2004. Pastor Trevor has an interesting way of looking at the book of Ruth. He says Elimelech, meaning "My God is King", should not have married Naomi, "Pleasure" (here he changes the meaning of Naomi's name from "Pleasant" to "Pleasure"), because Christians should not be seeking pleasure over serving God. Seeking pleasure in the world can lead to sickness (Mahlon) and bitterness (Mara). Other sermons in the series (which are just titled "Part 1", "Part 2", etc.) deal with "Spiritual Famine", "Worldly Pleasure", "A Sick World", Return from Sin or Die", "Spiritual food", and "Our Redeemer, Jesus Christ". Each sermon is about a half hour long, and uses Scriptures from both the Old and New Testaments to prove his points.

Moore, Beth. <u>The Kinsman Redeemer: A Study of Ruth</u>.
Houston, TX: Living Proof Ministries, 2005.

This three CD set of Beth Moore's speaking engagement, shows a very good grasp of the Kinsman Redeemer concept not only from Ruth but from the whole Bible. She is conservative and knowledgeable about the book of Ruth. The first CD deals with Naomi's bitterness. The second CD deals with Boaz as the Kinsman Redeemer and how God often uses people as examples of His own attributes: King David showing us that God is King of the universe; Aaron showing us that God is our High Priest; and Boaz showing us that God can and does redeem us from wherever and whatever we have gotten ourselves into. There is nothing that God cannot redeem us from if we ask for His redemption. Disc 3 deals with Boaz's court scene to confront the nearer kinsman and how we should be happy to say "I know that my redeemer lives."

Roby, Tracy. <u>Sermons on Ruth</u>. **Overland Park, KS: Overland Park Baptist Temple, 2005. (http://www.sermonaudio.com/main.asp)**

This is a four-sermon series from the book of Ruth. They are free to download from the website at http://www.sermonaudio.com/main.asp in audio format. The first sermon is called "It's Time to Come Home" and deals with chapter one of Ruth. In this sermon we see Naomi's willingness to go home to Bethlehem after all that had happened to her. The idea that we can all go home to Jesus at any time, no matter how far we have strayed from Him and he will welcome us back, is the central theme of this sermon. Sermon Two is called "The Hand of God I See". It deals with chapter 2 and emphasizes that Ruth is a type of sinner who seeks grace. She goes to Boaz who is a type of Jesus Christ, and finds grace everywhere. Boaz offers her protection, comfort, kindness, food, and water. He takes care of all her needs. Sermon 3 is called "Resting in Redemption." Again, Boaz is shown as a type of Christ and Ruth as a type of sinner. Naomi is a type of the person who leads or shows the way for a sinner to find Christ the redeemer. She tells Ruth in verse one of chapter 3 that she wants to find rest for Ruth, and in the last verse of the chapter Naomi tells Ruth that Boaz will not rest until the matter is settled (his work is done). "Redemption Draweth Nigh" is sermon four. This sermon continues with the theme that Christ is our redeemer just as Boaz was the redeemer of Ruth. It goes into what a redeemer is, what he has to do, what the qualifications to be a redeemer are, and what the outcome of redemption is. At the same time, it is a look at what our response to our redeemer Jesus Christ should be.

Rogers, Adrian. <u>Redeeming Love from the Book of Ruth</u>. Memphis, TN: Love Worth Finding Ministries, 1999.
The four sermons, presented on two CD's, each deal with a different chapter of Ruth. Although the sermons preach well, they do not necessarily follow Ruth very well. For instance, in the second sermon Adrian Rogers says Mahlon means song and Chilion means perfection and this along with Elimelech (My God is King) and Naomi (Pleasant) makes the family a wonderfully blessed family. I cannot find one Hebrew lexicon that says Mahlon and Chilion mean these things. Most say they mean weak and pining or something similar. While the overall points of his sermons are true to the overall Bible, he takes things out of Ruth and changes them to mean what he needs for his sermon content. He might have been better off choosing other scriptures to represent his sermon, but then it would not be a series of sermons about Ruth. "It is Decision That Determines Destiny" shows us decisions made by various

people in chapter one. Elimelech made a bad decision, while Ruth made a good decision. Sermon two (God's Amazing Grace) deals with chapter two of Ruth. In this sermon Mr. Rogers uses Boaz as a type of Christ, because Boaz shows Ruth grace while working in his fields, just as God shows us grace when we come to work for Him. Continuing on the theme of Boaz being a type of Christ, sermon three shows us "Five Ways to Draw Closer to Jesus", by using five examples from chapter three of how Ruth drew closer to Boaz.   Sermon four is about "Redeeming Love" and compares Boaz's love for Ruth to Christ's love for us.

Tomlinson, Glenn. A House Raised Up. Ontario, Canada: Sovereign Grace Community Church, 2007. (http://www.sermonaudio.com/main.asp)
This four-part sermon series was preached by Tomlinson at the Sovereign Grace Community Church in 2007. The four sermons deal with the fall of the house of Elimelech who according to Pastor Tomlinson is a type of Adam. Tomlinson compares Elimelech to Adam because Adam's house has fallen into sin and needs to be saved by the second Adam, Jesus Christ. The first sermon is called "The Fall of a House" and deals with Ruth chapter 1. The second sermon "Descending to Raise the Fallen" is from Ruth 1:16-17. "Designing to Raise the Fallen" uses Ruth 3:1-6, and "Delivering to Raise the Fallen" is taken from Ruth 4:1-10.

OTHER BOOKS:

Vance, Donald R. <u>A Hebrew Reader for Ruth</u>. Peabody, MA: Hendrickson Publishers, Inc., 2003.

This book, written by an associate professor of Biblical languages at Oral Roberts University, is designed mostly for the student of Hebrew. It contains a verse by verse and word by word look at the Hebrew text of the entire book of Ruth. Each verse is first shown in the Hebrew. Then an English translation is provided for the verse. Lastly is a word by word look at the Hebrew within the verse showing parts of speech, translation, root word, and any peculiarities about the word itself.

Young, G. Douglas. <u>Grammar of the Hebrew Language</u>. Grand Rapids, MI: Zondervan Publishing Company, 1951.

Professor Young offers a "new" way of teaching Hebrew by immersing his students directly into translating the Bible, rather than learning grammar first and memorizing vocabulary. Grammar and vocabulary are learned as the student translates. He uses the entire book of Ruth for his lessons showing a word study of each word. Also used is a transliteration of the Hebrew words rather than learning the Hebrew alphabet in the beginning. According to Young it is easier to transfer the students to the actual Hebrew letters latter in their studies, than to take time to teach them the Hebrew from the beginning.